THAI COOKING

KNACK®

THAI COOKING

A Step-by-Step Guide to Authentic Dishes Made Easy

DARLENE ANNE SCHMIDT

Photographs by Emily Heller

Guilford, Connecticut
An imprint of Globe Pequot Press

Editor in Chief: Maureen Graney
Editor: Katie Benoit
Cover Design: Paul Beatrice, Bret Kerr
Text Design: Paul Beatrice
Layout: Maggie Peterson
Cover photos by Emily Heller
Edited by Linda Beaulieu

All interior photographs by Emily Heller

Library of Congress Cataloging-in-Publication Data is available on file.

ISBN 978-1-59921-782-6

The information in this book is true and complete to the best of our knowledge. All recommendations are made without guarantee on the part of the author or Globe Pequot Press. The author and Globe Pequot Press disclaim any liability in connection with the use of this information.

Printed in China

10 9 8 7 6 5 4 3 2 1

Dedication

To my mother-in-law, Lena Lee, who has so openly shared with me her vast knowledge of Thai and Southeast Asian cuisine—with love and gratitude.

Acknowledgments Darlene

I'd like to acknowledge the help and support of my agent, Barb Doyen, without whom this book would not exist. Thanks also to Linda Larsen, who provided sage advice when I needed it, and to my editor Keith Wallman, who was always so encouraging. Finally, I'd like to thank my husband, Bertrand Lee, for his constant support, and for the ready use of his "super taste buds" in developing these recipes.

Acknowledgments Emily

I appreciate everyone who helped and supported me while shooting all these delicious Thai food recipes. Thanks to Courtney Katz and Katherine Wilson for their fantastic cooking and food styling skills. Thanks Linda Connor for the loan of props from all over the world. And thank you to those who ate the dishes after the shoot.

CONTENTS

Chapter 11: Shellfish

Chapter 12: Vegetables

Chapter 13: Rice

Chapter 14: Noodles

Chapter 15: Curry

Chapter 16: Salad

Chapter 17: Dessert

Chapter 18: Drinks

Chapter 19: Dips and Sauces

Chapter 20: Resources

INTRODUCTION

Cooking Thai food is like embarking on a culinary adventure. Along every step of the way, from preparation to cooking to tasting, Thai cuisine never ceases to tantalize and astound. An incredible variety of flavors mingle and dance across the taste buds, while various textures and aromatic notes both seduce and satiate the senses. A well-prepared Thai meal should leave you not only truly satisfied, but also inspired to delve further into this rich and diverse cuisine.

The four main flavors in Thai food are spicy, salty, sweet, and sour. Another flavor, bitter, is often added for additional depth; for example, the fresh Thai basil used to garnish curries, stir-fries, and noodles. The best Thai dishes achieve a balance of these flavorings while also offering a variety of textures such as crisp, soft, crunchy, chewy, and even gritty. All such textures are found in Thai food, sometimes even within the same dish. Nuts and fresh herbs help add some of this texture, but oftentimes it is the ingredients themselves that provide textural variety. Stir-fries are a good example of this, with the meat cooked to tenderness while the vegetables remain crisp and crunchy.

The country of Thailand, much like its cuisine, is rich and varied, with plenty of coastal fishing areas as well as mountainous regions, jungles, and plains, plus urban areas.

Known as one of the great rice bowls of Asia, the central

plains make up the heartland of Thailand, consisting of fertile rice farms. Originally this region was a swamp, and it is still prone to flooding during monsoon season. However, this abundance of water also allows for easier rice production. From this region, tons of fragrant, jasmine-scented rice are exported around the world each year. The cooking in this region includes rice noodle dishes, usually eaten for lunch or as a snack, the most famous of which is Pad Thai. Protein in this region varies from beef to chicken and fish, and desserts made with banana and mango are very popular.

The north of Thailand, including the city of Chiang Mai, is a very different type of culinary region. Until the late 1800s, the north existed almost as a separate kingdom; it was like a fortress consisting of rivers, mountains, and trees. Within this isolation, the northern Thai people developed a distinct dialect as well as their own unique style of cooking.

Unlike the south, here there are no coconut trees—hence no coconut milk. Fish is also hard to come by in this landscape of hills, valleys, and farmland. Red meat of all kinds is more common here, along with various vegetable dishes (both raw and cooked). Sticky rice is eaten daily, not necessarily as a dessert (like in other regions), but to accompany these spicy meat dishes. Jungle Curry is an example of this type of cooking.

While northern Thailand has traditionally been associated with a diet based on various red meats, these days the northern city of Chiang Mai is becoming known as a kind of spiritual retreat for those seeking peace and serenity (as well as a little more of the traditional Thai culture and atmosphere that can still be found in this mountainous city). Hence, Chiang Mai now boasts a number of vegetarian and vegan restaurants, which many Western tourists to the region appreciate and are helping to support.

The northeast is probably the poorest region of Thailand, also known as Issaan. Droughts are common, and the heat during the day can be oppressive. Like in the north, fish and coconut milk are not readily available for everyday home cooking. When animals are eaten, no part is left to waste. Beef (including tongue, stomach, intestines, heart, and liver) is common, as are chicken, pork, and even boar. Cooking methods here include much roasting or broiling. Clear curries are popular, while the most famous dish of the region is Green Papaya Salad, often eaten with sticky rice.

The region south of the capital forms a long peninsula that joins with Malaysia. A long mountain range follows the peninsula from north to south, while palm trees and white-sand beaches line the coast. Just off the western side of the peninsula lie a plethora of islands, many of them famous (such as Phuket) for attracting millions of international tourists each year who seek white-sand beaches and clear azure waters. Aside from tourism, fishing is another main industry. The coastal area on the eastern, gulf side is known both for fishing as well as the large-scale production of fish sauce—one of the most important of Thai cooking ingredients. With its abundance of fresh fish and coconuts, southern cooking tends to be rich in fish and seafood dishes cooked a number of different ways. Coconut-based curries (served with jasmine-scented rice or coconut rice) and whole deep-fried or grilled fish (usually smothered in a tangy tamarind-based sauce) are good examples of southern cooking.

Dessert in this region is very simple, consisting mainly of fresh tropical fruit, which is so abundant in the region. Fresh pineapple, mango, papaya, mangosteen, and many others are often served, either on their own or with sticky rice, tapioca, or coconut milk.

It should also be noted that every year the southern island of Phuket hosts a wildly popular vegetarian and vegan festival (usually in November—the date changes slightly from year to year). This is the perfect time of year for vegetarians to visit Thailand and partake of true vegetarian Thai food, as well as a number of traditional cultural rituals related to food.

Bangkok could be called a meeting place of the various types of Thai food from all of these regions, so it's always a good place to visit if you're planning a culinary tour of Thailand. Because Thailand has no colonial past, the country has managed to retain much of its original culture and, when it comes to food, its original flavor. A large Chinese immigrant population has been present in Thailand for numerous centuries, and this influence is evident in Bangkok, especially in many of the Thai noodle dishes and sauces used to marinate and add flavor (such as soy sauce, oyster sauce, dark soy sauce, and sesame oil).

But it is the Portuguese who gave Thailand its most distinctive ingredient: the chili pepper. Before Portuguese traders arrived, the Thais added heat to their foods with white and black peppercorns, both of which are still evident in Thai cooking to this day.

In addition to its incredible visual, taste, and aromatic appeal, Thai cuisine also offers many important health benefits. With an abundance of fresh fruit and nutritious vegetables combined with leaner meats plus rice and gluten-free rice noodles, Thai food is said to be one of the healthiest cuisines in the world. Both the fresh and dry spices used to flavor these foods provide the body with numerous antioxidants in addition to vitamins and minerals. Lemongrass, chili, coriander, galangal, turmeric, garlic, and lime leaf are all key ingredients that help boost the immune system, aid digestion, assist the heart, and may even help you sleep better.

If cooked correctly, Thai food is lower in fat and calories than most Western cuisines. Where cream, cheese, or milk might be added to a North American dish, in Thai cooking heart-healthy coconut milk is used.

In addition, Thai cooking methods, such as stir-frying, allow fruits, vegetables, and herbs to retain most or all of their vitamin and mineral content. And because of its satisfying mixture of flavors and textures, when eating a Thai meal, you may well find yourself requiring less food to feel sated, helping you achieve or maintain a healthy body weight.

Because cooking this marvelous cuisine can seem a bit daunting at first, the following recipes have been laid out in such a way as to make the process simple and straightforward. Considering Thai cuisine offers such delicious ingredients to work with, there is also quite a lot of room for experimentation and creativity within the various dishes presented here. Like all good Thai chefs, you will soon find the culinary journey from raw ingredients to exquisite Thai food is all in the taste buds—just let your senses be your guide.

THE WOK

Equip yourself with a good wok, and your Thai kitchen is nearly complete.

A wok is the Asian equivalent of the frying pan, with high, curved sides and a rounded or flat bottom. The wok originated in China and was brought to Thailand many centuries ago by Chinese immigrants. Although a large frying pan may be an adequate substitute for some recipes, a wok will get the job done better, faster, and easier.

Once you become accustomed to using a wok, you may well find it replaces not one but several of your standard pots and pans. Its versatility is one of its greatest advantages. A wok can be used not only for stir-frying, but also for boiling, searing, deep frying, steaming, and braising. You can even use it to toast dry herbs, spices, and seeds.

Traditional Round Bottom Woks

- This type of wok requires a circular ring that fits around your stovetop burner (usually included with the wok when you buy it).
- Because of its shape and the fact that is can be tilted so easily, those new to stir-frying may find a round bottom wok somewhat awkward and unwieldy at first.
- It is better suited to those already accustomed to Asian cooking techniques, but if you're up for a challenge, cooking with a traditional wok can be a wonderful learning experience.

Flat Bottom Woks

- The flat bottom wok is recommended for anyone starting out in Thai cooking.
- Unlike iron, stainless steel does not require seasoning and is easy to care for.
- Look for a stainless steel wok that is sturdy and heavy-duty enough to last many years.
- Also be sure to read any instructions that come with your wok, as some models are made to retain heat and therefore require lower temperatures than one might expect (an energy-saving feature!).

Woks are made of various materials, from cast iron to carbon steel and stainless steel. They also come in two different shapes: either with a round bottom or a flat bottom. The main advantage of a round bottom wok is in its "pooling" effect: liquids such as hot oils are not distributed across the entire cooking surface but remain in one small area. Foods can then be maneuvered into or out of the oil as needed. The same principle is at work when stir-frying—ingredients that are already cooked can be pushed aside, preventing overcooking.

A flat bottom wok is a good compromise between a traditional wok and a frying pan—foods can still be distributed or pushed out of the way as needed.

For health reasons, cast iron, stainless steel, or carbon steel is recommended over non-stick and aluminum. Non-stick surfaces scratch easily and break down, especially when cooking over the high temperatures required in Thai cuisine. Iron or stainless steel makes a far better choice.

Carbon Steel Woks

- Traditional Asian woks are made of carbon steel and need to be "seasoned" before use.
- Unfortunately, you can't simply coat the wok with lard and place it in the oven as you would with a cast iron frying pan.
- A wok has to be evenly heated over your stovetop, so all surfaces are equally seasoned. It is then wiped out and the process repeated.
- Consider buying a stainless steel wok, a healthy and efficient choice. If it's well made, it will last many years.

Cast Iron Woks

- There are two types of cast iron woks: Asian style and Western style.
- Of the two, the Asian iron wok is recommended, since it is thinner and lighter. It will heat up quicker and also allow for easier lifting, tilting, and tipping than the heavier Western version.
- A further option is the enameled cast iron wok. This type is popular in Europe, and while of excellent quality, these woks do tend to be far more expensive than a good stainless steel wok.

PESTLE & MORTAR

This ancient kitchen tool remains a useful part of the modern Thai kitchen.

Like the wok, a pestle and mortar have the advantage of multipurpose versatility: they can be used for grinding whole spices such as coriander seeds, for pounding smaller pieces of meat to tenderize them, for bruising or mashing fresh lemongrass, or for creating pastes out of a mixture of herbs and spices. It is also useful for grinding nuts, or for mincing garlic, shallots, ginger, and other fresh spices for stir-frying. Some Thai recipes also call for dry ground rice, which the pestle and mortar can handle beautifully.

Pestle and mortar sets come in various materials, from ceramic to porcelain to glass, metal, marble, wood, and stone. For Thai food preparation, a stone pestle and mortar are

Grinding Dry Spices

- Like fresh-ground coffee, dry spices taste their best when freshly ground.
- The sheer weight of a stone pestle does a fine job of this task, easily pounding Thai spices like dried coriander seeds into a powdery consistency.
- Other spices that can be ground with a pestle and mortar for Thai cuisine include cumin, star anise, cinnamon bark (or sticks), and fennel seeds.

Grinding Nuts, Rice, or Coconut

- The pestle and mortar can easily grind up nuts like peanuts and cashews, which are common garnishes in many Thai dishes.
- Toasted coconut is another ingredient that sometimes needs to be ground, as is toasted sticky rice. Such jobs are easily tackled by the pestle and mortar.
- To clean your mortar, wipe it out with a dry cloth, or place both pestle and mortar in your sink and wash with warm soapy water.

recommended. Other materials may break easily with use or become stained by colorful spices such as turmeric. One made of granite, basalt, or other stone-derived material is best.

While using a pestle and mortar, always begin with small amounts, pounding a little at a time to prevent items from flying out of the mortar, then adding more until everything is ground or mixed together. Any liquids should be added last. Using a dropping or pounding motion combined with a mixing and stirring motion allows you to both grind and blend items together.

ZOOM

The pestle and mortar are one of the oldest kitchen tools in existence. Although they have been replaced to some extent by the modern food processor, chopper, and grinder, the pestle and mortar are still preferred by many Thai chefs, especially for making fresh spice and curry pastes. They are also more economical, since a good pestle and mortar can do the job of two or three electronic gadgets.

Bruising and Mashing Lemongrass

- Slicing up a lemongrass stalk isn't enough preparation for cooking it.
- Because lemongrass is so densely fibrous, it needs to be broken down into softer, smaller pieces in order to make it palatable.
- Pounding slices of lemongrass with a pestle and mortar is a good way to do this, and you'll find it also brings out the wonderful aromatic qualities of the herb, which otherwise might remain in the stalk.

Making Curry Paste

- When making a Thai curry paste in a pestle and mortar, always start with any dry spices that require grinding, such as coriander or cumin seeds.
- Once these are pounded into a powder, add your fresh spices, like garlic, ginger, or fresh coriander, pounding and mashing everything together as you go.
- Add any liquids last and in small amounts at a time, stirring well to mix everything together.

FOOD PROCESSOR

The food processor makes light work of Thai food preparation.

The modern equivalent of the pestle and mortar is the food processor. Because most Thai recipes start with a spice paste or sauce mixture—usually made up of a combination of fresh and dry spices and herbs—a food processor will save you time and effort by doing the chopping, mixing, and blending for you.

Curry pastes and sauces are really where the food processor shines, as this gadget can whip up a mixture of seemingly disparate ingredients into a fragrant Thai curry paste or sauce in just minutes. However, most food processors (unless they are top of the line) cannot completely replace a grinder or pestle and mortar, which can finely grind up and mince spices or seeds (such as coriander or cumin seeds), as well as ground roasted rice with superior results.

Basic Food Processor

- Today food processors are made to tackle nearly any type of food preparation task, from making bread dough to shredding cabbage.
- But when it comes to cooking Thai food, all you really need are the basics. Look for a standard processor that can chop and blend, and you'll be able to handle nearly any Thai recipe.
- Buying anything extra is optional and entirely up to you and your daily cooking needs.

Making Curry Paste

- The food processor does an excellent job of making Thai curry pastes. Simply place all the paste ingredients together in the processor and blitz.
- Be sure to add a little liquid (coconut milk usually) in order to keep the blades moving smoothly.
- Also, add only ground spices (such as ground coriander), not whole spices. Unlike the pestle and mortar, the food processor will not be able to both grind and chop/blend at the same time.

Although food processors can be pricey (up to $400), less expensive models (as low as $50) can do an equally efficient job of chopping, mixing, and blending most Thai ingredients. While a more moderately priced processor may not be able to grind up all your spices and other dry ingredients, an inexpensive pestle and mortar set or a coffee grinder (about $12) can take over this particular task.

For some Thai recipes, a blender can be substituted for a food processor, especially when there are enough liquids involved.

ZOOM

Traditionally, it was common to have several cooks and helpers in the Thai kitchen to prepare ingredients. Today you can still see kitchen helpers preparing food by Thai road stalls or in marketplaces. In the absence of so many helping hands, we in the West have come to rely on the food processor as our most reliable kitchen companion, and many urban Thai cooks are now doing the same.

Making Curry Sauce

- The difference between making a curry paste and a curry sauce is minimal; oftentimes the two vary only in the amount of liquid added.
- To make a curry sauce, simply place all the ingredients—including liquid ingredients, such as coconut milk—together in the processor and blitz to a smooth sauce.

Making Dips and Sauces

- The food processor can easily tackle Thai stir-fry sauces, marinades, and dipping sauces of all kinds.
- Fresh fruit purees, such as this fresh mango dip, can be put together in mere minutes, and even fresh fruit drinks can be made with your food processor.
- There's no need to buy a blender for these tasks if you don't already own one—your food processor can handle all of this perfectly well.

MINI FOOD CHOPPER AND GRINDER

These two small and inexpensive gadgets prove useful in the Thai kitchen.

There are times when nothing but a grinder will give you the results you're looking for, especially when it comes to preparing dry spices or spice mixtures. By the same token, there are other times when a mini food chopper will do the job better than a grinder—for example, when mincing up fresh spices and herbs like garlic—without the need to resort to a food processor. In fact, many Thai cooks manage to do all their ingredient preparation with only a mini food chopper in combination with either a grinder or a pestle and mortar. This saves both money and storage space, as mini choppers are small and inexpensive.

For this reason, budget-conscious cooks may wish to

Mini Food Chopper

- For the most part, mini food choppers are inexpensive and small enough to easily store in a cupboard or drawer.
- This kitchen gadget does an excellent job of mincing fresh spices like garlic and galangal or ginger (which form the base of most Thai recipes), and is equally efficient at creating curry pastes and sauces.
- If you're watching your budget, a mini chopper can provide an adequate substitute for most Thai recipes.

Making Stir-Fry Sauce

- Because the mini chopper does such a good job of finely chopping even the most difficult items (like slippery lime leaves and fibrous lemongrass), it is perfect for making stir-fry sauces and curry pastes—anything that requires finely minced and/or blended ingredients.
- If the recipe calls for more liquid ingredients (such as coconut milk) than your chopper has room for, simply add as much as you can; any additional liquids can be mixed into the paste or sauce afterward.

experiment first with a mini food chopper before investing in a food processor, as the mini chopper can perform the same basic function at a fraction of the cost.

In terms of grinding, a coffee grinder can perform double duty, grinding coffee beans in the morning and Thai spices in the evening. In fact, some manufacturers are now producing grinders made for both coffee and spices.

In the Thai kitchen, pulverizing whole spices is the grinder's main function, but some recipes also call for finely ground shrimp, nuts, toasted rice, and sesame seeds.

GREEN LIGHT

Cleaning a grinder can be done two ways, both of them environmentally friendly. To remove any residual coffee grounds, simply wipe the grinder out with a dry cloth. To clean away any residual spices, add 1 Tbsp. uncooked white rice and grind up. Throw away the ground rice. Any residual scent or flavor will be absorbed and taken away by the rice.

Coffee and Spice Grinder

- A coffee grinder works well for grinding up dry whole Thai spices, such as coriander and cumin seeds, or even dried red chilies.
- If you'd rather not be bothered with cleaning your grinder after every use, consider purchasing a second grinder just for your spices (grinders can cost as little as $12).
- A third option is to buy one of the new two-in-one grinders designed for both coffee and spices.

Grinding Whole Spices

- Though most Thai spices can be purchased already ground, freshly grinding your own makes for better, fresher spice flavor.
- Whether you own a coffee grinder or a spice grinder, both gadgets do a wonderful job of grinding up dry whole spices.
- Grinders also allow you to make your own freshly ground spice mixtures. Experiment with creating your own curry powder, barbecue rubs, or other dry spice mixtures.

RICE COOKER

The electric rice cooker can tackle more than plain steamed rice.

While it's true that rice can be cooked in a pot on your stovetop, a rice cooker does make the job easier. For one thing, you don't have to keep checking the rice pot to make sure it isn't burning or boiling over; and with a rice cooker, you get perfectly cooked rice every time. The other benefit of using a rice cooker is its portability: it can be plugged in nearly anywhere, which means your stovetop can be freed up for cooking the main dish.

In addition, most rice cookers have a "keep warm" feature, allowing you to make the rice several hours ahead of time, if you so wish. This is convenient when having a dinner party, but it's also useful for everyday dining, keeping the rice warm for second helpings or that late-comer to your table.

Rice Cooker

- There are numerous rice cookers available, with varying prices and features. But all you really need in a rice cooker are the basics: a sturdy design, a tight-fitting (or snap down) lid, a "keep warm" feature, and preferably a retractable cord.
- Be sure to buy one that isn't too large for your needs—even some of the smaller rice cookers can make 6–8 cups of steamed rice, perfect for two to four people.
- A smaller rice cooker is easier to clean and takes up less space.

Coconut Rice

- To make coconut rice in your rice cooker, add 2 cups jasmine rice (this will serve 5–6 people), plus 1½ cups water, and 1½ cups good-quality coconut milk. Also add ½ tsp. salt and ½ tsp. sugar.
- Stir gently to break up any lumps of coconut milk (cream) and to dissolve the sugar. Turn on your rice cooker.
- When the rice is done, fluff with chopsticks or a fork. Do a taste test, adding more salt (if needed) before serving.

ZOOM

With the rice cooker, manufacturers usually include a recommended rice-to-water ratio: usually 1 to 1. But, this makes for a rather dry-tasting rice. Instead, try increasing the amount of water slightly. For example, for a small pot of rice, add 2 cups Thai jasmine-scented rice with 2½ cups water. Turn on your rice cooker, and you'll have fluffy steam-textured rice in about 20 minutes.

YELLOW LIGHT

Most rice cookers feature a non-stick coating, which can gradually scrape off if metal spoons or other abrasive utensils continually scratch the surface. Ingesting these coatings is harmful to your health; therefore, use only soft spatulas or wooden or plastic spoons inside a rice cooker. When cleaning up, place the rice cooker container in the dishwasher, or use a soft cloth.

Saffron Rice

- To make saffron rice, simply replace the amount of water you would normally add with a good-quality chicken or vegetable broth.
- Then add ¼ to ½ tsp. turmeric, ½ to 1 tsp. salt, and ¼ to ½ tsp. saffron threads, adjusting the amounts according to how much rice you're making.

Sticky Rice

- To make sticky rice in your rice cooker, place 2 cups of sticky rice in the rice cooker with 2⅔ cups water.
- Let rice sit 30 minutes, then add ¾ tsp. salt and stir. Cover and turn on your rice cooker.
- When rice is done, allow it to sit an extra 10 minutes before removing the lid.
- (Note: If desired, you can line your rice cooker with a banana leaf.)

STEAMER

The steamer is an essential piece of equipment in the Thai kitchen.

The basic bamboo steamer is an inexpensive item that serves many purposes in the Thai kitchen. While more expensive electric steamers may be purchased, owning one isn't a necessity. Traditional Asian steamers work equally well, and are much easier on the budget.

Stainless steel steamers can also be used for most Thai dishes. Sometimes woks are sold with simple stainless steel steaming units that sit inside the vessel, or you might have your own stainless steel steamer designed for vegetables.

If you don't have a steamer, a colander can make a passable substitute. Some items, like dumplings, will stick to stainless steel, so be sure to line your colander with banana leaves.

All of this being said, traditional bamboo steamers work best for Thai food. Their flat bottom allows you to steam more

Electric Food and Rice Steamer

- If you're in the market for a rice cooker, consider purchasing one that doubles as a steamer.
- Compared to traditional bamboo steamers, the main advantage of this kind of steamer is that you needn't worry about the water level.
- Most are made for high capacity, and can steam more than one batch at once, which makes this appliance an energy-efficient choice.

Traditional Bamboo Steamer

- Traditional bamboo steamers can be found at most Asian food or supply stores. They cost very little and are made to last.
- When purchasing, make sure the lid fits snugly, and that the bamboo is tightly woven.
- The largest bamboo steamers are made to fit over a soup pot, while the smaller ones can sit over a regular pot or inside a wok.

food at once, and you can buy a stackable set, allowing you to steam several batches of food at once. Note that the bamboo steamer is also very adaptable: you can place it over a soup pot or wok, or even a frying pan so long as it sits securely and there is enough room for water to boil beneath it.

GREEN LIGHT

Because bamboo is one of the fastest growing trees in existence, it has become known as an environmentally friendly material. The design of the bamboo steamer is also very energy efficient, with the slats on the bottom allowing for more steam to penetrate the cooking surface than most Western-type steamers. And its stackable option means you can cook several batches at once, saving even more time and energy.

Stackable Bamboo Steamer Set

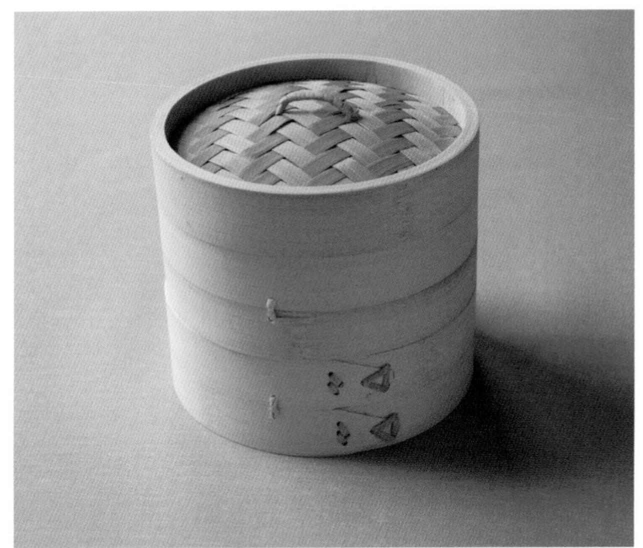

- For anyone who enjoys dim sum, stackable sets of bamboo steamers are a familiar sight. The main advantage of this kind of steamer lies in its ability to cook a variety of steamed dishes at the same time.
- For home cooks, one might want to steam two or more batches of the same dish at a time. This saves both time and energy.

Classic Colander

- In the absence of an electric or bamboo steamer, a colander can be used for steaming. Simply set it inside a large soup-type pot, and have a lid that will fit tightly.
- Consider lining your colander with banana leaves. Being porous, banana leaves allow the steam through while preventing food from sticking.

RICE

Though by far the most famous, Thai jasmine-scented rice is just one of several possibilities.

Thailand is one of the world's largest producers of rice. Aside from its jasmine fragrance and long grains, Thai rice is also among the healthiest of all white rice varieties. Once cooked and refrigerated, Thai rice also tends to store better and last longer than other varieties. This makes it an excellent choice for fried rice.

Due to the recent demand for healthier rice, it is now possible to find Thai whole-grain brown rice with the same familiar jasmine scent. Look for it in health food or organic food stores.

Aside from jasmine-scented rice, another common variety in Thailand is sticky rice, or "sweet rice." It is also sometimes

Thai Jasmine-Scented Rice

- Thai jasmine-scented rice is known the world over as a high-quality rice that is also pleasantly fragrant (hence the descriptive name "jasmine-scented," or simply "jasmine rice").
- Note, however, that the quality can vary greatly depending on the brand and the region in which the rice was grown. Look for top grade jasmine-scented rice sold in 25- to 50-pound sacks.
- It should fluff up nicely when cooked, taste slightly chewy, and have that wonderful characteristic fragrance, especially when first steamed.

Thai Brown Jasmine-Scented Rice

- Thai brown jasmine-scented rice is a healthier option than white, containing far more nutrients plus beneficial fiber.
- It is basically the same strain of rice, but without the last stage of polishing. This means the bran layer is still on the rice, making it chewier and slightly denser.
- To cook Thai brown rice, double the amount of water you would normally use to steam white rice. Brown rice also takes twice as long to cook, but the extra health benefits make it well worth your while.

referred to as "glutinous rice" due to its gluten-like consistency (note, however, that sticky rice does not contain gluten, and is therefore safe for gluten-free diets). While most people in the West associate sticky rice with Thai desserts, in the north and northeast of Thailand, sticky rice is regularly eaten with savory dishes.

A fourth type of Thai rice is black sticky rice. Uncooked black sticky rice may remind some of wild rice, since it contains grains of varying color and texture. However, it is easier to grow than wild rice and therefore costs a fraction of the price.

ZOOM

Black sticky rice has a distinctive flavor that lends itself well to rice pudding and other desserts. In Thailand, black sticky rice is often cooked with coconut milk, sugar, and pandan leaf (a natural flavoring), and enjoyed as a common street food, either as a snack or dessert. It is served up on a banana leaf and topped with shredded coconut.

Thai Sticky Rice

- Also known as glutinous rice, Thai sticky rice can be purchased at Asian food stores. In Thailand, sticky rice is usually steamed in a funnel-shaped woven basket.
- Here in the West, the easiest way to steam sticky rice is using a bamboo steamer or colander lined with banana leaf. Although not strictly authentic, sticky rice can also be made in a rice cooker (see previous chapter).
- Before cooking, always soak sticky rice in water for at least 30 minutes.

Black Sticky Rice

- Black sticky rice is also known as black glutinous rice or black sweet rice. It looks similar to North American wild rice, but costs far less.
- Some people are leery of black sticky rice because, when they cook it, the water colors to a dark purple; however, this is not a result of artificial colorants.
- Like turmeric, blueberries, and other fruits and vegetables with high pigment content, the intense natural coloring of black sticky rice means it is rich in nutrients and antioxidants.

NOODLES

Rice noodles are just one of many options available to the Thai cook.

Although Thailand is known for its rice noodles—the most famous dish being Pad Thai—numerous other types of noodles are also used, including wheat noodles, egg noodles, and even mung bean noodles, which are known as glass or cellophane noodles. Then there is the choice between buying fresh or dry noodles. Some noodles, such as river noodles, are best bought fresh, while most other types are normally purchased dried.

It seems there is no end to the various types of noodle dishes available in Thailand, and, indeed, each Thai chef or street food hawker serves up his or her own special creation.

Noodles were first brought to Thailand by Chinese immigrant workers, and therefore a good many Thai noodle dishes bear similarities to Chinese noodles (Pad See Ew, for example,

Classic Thai Rice Noodles

- Rice noodles come in a variety of thicknesses, from very thin (vermicelli type) to medium width (linguini type) to broad (river noodles). The type shown here are those used for Pad Thai—they are flat and of linguini thickness.
- The best way to cook these noodles is to soak them first in hot water until they are edible but still very chewy; they will finish cooking when you stir-fry. This process is what gives Pad Thai noodles their wonderfully chewy texture.

River Noodles

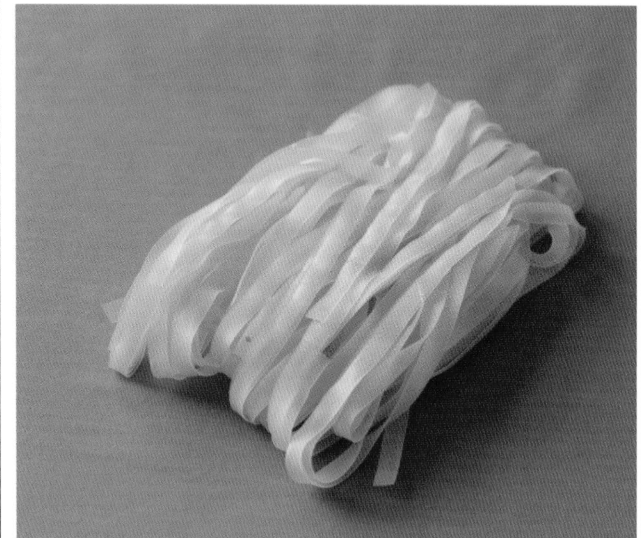

- Thai river noodles are made of rice flour and are broad and flat in shape.
- While it's possible to buy these noodles in their dried form, they are best purchased fresh. Look for them in the deli or fresh food section of your local Asian food store.
- Since these rice noodles are freshly made, they do not need to be soaked; however, they may come in compressed packages and need to be separated before stir-frying.

is similar to Chinese chow fun noodles).

Most North American cooks are accustomed to working with egg or wheat noodles. Rice noodles, however, can present a challenge. Unlike those made of wheat, dry rice noodles require two stages of preparation in order to taste their best: soaking, followed by stir-frying. Although this may seem like a lot of work, the wonderful results you can achieve with this method will encourage you to cook rice noodles again and again.

ZOOM

In Bangkok, food hawkers can be seen selling noodles of all type and description from roadside stalls any hour of the day or night. Aside from being a common lunch or snack food, noodles are often eaten for breakfast, something that most foreigners find hard to fathom; that is, until they try it and realize how energizing noodles (fried up with a little meat, seafood, tofu, or egg) can be.

Vermicelli Rice Noodles

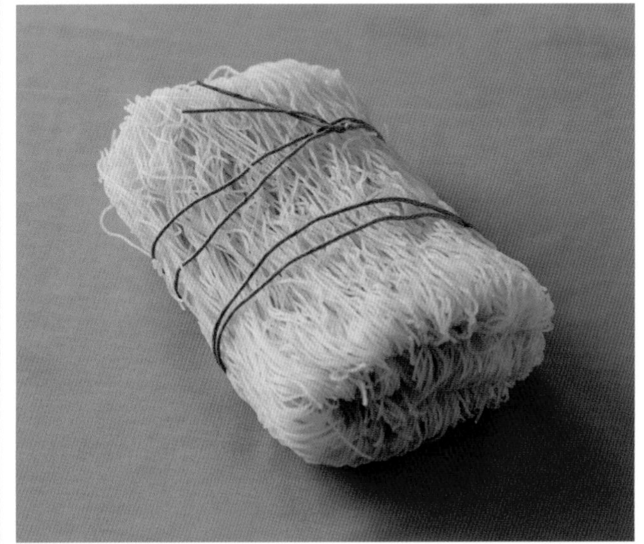

- These rice noodles are the Asian equivalent of vermicelli pasta. Because they are so thin, they cook very quickly.
- Like Pad Thai noodles, vermicelli noodles taste best when soaked in hot water rather than boiled, allowing them to retain their chewiness.
- Vermicelli rice noodles can be cooked up in a variety of ways. They may be served in soups, or as one of the main ingredients in spring rolls or fresh rolls. They also make very good stir-fried noodles.

Glass or Cellophane Noodles

- Thai glass or cellophane noodles are so named because, when cooked, they turn translucent as glass.
- They are sold tied in bundles and look very similar to vermicelli rice noodles—often, the only way to tell them apart is to read the ingredients.
- Glass noodles are made from bean flour (mung bean or pea flour, or a combination of both). They are therefore safe for gluten-free diets.
- Note that glass noodles are very absorbent and will grow much thicker once cooked.

DRY HERBS & SPICES

Stock your pantry with these key Thai herbs and spices.

Thai recipes tend to call for many of the same dry spices over and over again, which means you needn't buy a lot of extra supplies to cook Thai food. In fact, if you're an avid cook you may already have many of these spices in your pantry.

The most common herb or spice used in Thai cooking is coriander. In fact, Thai cuisine uses coriander in all its myriad forms: fresh coriander and coriander root, as well as dried coriander seeds and ground coriander, are all common ingredients in classic Thai cuisine.

Other dried herbs and spices you will want to have on hand include the following: cumin, turmeric, cinnamon, star anise, pepper, cayenne pepper, dried chili flakes, and possibly dried whole red chilies (which you can then grind up into your own Thai-style chili powder).

Coriander

- While ground coriander is readily available in most supermarkets these days, you may want to consider buying the whole form of this spice (coriander seed) and grinding it yourself. This makes for the freshest possible taste.
- Simply place whole coriander seeds in a coffee grinder and grind up, or use a pestle and mortar to pulverize the seeds into a powder.
- Like freshly ground coffee beans, you'll be able to smell the difference freshly ground spices make (not to mention the taste).

Dried Chili

- In most areas of North America, fresh Thai red chilies are not readily available. In place of fresh chilies, the dried version comes to the rescue.
- Dried chili flakes can be found in virtually every grocery store. And for those with stomach sensitivities, cayenne pepper makes an excellent option for adding chili heat and flavor.
- Unlike other types of chili, cayenne pepper has numerous healing properties and is actually beneficial for your stomach as well as your overall health.

Before Portuguese traders brought chili peppers to Thailand, Thai cooks added heat to their food by using pepper—not only black pepper, but white and green peppercorns continue to be common ingredients in Thai cooking. If you don't already have it, be sure to add white pepper to your pantry (luckily ground white pepper is readily available in most North American supermarkets).

ZOOM

North American chili powder originated in Mexico and is different from Thai chili powder. If you prefer authenticity, consider making your own chili powder by grinding up a handful of dried red chilies (available at Asian stores). Or, if you're up for a challenge, lightly roast the chilies in your oven before grinding—this will give you that smoky Thai chili sometimes referred to as "gun powder."

Turmeric and Curry Powder

- Dried turmeric is called for in various Thai recipes, from fried rice to curries.
- For those who follow a gluten-free diet, note that many of the less expensive turmeric powders contain wheat (as a bulking agent). The same holds true for many curry powders.
- For this reason—as well as for the quality and taste of the product—it is well worth seeking out a superior brand from an Asian or Indian food store.
- Madras curry powder works especially well with Thai food, and is highly recommended.

Cumin

- Cumin is another common spice that, like coriander, can easily be purchased ground.
- Feel free to use it in this form, but also consider grinding your own from seed.
- Whole cumin seed can be found in most supermarket chains, and has superior aroma and taste when freshly ground up in a coffee or spice grinder.

SAUCES & CONDIMENTS

These special items are "must-haves" in the Thai kitchen.

Thai cooking calls for various sauces and condiments. Some of these bottled concoctions perform double duty as both an ingredient in cooking and a condiment in serving.

By far the most important is fish sauce. Made from fermented anchovies, fish sauce has a salty and slightly sour flavor, and can be used to enhance nearly any Thai dish you might be cooking.

Other sauces that have become important in Thai cooking were first brought from China, such as soy sauce, oyster sauce, sesame oil, rice vinegar, and various soy bean sauces, such as ground bean or yellow bean sauce.

Tamarind fruit is grown in Thailand, and is used in cooking for its sour properties and rich taste. Shrimp paste, similar to fish sauce in flavor (except more intense), is another

Fish Sauce

- Fish sauce (*nam pla*) is one of the most important ingredients in Thai cooking. It has a rich translucent reddish-golden-brown color, and is used liberally in nearly all Thai dishes.
- Good fish sauces are made from a mixture of fish and salt that has been allowed to ferment for 1 year to 18 months.
- Vegetarian fish sauce exists—and is quite good—but may be difficult to find. Vietnam is the main exporter of vegetarian fish sauce, so try looking for it at Vietnamese food stores.

Sweet Chili Sauce

- These days, Thai sweet chili sauce is available at nearly all major supermarket chains across North America.
- Sweet chili sauce was originally paired with roasted chicken, but has since become a popular dip for all kinds of Thai snacks.
- Thai sweet chili sauce may also be used in cooking, and is especially good in stir-fry sauces or in marinades for chicken, fish, pork, or tofu.
- Once you try it, you'll find myriad uses for this flavorful Thai sauce.

ingredient you will want to have on hand.

Finally, no Thai pantry would be without a good supply of chili sauce. Because of its growing popularity, Thai sweet chili sauce is available in most supermarkets these days. It is a delightful sauce used both in cooking and serving. While sweet chili sauce is mild in flavor, nam prik pao is hot and savory. This chili sauce can be purchased at most Asian food stores, but is also easily made at home (see Chapter 19).

ZOOM

Shrimp paste has a very potent taste and smell, so some North Americans find it repulsive and refuse to use it. But once combined with other Thai ingredients, shrimp paste adds wonderful flavor and depth. It may help to think of it as very concentrated shrimp stock (like chicken stock cubes), because it has that same kind of flavor-enriching effect upon your cooking.

Shrimp Paste and Tamarind Paste

- Shrimp paste (*kapi* in Thai) is a common ingredient in many dishes, from curries to fried rice to salads. It is made from sun-dried shrimp and therefore has a very potent taste and scent. It is sold both in tubs and in small jars.
- Tamarind paste is much easier to work with than fresh or dried tamarind, which has to be softened and mashed (stones removed) before it can be used in cooking. Tamarind paste can be purchased at either Asian or Indian food stores.

Nam Prik Pao

- The most popular type of savory chili sauce in Thailand is known as nam prik pao.
- This chili sauce is very strong flavored and spicy hot. It is used as a condiment for many (nearly any) Thai dishes, including Tom Yum soup, all types of Thai noodles, and nearly any type of Thai finger food. Some Thais even eat it as a kind of jam, spreading it over toast for breakfast!
- Thai chili sauce also makes a good stir-fry sauce for shrimp and other seafood.

COCONUT

Coconut in all its myriad forms is used extensively in Thai cuisine.

The coconut tree must be one of the most useful of trees known to humankind, producing a plethora of coconut-based products that help sustain life. For this reason, in fact, it is sometimes called the "tree of life." In Thailand, every part of the coconut tree is used, including the roots, trunk, branches, husk, shell, bud, and, of course, the coconut meat and water (used to make coconut milk). As a crop, coconut is thus of prime importance to the Thais, and for this reason coconut plantations can be found across much of southern Thailand.

It's no surprise, then, that coconut milk and meat are such common ingredients in Thai cooking (especially in southern Thai cuisine). Coconut oil is also preferred over other types of oil for both stir-frying and deep-frying.

Unfortunately, for many years, coconut milk and oil suffered

Coconut Milk

- In Thailand coconut milk is made by squeezing fresh coconut meat (by hand).
- Here in the West, canned coconut milk has greatly improved with even organic varieties now available for purchase.
- Another option is "lite" coconut milk, which is much thinner and lower in calories. However, for most Thai recipes, full fat coconut milk works far better, making your curries and sauces thicker (not watery) and full of flavor.

Coconut Cream

- Like dairy cream, coconut cream is the thick layer of coconut milk that rises to the surface of coconut milk.
- If you are able to buy a good-quality coconut milk, you will find the top third of the can contains thick coconut cream, while the remainder of the can is more watery (coconut milk).
- Some manufacturers have tried to reproduce coconut cream in the form of a powder; however, this product doesn't replace real coconut cream in terms of quality or health benefits.

from a bad reputation; it was known as being cholesterol laden and therefore an unhealthy food choice. More recently, however, studies have shown the opposite to be true: that coconut actually lowers bad cholesterol levels and raises good. It is therefore now being promoted by health professionals and health food stores as both a healthy substitute for butter as well as the best choice for frying at both low and high temperatures.

ZOOM

In Thailand, large coconut plantations are now using monkeys to harvest coconuts. The chosen monkeys are sent to a training school for up to six months where they learn to pick only the ripest coconuts. The monkeys are treated well and it is even said the pigtailed macaque monkey might well be extinct were it not for the fact that they have "jobs" in the coconut plantations.

Dry Shredded Coconut

- In Thailand, fresh coconut meat is widely available and is often shredded for use in various sweet and savory dishes.
- Here in North America coconut meat is difficult to find, although it is sometimes available at Asian food stores (if not fresh, then sometimes frozen).
- Depending on the recipe, dry shredded coconut can often be used in place of fresh coconut. Toasting the shredded coconut helps bring out the flavor and add a pleasurable touch of crunch to many Thai dishes.

Coconut Oil

- Recently, coconut oil has been found to be one of the healthiest oils we can eat. Coconut oil lowers "bad cholesterol" levels and is safe for all types of cooking and baking.
- It is also one of the best options for deep-frying, as it doesn't break down like other oils do, nor does it smoke easily.
- Note that, unless it is a very hot day (above 80 degrees), coconut oil appears as a solid (like butter), but quickly dissolves into a liquid when heated.

LIME LEAVES

Lime leaves provide a distinctive Thai flavor to curries and stir-fry dishes.

When shopping for Thai food ingredients, be sure to place lime leaves at the top of your list. Most people enjoy the distinctive taste and aroma of Thai cooking without really realizing what it is they are tasting or smelling—and oftentimes the unknown ingredient is lime leaf.

Widely known as "kaffir lime leaves," these gorgeous leaves have a wonderful aroma, especially when torn or cut into small pieces. In Thai cooking, both whole and shredded lime leaves are used, often within the same dish.

Lime leaves can sometimes be purchased fresh in Asian or Chinese food stores. If you can't find them in the fresh produce and herb section, look for them in frozen packets.

Kaffir Lime Leaves

- If you can find fresh kaffir lime leaves at your local Asian food store, by all means buy them. However, more often than not you will have to wander over to the frozen foods section and seek them out there.
- Fortunately, lime leaves freeze extremely well and will keep in this way for 6 months to a year (especially when wrapped up tightly).
- If you happen to purchase fresh lime leaves, remember to freeze any leftover leaves for use in the future.

Preparing Lime Leaves

- To quickly thaw frozen lime leaves, give them a quick rinse under hot running water. The hot water will not only thaw the leaves, but it also brings out the natural aromatic qualities (oils) of the leaf.
- Note that while whole lime leaves have two sections (they are said to be hourglass-shaped), in most Thai recipes, one lime leaf is actually a "leaflet"—just one of these double leaves.

Fortunately, lime leaves keep very well when frozen, which makes storing them a cinch. Just be sure to wrap them up tightly before freezing—this will help them last even longer.

Note that kaffir lime leaves are not the same as leaves from young lime trees; rather, they come from the Thai magroot (or makrud) plant, a common shrub found in many Southeast Asian countries. You can distinguish this type of lime by its leaves, which are hourglass-shaped (with 2 distinct sections joined by a central stem), and also by its fruit, which have very bumpy skin.

ZOOM

In many world cultures, the word "kaffir" is a derogatory term and considered rude. For this reason, most South Africans refer to kaffir lime as "K-lime." Other chefs and food writers prefer to drop the word "kaffir" altogether in favor of simply "lime leaves." But despite all such attempts at change, the term "kaffir lime leaves" continues to be the standard term of use in Thai cooking.

Removing Stem and Vein

- Thai recipes often call for shredded lime leaf.
- In this case the lime leaf will be eaten, which means the leaf will have to be cut into sliver-like pieces and the stem will need to be removed.
- To remove the stem quickly and easily, simply tear the leaf in half (along the stem), then tear the stem away from the leaf.
- This task can also be accomplished with scissors or a knife.

Shredding Lime Leaves

- There are two easy ways to shred lime leaves.
- The first is with a pair of clean scissors (note that scissors are a common kitchen tool in Asia where they are used not only for shredding, but also for slicing up green onions, cutting noodles, and myriad other tasks). Simply cut the lime leaf into very thin strips.
- Another way of preparing lime leaf is to place the torn leaves (stems removed) in a food processor or mini chopper and blitz until minced.

LIME & MANGO

Both sweet and sour fruits have important roles to play in Thai cooking.

In Thai cooking, sour flavors are balanced with sweet to achieve a tantalizing taste effect on the palate. Lime juice is one of the key sour ingredients. While lemon juice is sometimes added, lime is by far the more popular choice, with the smaller key lime type of fruit being the norm.

Lime zest may also be called for in some Thai recipes, though more often it is the zest from the makrud lime that would be used in Thailand. Lime is also frequently used in serving, with lime wedges placed at the side of soups or noodle dishes. This is done not only as a decorative element—the lime is meant to be squeezed over the food before eating.

Fresh mango offers the Thai cook both sweet and sour

Limes

- The limes used in Thailand are similar to American key limes, so if your supermarket carries this type of lime, be sure to pick up a bag for your Thai cooking.
- Smaller limes tend to be less acidic and slightly sweeter in flavor, although you do have do deal with seeds.
- In place of key limes, regular (large) limes make a fine substitute, and are readily available all times of the year.

Lime Juice and Zest

- It's always a good idea to have 2–3 limes at your disposal, even if the recipe only calls for 1. Adding extra lime juice is one of the things you can do to adjust the final flavor of Thai dishes.
- Lime juice can easily fix an over-salted or over-sweetened dish—just 1–2 tablespoons is usually all it takes.
- Lime zest is also sometimes called for in Thai cooking, and can be used (in a pinch) as a substitute for kaffir lime leaf.

flavors. When used in its unripe form, mango has an appealing sourness and makes for excellent salads. Green Mango Salad is by far the most famous of these dishes, the sourness of the mango being balanced out by a sweet and salty dressing.

Ripe mango is mainly featured in Thai desserts, but may be used to add sweetness to a stir-fry or condiment. Ripe mango is also used juiced for fruit drinks, or may simply be cut up and enjoyed as a treat unto itself.

ZOOM

Over 12 different varieties of mangos are grown each year in Thailand (April to June). Thai mangos vary in shape, size, and color: some are oval, others are oblong with tapered tips. Mangos are ripe when they are no longer entirely green and red on the outside, but are orange or yellow, and can be indented with your thumb. Mangos should be fragrant when you hold them to your nose.

Mango

- When cutting a mango, remember there is a stone at the fruit's center.
- The easiest way to cut a mango is to turn it on its side and make an off-center slice down through the fruit. Then turn the mango and do the same on the other side: this will give you 2 wide, cup-shaped pieces of fruit.
- Using a tablespoon, scoop the flesh out of each portion, or use a knife to cut the flesh into cubes before scooping it out.

Green Mango

- Green, unripe mangos can usually be found in supermarket fruit stalls among the ripe mangos.
- If you're planning to use the green mango for salad, be sure the mangos you choose are green (they may have tinges of red) and firm. If you can indent the flesh with your thumb, the mango is too ripe.
- To shred the green mango, simply peel away the skin, then either use a large-size grater to grate the flesh or a knife to cut it into thin shards or matchstick-like pieces.

PINEAPPLE & PAPAYA

These sweet and succulent fruits are used in many savory Thai dishes.

Pineapple and papaya: two incredible Thai fruits that are both healthy and undeniably delicious. Once you start using these two tropical fruits in your cooking, it seems there is no end to the kinds of Thai dishes you can create with them.

When visiting Thailand, one of the first dishes you are likely to try is Pineapple Fried Rice—often it is served in a pineapple boat (a carved-out pineapple). Pineapple is also used in other savory dishes, such as salads, stir-fries, and curries. It is especially beautiful when paired with shrimp.

While fresh pineapple is mainly used to add natural sweetness to various Thai dishes, papaya is used for both its sweet and sour properties. Like mango, papaya is sometimes eaten

Choosing a Fresh Pineapple

- When shopping for a pineapple, look for flesh that is still firm but may be slightly indented with your thumb.
- When ripe, the skin of the pineapple turns from green to yellow, so look for a pineapple that is between these two colors. If the flesh is very soft, the pineapple is overripe.
- One of the best tests for choosing a pineapple is to try lifting it by one of the uppermost leaves. If the leaf separates from the fruit, the pineapple is ready to be eaten.

Cutting a Fresh Pineapple

- There are several ways to cut a pineapple.
- One is to simply slice off the skin and cut the fruit up into chunks, with the core of the pineapple normally cut out and discarded (though it is also edible).
- Another way is to slice off one side of the pineapple, then use your knife to cut around the perimeter of the fruit. Use a tablespoon to scoop out the fruit. You will be left with a hollow pineapple "boat" that can be used for serving.

when not yet ripe, and is especially popular in salads. In fact, the most popular salad in Thailand is made with unripe shredded papaya, known as Green Papaya Salad (or, as it is sometimes called in Thailand, Paw Paw Salad).

But ripe papaya is also used in Thai salads, and is especially good when paired with shrimp or chicken. Fresh papaya may also be served as a side dish at breakfast, or as a simple but delicious dessert.

ZOOM

In North America, there are two types of papaya sold in most supermarkets. One is very large and long (Caribbean type), while the other is quite small and rounded (Hawaiian type). Both are delicious when fully ripe. To make fresh papaya taste even better, drizzle over a little lime. Freshly squeezed lime juice magically brings out the taste and sweetness of fresh papaya.

Choosing a Ripe Papaya

- Papayas are ripe when the skin turns from green to orange, and the outside can be indented with your thumb.
- To prepare papaya for eating, simply slice the fruit in half lengthwise. Crack open the papaya and scrape out the seeds.
- Now you can either scoop out the flesh, or slice up the fruit.
- Eat as you would watermelon slices, or cut off the skin and slice the flesh up into cubes. Drizzle over freshly squeezed lime juice, and enjoy.

Green Papaya

- Since it is often difficult to tell a green papaya from one that is ripening, green papayas are best purchased from an Asian food store or market (where they are labeled as green).
- To prepare a green papaya, simply cut it in half, scrape out the seeds (which are white when unripe, and black when ripe), and then peel off the skin.
- Grate or shred the flesh for salad, or cut it into bite-size pieces for curries, soups, or other savory dishes.

SHALLOTS & CUCUMBERS

Add these two fresh ingredients to your Thai shopping list.

Shallots are a small type of allium with garlicky overtones that pair beautifully with Thai food. Here in the West, shallots are still considered a kind of gourmet item that is often only purchased when cooking special gourmet dishes. In Thailand, however, shallots are an everyday item that is preferred over onions for their milder flavor and lower acid content. In fact, shallots are thought to have originated in Asia, and are more of a commonplace item in the marketplaces there than they are here.

Cucumber is another fresh item that should be added to your Thai shopping list. It is especially valued in salads, but cucumber also makes an appearance in hot dishes, being added right at the end of the cooking process in order to keep the fresh crispness and flavor present. Cucumber is

Shallots

- In Thailand, shallots are called hom, which means "fragrant."
- The preferred type of shallot is the red-purple variety, which is fortunately available here in North America.
- Although shallots are a little pricey, usually only ½ to 1 shallot is needed to flavor a dish, plus shallots store well: when refrigerated, they will keep for many months.
- If you can't find shallots or happen to run out—or you're watching your budget—the best substitute is purple onion.

Preparing Shallots

- Diced or minced shallots form the basis of many Thai dishes; in fact, along with minced garlic, shallots form the start of most Thai stir-fry recipes.
- Shallots are also commonly minced and pounded (or processed) as part of a curry paste or sauce.
- Sometimes minced shallots are fried until crispy and used as a crunchy, flavorful topping (this is also true for garlic).
- When shopping for shallots, seek out red-purple shallots with tight (not loose) skin.

especially refreshing when added to spicy soups or a hot shrimp curry, for example.

In Thailand, cucumber slices are also often used as a garnish for fish and seafood, or any dish that is laid out on a platter and meant to be shared (steamed or whole fish, or grilled or broiled beef, for example).

Sometimes cucumbers and shallots are pickled together in bottles and enjoyed as a side dish or condiment.

ZOOM

In traditional palace-style Thai cuisine (specially prepared dishes for the royal family), cucumber is one of many vegetables that are carved into beautiful flowers and other decorative designs for garnishing. In fact, vegetable carving has been elevated to a kind of art form in Thailand, with special tools used for the task. It is a skill that requires much patience and creativity.

Cucumbers

- In Thailand, cucumbers are eaten both fresh and as a last-minute addition to cooked dishes such as curries.
- Oftentimes they are carved into fancy shapes and used to garnish special Thai dishes, or they may simply be sliced or cut into chunks and enjoyed as part of a vegetable platter (together with a spicy or flavorful dip).
- When adding cucumber to soups or curries, cut the cucumber lengthwise, then chop it into chunks (rather than slices). This helps keep the seeds (and juice) from falling out.

Preparing Cucumber

- In Thailand, presentation is very important, and oftentimes the cucumber will be carved into leaf-like designs.
- An easier alternative is to make cucumber "ribbons." Be sure to wash the outside of the cucumber well and dry it. Then, using a potato peeler, create ribbon-like strips by peeling it, working from the outside of the cucumber in. If the ribbons are too wide to be eaten easily, simply slice them in half lengthwise.

CHILIES & LEMONGRASS

These two ingredients have become synonymous with Thai cooking.

Thai red chilies, sometimes known as "bird's eye chilies," are not, as some would assume, native to Thailand. Chilies were brought to Thailand by Portuguese traders many centuries ago, and have been an important part of the cuisine ever since. Before the arrival of chilies, Thai food was still fairly spicy, with cooks using black, white, and green peppercorns to add the desired level of heat. These days, however, one can't imagine eating Thai food without seeing (or tasting) at least a little fresh-cut chili. Red chilies are the most popular, but green and yellow chilies are also used.

Chili may be added to a Thai recipe in various forms: as a whole chili, as finely minced or sliced chili, as ground-up chili

Fresh Thai Red Chilies

- Most Asian stores sell fresh red chilies either in small packets or in bulk.
- Unlike the plumper American red chilies, Thai red chilies are small and thin, and are often called "bird's eye chilies" because the part where the stem meets the pepper looks like a bird's eye.
- Because these chilies are extremely hot, many Thai recipes will suggest removing the seeds and cooking (or garnishing) only with the red chili casing.

Dried Chilies

- If you can't find fresh red chilies at your local Asian food store, look for them in their dried form—in clear plastic packets.
- In Thailand, chili powder is made from dried red chilies such as these (usually they are roasted first).
- If you'd rather not be bothered with grinding up dried chilies, all supermarkets sell both dried chili flakes and cayenne pepper.
- Both of these items can be used to spice up a variety of Thai dishes, especially if you can't find fresh red chilies.

powder, or as fresh-cut chilies as part of a condiment (often together with soy sauce or fish sauce).

Lemongrass is another ingredient that we have come to associate with Thai cooking, though it is also used in Malaysia, Singapore, Indonesia, Vietnam, and other Southeast Asian countries. Lemongrass is a very fibrous herb and therefore requires preparation before use. Sometimes whole pieces of lemongrass are added for a touch of flavor to soups and curries, while at other times only finely minced lemongrass will give you the strong lemony taste you are looking for.

ZOOM

For some people, too much chili irritates the stomach, which makes it difficult to enjoy spicy Thai dishes. If you suffer from a sensitive stomach, ulcers, or heartburn, consider substituting your regular chilies and chili powder with cayenne pepper. Unlike regular chili, cayenne actually helps heal the stomach. Cayenne chilies can also be grown fresh in your garden or in pots on a warm patio.

Lemongrass

- Lemongrass is sold both fresh and frozen—look for it at your local Asian food store.
- Frozen lemongrass comes either as stalks chopped down to half their size, or already minced and ready for cooking. The latter is sold in small plastic (frozen) tubs.
- Lemongrass is also easy to grow and makes a beautiful house or garden plant. Simply buy a few fresh stalks and set them in water (as you would flowers). Roots will eventually grow; then plant the stalks in a pot or the ground.

Preparing Lemongrass

- Because lemongrass is very tough and fibrous, when purchasing it fresh you will need to do some prep before adding it to your recipe.
- To prepare fresh lemongrass for cooking, first remove the bulb and upper stem. Cut the remaining stalk into thin slices. Then either pound the slices with a pestle and mortar or process them with a mini chopper or food processor.
- You will end up with small, softened bits of lemongrass, which can be cooked and consumed.

EGGPLANT & BOK CHOY

These healthy vegetables are enjoyed either as a side dish or as part of a main entrée.

Not all of the vegetables used in Thailand are available here in North America, but two that are plentiful no matter where you live are eggplant and bok choy. Both work well with a variety of Thai dishes, including soups, stir-fries, and curries.

There are many different types of eggplant to choose from in stores these days. While Thai eggplants are not always available, both the Chinese and American varieties can be found in most large supermarkets.

Bok choy is a kind of Chinese cabbage, and is a good standard green vegetable that works well as a side dish, or as part of a main entrée. Bok choy actually belongs to the turnip family, though it is also a distant relative of American cabbage. It

Thai Eggplant

- If you live in the vicinity of a good Asian market, you may be able to find Thai eggplant.
- This variety is very small and round—roughly the size of golf balls. They may be white or green, and are sometimes called "pea eggplant."
- A second type of Thai eggplant is long and thin, like those in American stores, except they are light green in color. This type is called *makua* in Thai. The taste of these eggplants is very similar to American or Chinese eggplant.

American and Chinese Eggplant

- The most common eggplant found in North American supermarkets is a large, pear-shaped eggplant with very dark purple skin. It is usually called American or globe eggplant.
- A second type of eggplant, which is just as long but thin and with light purple skin, is called Chinese eggplant.
- Chinese and Japanese eggplants are very similar, with the Japanese being slightly thicker but with the same long shape.

is very nutritious, and has the advantage of storing well in the refrigerator.

Bok choy comes in different sizes and even different shades of green, from baby bok choy (the smallest leaves) to standard size bok choy, which is closer to cabbage in size, except oblong in shape. It is thought that bok choy, among other Chinese cabbages, has been cultivated in Asia for more than five thousand years. Recently it has also become a popular vegetable in North America, with seeds now available for our own home gardens.

ZOOM

For several centuries in Europe, eggplant was blamed for a variety of illnesses. Its "bad reputation" was carried to England and then on to the United States. All of this changed when Thomas Jefferson began experimenting with the vegetable in his Virginia garden, trying out different varieties to see which would flourish. He is now credited with introducing eggplant to North America.

Bok Choy

- Bok choy is available in various sizes and varieties. Standard bok choy looks similar to Napa cabbage, except it is narrower at the bottom and fans out into leaves at the top.
- Bok choy may also be labeled as Chinese chard or Chinese mustard cabbage.
- When preparing bok choy, remember that the lower white stem will require more cooking that the thin upper leaves; it is therefore a good idea to chop up each piece into sections, cooking the white parts first, and adding the green leaves last.

Baby Bok Choy

- Because it isn't as large as regular bok choy, baby bok choy is a wonderfully easy vegetable to cook with, and because its leaves are so small, one can often simply cook them whole, without the need for a lot of chopping.
- Like regular bok choy, baby bok choy has a natural crunchy texture that is highly valued in Thai cooking.
- At the same time, it is also more tender than larger varieties, so be sure not to overcook it or you will lose its delicious crunchiness.

FRESH HERBS: CORIANDER & BASIL

Used often in Thai cooking, these herbs add flavor, freshness, and visual appeal.

By far the most common fresh herbs used in Thai cooking are coriander and basil. Coriander has several names, including cilantro (from the Spanish) and Chinese parsley. In Thai cooking, all parts of this herb are used, including the roots, stems, leaves, and the dried seeds (for ground coriander).

Fresh coriander is not only used for garnishing Thai dishes, but is also frequently added as part of a spice or curry paste.

Basil is another quintessential Thai ingredient that provides an extra note of flavor to many Thai dishes. There are various types of basil being grown and sold these days, from Italian basil (sweet basil), to Greek basil (a globe-shaped plant with tiny leaves), lemon basil (which has a lemony

Fresh Coriander

- Fresh coriander is usually sold in a bundle—look for it in the fresh herbs section of your local supermarket.
- Be sure to wash coriander well, as the leaves make it easy for sand and grit to get caught and find its way into your food.
- Like basil, coriander is a very easy herb to grow; it isn't invasive, but will readily replant itself. To avoid this, be sure to pick the seed heads before they drop (the fresh seeds make for wonderful Thai green curry!).

Coriander Paste

- In Thailand, coriander root is routinely used to add a strong coriander flavor to various dishes.
- For most North Americans, coriander root can be difficult to find, but making a fresh green paste with the stems and leaves of fresh coriander works as a good substitute for curries, sauces, marinades, and other Thai recipes.
- This can be done easily by pounding the coriander with a pestle and mortar, or processing it with a mini food chopper or food processor.

scent), and traditional Thai basil.

Among Thai basils, there is the standard variety (with purple stems and a slightly minty flavor), Thai lemon basil (lemon scented and flavored), and Thai holy basil. Depending on which type you use, the flavor might be sweet (especially if you use Italian basil) or slightly bitter (most Thai basils).

Both basil and coriander are easy to grow, either in pots on a sunny windowsill, or in your garden. The most popular cultivar of Thai basil in North America is called Queen of Siam. Look for the seeds at any reputable garden center.

ZOOM

While holy basil is associated with Thai cooking, the name actually refers to a different herb native to India known as tulsi. This herb has been used for centuries in traditional Indian medicine, and can often be seen in mass planting around Indian temples. It is called "holy" is because of its use in meditation: this herb is said to calm and assist spiritual seekers toward enlightenment.

Thai Basil

- Oftentimes basil isn't identified as being a certain kind; however, you can recognize Thai basil by its purplish hue.
- The stem, plus any flowers that might be present, are purple in tone. The leaves tend to be long and not as broad as other types of basil, and also darker green in color.
- Thai basil has a slight licorice taste, and may also have a minty flavor. It is not as sweet as other types of basil, but the slight bitterness works incredibly well with Thai food.

Sweet Basil

- Sweet basil is by far the most common variety found in North American grocery stores and also at fresh food markets.
- The leaves of sweet basil are bright, light green, and broad compared to those of Thai basil.
- Sweet basil works well for Mediterranean fare, and may also be used in Thai cooking, especially if you prefer sweet over bitter tastes. However, be sure to use a generous amount; you will need much more sweet basil (than Thai basil) to make its presence known.

THAI SPRING ROLLS

Served as appetizers in North America, in Thailand spring rolls are also enjoyed as snacks.

Spring rolls are a common street food in Thailand and are enjoyed as snacks nearly any time of day or night. They are fried up in large batches with a variety of fillings ranging from shrimp to chicken and vegetables.

Oftentimes standard spring rolls fail to live up to one's taste expectations, but not these! You'll find the filling has loads of flavor, mainly because it isn't just tossed together, but is actually stir-fried before being rolled up and fried.

You want the vegetables in the filling to retain some crispness, so do not overcook when stir-frying; everything will be heated through thoroughly when the rolls are deep-fried. *Yield: Serves 4–8*

Ingredients

2-3 Tbsp. oil, plus 1 cup oil

2 cloves garlic, minced

1 Tbsp. grated galangal OR ginger

3 green onions, sliced

1 red chili, minced, OR 1/2 tsp. cayenne

1/2 cup shredded cabbage

1 cup shiitake mushrooms, chopped

1/2 cup raw or cooked baby shrimp

2 1/2-3 cups bean sprouts

1 pkg. spring roll wrappers

1/2 cup fresh coriander, chopped

1/2 cup fresh basil, roughly chopped

Stir-Fry Sauce:

3 Tbsp. soy sauce

2 Tbsp. fish sauce

2 Tbsp. lime juice

1/2 tsp. sugar

Thai Spring Rolls

- Stir together the stir-fry sauce ingredients and set aside.
- Warm your wok over medium-high heat. Add 1–2 Tbsp. oil, then the garlic, galangal or ginger, green onion, and chili (if using). Stir-fry 1 minute. Add a little water to the wok when it becomes dry.
- Add cabbage, mushrooms, shrimp, and stir-fry sauce. Stir-fry 1–2 minutes, until the shrimp and mushrooms are cooked. Remove from heat and add bean sprouts. Toss, then taste test for salt, adding 1 Tbsp. more fish sauce if desired.

• • • • RECIPE VARIATION • • • •

To make this recipe vegetarian, replace the shrimp with ½ cup medium-firm tofu. Finely chop the tofu so it absorbs the flavors of the stir-fry. When making the stir-fry sauce, replace the fish sauce with vegetarian fish sauce OR 1–2 Tbsp. vegetarian oyster sauce. If you can't find either of these, use the following combination: 4 Tbsp. soy sauce, 1 Tbsp. sherry, 2 Tbsp. lime juice, and ½ tsp. sugar.

Making spring rolls is a great way to use up leftover roasted chicken or turkey, but you can also use fresh chicken, turkey, or pork. Chop the meat up well, or use the ground variety. For cooked meat, follow the recipe exactly, adding it when you would normally add the shrimp. If using fresh chicken or pork, add it at the beginning of the recipe, together with the garlic, ginger, green onion, and chili.

Wrapping the Spring Rolls

- Place the first wrapper on a clean working surface. Scoop a heaping tablespoon of the filling onto the wrapper (if using large wrappers, you will need more). Try not to include too much of the liquid.
- Spread the filling along the width of the wrapper. Sprinkle with some fresh coriander and basil.
- Fold the left and right sides of wrapper over filling. Lift up the bottom of the wrapper, tuck over, and roll to the other end. Secure the roll by wetting the tip with water or a little beaten egg and pressing firmly.

Frying the Spring Rolls

- Place 1 cup oil or more (it should be 1 inch deep) in your wok over medium-high heat. To test whether the oil is hot enough, dip one corner of a spring roll into the pan. If the roll begins to sizzle and cook, the oil is ready.
- Fry spring rolls 1 minute on each side, or until they turn light to medium golden-brown.
- Drain the rolls on paper towels while you finish frying the rest.
- Serve with Thai sweet chili sauce for dipping.

EGG ROLLS

These mini egg rolls make a great party finger food.

Like spring rolls (which are made with a thin, wheat wrapper, egg rolls (made with an egg-based wrapper) are a common snack food in Thailand and can be purchased from food stalls along the roadside, on the street, or in the marketplaces. Here in the West, egg rolls are more likely to be enjoyed as an appetizer. Because this egg roll recipe makes mini-sized rolls, they're also perfect for serving at parties as a finger food.

Egg rolls can be made vegetarian or with shredded chicken—they are delightful both ways. If your children will be eating these egg rolls, serve them up with traditional Chinese plum sauce in place of Thai sweet chili sauce, which, although mild, is still too spicy for most young taste buds.

Yield: Serves 4–6

Ingredients

1 Tbsp. oil for stir-frying, plus 1 cup or more for deep-frying

3 cloves garlic

1 red or green chili, minced (optional)

5–6 fresh shiitake mushrooms, chopped

1/4 cup white wine or sherry

1 cup grated or finely chopped cabbage

3 green onions, sliced

1 egg

3 cups fresh bean sprouts

1 package small egg roll wrappers

Stir-Fry Sauce:

2 Tbsp. fish sauce (plus more to taste)

1 Tbsp. soy sauce

1 Tbsp. lime juice

1 tsp. brown sugar

Egg Rolls

- Mix all stir-fry sauce ingredients together in a cup and set aside. Place a wok or large frying pan over medium-high heat. Add 1–2 Tbsp. oil and swirl around, then add the garlic and chili (if using). Stir-fry 30 seconds to release the fragrance.
- Add the mushrooms plus 1–2 Tbsp. wine or sherry. Stir-fry 1–2 minutes, or until mushrooms have softened.

RECIPE VARIATION

To make these egg rolls with chicken, add ½ cup finely chopped fresh or cooked chicken and only ½ cup of shredded cabbage. Add uncooked chicken at the beginning of the stir-fry, with the garlic and chili. Stir-fry 2–3 minutes, adding sherry if your wok or pan becomes dry. Then add the mushrooms and continue as written. If using cooked chicken, add it with the cabbage and green onions.

MAKE IT EASY

Knowing when oil is hot enough for deep-frying takes experience, but even seasoned chefs have to test it to make sure. One of the ways to do this is to drop in a small cube of bread. If the oil is ready, the bread will brown in 30 seconds or less. For this recipe, you can also try dipping a corner of one of the egg rolls into the oil. If it begins to sizzle and cook, the oil is hot enough for cooking.

Stir-frying the Filling

- Add the cabbage and green onions, and continue to stir-fry in the same way 2 more minutes. Add more wine or sherry if wok becomes dry.
- Push ingredients aside and break the egg into the middle of your wok, quickly stir-frying to scramble it.
- Add the bean sprouts and stir-fry sauce. Stir-fry everything together 1 minute or less, allowing bean sprouts to remain crisp.
- Remove from heat and taste test. If not salty enough, add more fish sauce until desired taste is achieved.

Wrapping the Egg Rolls

- Place a wrapper on a clean work space with the pointy edge facing you. Place 1 heaping tablespoon of filling width-wise along the wrapper. Fold over the sides, then tuck over the end and roll away from you. Secure the tip by brushing with water and pressing firmly.
- Place 1 cup oil in a wok or small frying pan over medium-high heat (oil should be 1 inch deep). Fry the rolls until golden-brown and set on paper towels to drain.
- Serve hot with Thai sweet chili sauce.

MIANG KHUM

Pop one of these leaves into your mouth and experience an explosion of Thai flavors!

This special Thai finger food is not very well known in North America, but one day it is sure to be! Though it looks innocent enough, the taste of Miang Khum is truly explosive. Various flavors and textures all hit the palate at once, awakening the taste buds as well as all your other senses.

Though in Thailand this wonderful concoction would be placed on pieces of banana leaf (which are inedible), here leaves of spinach are used, which adds a healthy touch of greens to the dish. If you happen to have extra-large basil leaves on hand, they will work too—or make a combination of both spinach and basil leaves and see which one you prefer.

Yield: Serves 4–6

Ingredients

¼ cup dry unsweetened baking coconut

¼ cup dry sweetened baking coconut

¼ cup very small dried shrimp (the smallest you can find at Asian food stores)

¼ cup dry roasted unsalted peanuts, ground, plus some for serving

1 Tbsp. grated galangal or ginger

2 cloves garlic, minced

½–1 tsp. chili powder

1 tsp. fish sauce (or more to taste)

1 tsp. lime juice

1 bunch large spinach leaves and/or 1 bunch extra-large basil leaves

Optional: fresh-cut red chilies

To serve: 1 lime cut into wedges

Miang Khum

- Place both types of dry shredded coconut in a dry frying pan over medium-high heat. Stir continuously, dry-frying the coconut for 1–2 minutes or until it turns light golden-brown and is very fragrant.
- Immediately tip most of the toasted coconut into a mixing bowl, setting a little aside for the garnish.

RECIPE VARIATION

Another popular way to enjoy this finger food is to place the shrimp mixture in a bowl in the middle of the table. Provide small dishes of extra toasted coconut, ground peanuts, and fresh-cut chilies. Surround these bowls with leaves (lettuce leaves can also be used in place of spinach or basil), and garnish with wedges of lime. Now have each person assemble his or her own appetizer wraps.

ZOOM

The tiny dried shrimp in this recipe can be found at Asian food stores, usually sold in packets in the refrigerated section. If you happen to be in your local Chinatown, you can also check any stores selling dried bulk items, such as dried and salted fish. Usually these shrimp are sold by weight. They should be salmon in color and feel firm but slightly pliable to the touch (not crumbly).

Preparing the Dried Shrimp

- Using a pestle and mortar or food processor, pound or process the shrimp until you have powder-like bits (as fine as you can make it). Add this to the mixing bowl with the toasted coconut. Also add the ground peanuts and grated galangal or ginger.
- Finally, add the garlic, chili powder, fish sauce, and lime juice. Stir well.
- Do a taste test, adding more chili if you'd prefer it spicier, or more fish sauce for a saltier, more flavorful taste.

Spooning Mixture onto Leaves

- Rinse and spin-dry the spinach and/or basil. Arrange leaves face-up on a serving platter, pressing them open if necessary. Spoon some of the shrimp mixture onto each leaf. Top with a little more toasted coconut and ground peanuts, and serve with some fresh-cut chilies sprinkled over (if using) and wedges of lime on the side.
- To eat: Squeeze over a little lime juice, then pop the entire leaf into your mouth. Enjoy the wondrous mixture of flavors and textures dancing across your taste buds.

GOLDEN POUCHES

These bite-size Thai snacks make an attractive appetizer to serve guests.

This pretty Thai appetizer is also known as "golden purses," and, indeed, one can almost imagine these tiny bags being filled with money or gold. In Thailand, the pouches are made with various fillings, including ground chicken, pork, or shrimp. They are quite decorative, and therefore make a pretty appetizer to serve guests or to present at a party.

The pouches can be fried and eaten straightaway, or they can be tied with chives for a final finishing touch. If you don't have fresh chives, you can try substituting some of the thinner leaves from green onions. Just be sure to tie them very gently, or they will break.

Yield: Serves 6+

Ingredients

½ cup cooked chicken, crab, or shrimp

1 package fresh wonton wrappers

1 cup (or more) oil for deep-frying

Fresh chives to tie the pouches

Spice Paste:

3 cloves garlic

¼ cup fresh coriander leaves and stems

1 fresh red chili, minced, or substitute 1 tsp. chili sauce, or ½ tsp. cayenne pepper

3 green onions, sliced

¼ tsp. white pepper

1 Tbsp. fish sauce

2 Tbsp. soy sauce

Golden Pouches

- Place meat in a food processor or chopper. Add all the spice paste ingredients, and process well.
- Or simply slice up the meat as finely as you can and mix it together with the spice paste.
- Taste test this mixture, adding ½ Tbsp. more fish sauce if not salty enough. If too salty, add a generous squeeze of lime juice.

RECIPE VARIATION

Fried wontons are another popular snack food. To make them, follow the instructions for the filling as written. Lay out the wonton wraps and place about 1 tsp. of filling in the middle of each one. Moisten the outside of each wrapper with water and simply fold in half from tip to tip to make triangular-shaped wontons. Press firmly to secure, then fry and serve with Thai sweet chili sauce.

ZOOM

Thais are known to eat between meals, sometimes even preferring numerous snacks to the standard 3 meals per day. Luckily, there is always an abundance of finger foods available on Thai streets and marketplaces. In Bangkok, all types of Thai dishes are served up on the street, from snack foods to desserts, drinks, and even main course dishes like satay and curry.

Wrapping the Pouches

- Spread wonton wrappers over a clean surface. Place about 1 tsp. of filling in the middle of each wrapper.
- Using a pastry brush or your fingers dipped in water, wet 1 inch around the periphery of each wrapper.
- Now lift up the sides of the wrapper and pinch them together over the filling.
- If the pouch does not stay closed, you need more water. Moisten well and pinch to close.

Frying the Pouches

- Place oil in a wok or small frying pan over medium-high heat (oil should be at least 1 inch deep). To test the oil, dip in a wonton wrapper—if it starts to sizzle and cook, the oil is hot enough.
- Lay pouches on their sides in the oil and fry 30 seconds to 1 minute. Turn and fry the other side. When pouches are uniformly golden-brown, remove and drain on paper towels.
- Tie each pouch with a chive and serve with Thai sweet chili sauce.

FISH CAKES

These fish cakes are crisp on the outside and melt-in-your-mouth tender on the inside.

Fish cakes are sold all over Thailand, but especially in coastal areas where fish is fresh and plentiful. The following recipe is a slight departure from traditional Thai fish cakes, which tend to be rubbery in texture. These fish cakes are crisp on the outside, and deliciously tender on the inside. In order to get this kind of crisp coating, the cakes are rolled in rice cracker crumbs instead of flour.

Nearly any type of filleted fish will work for this recipe, from salmon to sole to tilapia. One of the key ingredients is lime leaf, which marries beautifully with the fish as well as the overall taste of these cakes.

Yield: Serves 4

Ingredients

7–8 oz. fresh or frozen fish fillets (such as salmon, sole, cod, tilapia, or snapper)

4 kaffir lime leaves, fresh or frozen

1 package plain or sesame-flavored rice crackers (3.5 oz.)

3 green onions, sliced

1 fresh red chili, OR 1–2 tsp. chili sauce

1 Tbsp. lime juice

1 Tbsp. fish sauce

1 Tbsp. oyster sauce

1 egg

Optional: 1 Tbsp. mayonnaise (not really Thai, but it makes the cakes more moist)

1 cup (or more) oil for deep-frying

To serve: Wedges of fresh lime or lemon, plus Thai sweet chili sauce for dipping

Thai Fish Cakes

- If using frozen fish, quickly thaw it by dunking it in lukewarm water. Prepare fresh fish by quickly rinsing and patting it dry.
- Run your fingers over both sides of the fillets and remove any bones you might find.
- If using frozen lime leaves, briefly rinse them under hot water. Use a pair of clean scissors to snip them into strips.
- Discard the stem and central vein of each leaf. Set the lime leaf strips aside.

MAKE IT EASY

Thai fish cakes can easily be prepared up to a day in advance. Just make the cakes and roll in the rice cracker crumbs, as instructed. Then cover and place in the refrigerator. When ready to cook, roll them once again in cracker crumbs and fry them up. Serve immediately, or keep them warm in the oven for up to 30 minutes.

GREEN LIGHT

Because of concern for depleting fish populations, it's good to keep in mind which types of fish are considered plentiful and which are being over-fished. Some safe bets include the following: herring, mackerel, tilapia, Pacific halibut, Pacific cod (not Atlantic), and white sea bass. The other alternative is to buy organic fish, which come from organic fish farms and are therefore sustainably grown.

Making the Rice Cracker Crumbs

- Place rice crackers in a food processor. Process well to create a fine consistency (similar to a powder).
- Place ½ cup of these rice cracker crumbs on a large plate. Leave the rest in the processor.
- Add the fish to the food processor, plus the lime leaf strips, onion, chili, lime juice, fish sauce, oyster sauce, egg, and mayonnaise (if using). Process well.

Frying the Cakes

- Scoop the fish mixture into your hands and pat to form individual cakes. If mixture is too wet to stick together, add a little flour.
- Once all the cakes are formed, roll them in the rice cracker crumbs to coat.
- Fry the cakes in hot oil (at least 1 inch deep) for 1–2 minutes per side, or until they are uniformly golden-brown.
- Drain the cakes on paper towels and serve while still hot with lime or lemon wedges and Thai sweet chili sauce.

LETTUCE WRAPS

These lettuce wraps make a fun appetizer, finger food, or main entrée.

Lettuce wraps make a wonderful appetizer, but are also equally satisfying as a main course dish. Crunchy and fresh, these warm lettuce wraps make a great way to get your greens, not only because of the lettuce that is used in place of rice or flour wraps, but also because there are plenty of vegetables in the filling.

The one complaint some people have with lettuce wraps is that they're a tad messy: one must eat them with one's hands rather than with a fork and knife (or spoon). But this is also what makes lettuce wraps so much fun to eat! The best way to serve lettuce wraps is simply to place all the ingredients (lettuce leaves, filling, and toppings) on the table and let everyone roll his or her own.

Yield: Serves 4

Ingredients

2 Tbsp. oil

2 shallots, diced

3 cloves garlic, minced

1 Tbsp. grated galangal or ginger

1 red chili, minced, OR 1 tsp. chili sauce

2 Tbsp. sherry or white wine

1/2 cup cooked chicken, OR cooked baby shrimp (fresh or frozen)

4–5 shiitake mushrooms, thinly sliced

1/2 cup shredded cabbage

3 green onions, cut into matchsticks

2 Tbsp. lime juice

2 Tbsp. regular soy sauce

2 Tbsp. fish sauce (or more to taste)

1 Tbsp. oyster sauce

1 egg

2 cups bean sprouts

1 head iceberg lettuce

Toppings: Fresh basil and ground peanuts

Thai Lettuce Wraps

- Place a wok or large frying pan over medium-high heat. When pan is hot, add oil. Swirl around, then add the shallots, garlic, galangal (or ginger), and chili.
- Stir-fry 1–2 minutes, or until shallots and galangal (or ginger) are soft.
- If wok or pan becomes dry, add 2 Tbsp. sherry or white wine to keep ingredients frying nicely.

• • • • RECIPE VARIATION • • • •

Vegetarian Lettuce Wraps. To make this recipe vegetarian, substitute ½ cup medium-firm tofu (plain or flavored) for the chicken or shrimp. Instead of oyster sauce, use vegetarian oyster sauce OR ground bean sauce (both are available at most large Asian food stores). In place of the fish sauce, use 2½ Tbsp. soy sauce, or look for vegetarian fish sauce, which is available at Vietnamese food stores.

Lettuce Wraps with Crunchy Noodles. To make a crunchy noodle topping (as served in many restaurants), heat 1 cup oil in your wok. When oil is hot enough to brown a cube of bread in 30 seconds or less, add a handful of rice vermicelli noodles straight from the package. If the oil is hot enough, the noodles will instantly puff up. Remove from the oil with tongs and use to top lettuce wraps (or other dishes).

Stir-frying the Filling

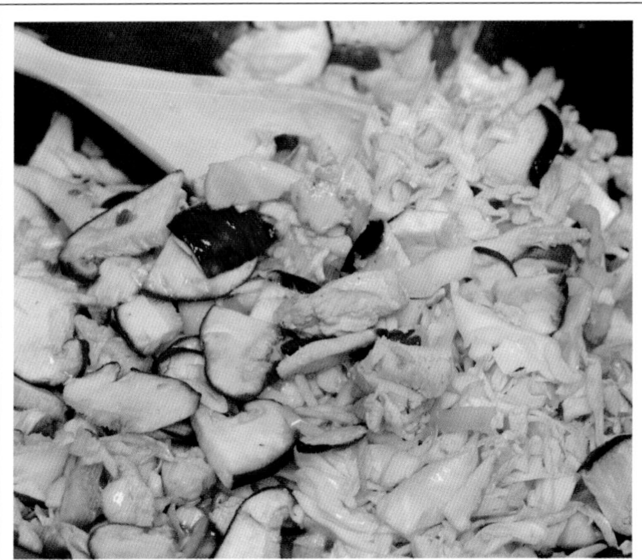

- Add the chicken or shrimp, plus shiitake mushrooms, cabbage, and green onions. Also add the lime juice, soy sauce, fish sauce, and oyster sauce. Stir-fry 2–3 minutes.
- Push ingredients to the side and crack egg into the center of the wok. Stir-fry quickly to scramble, then mix the egg with the other ingredients.
- Add bean sprouts and stir-fry briefly (to keep sprouts crisp). Remove from heat and taste test the stir-fry, adding up to 1 more Tbsp. fish sauce if not salty enough.

Assembling the Wraps

- Cut off the stem (but not all the core) from the head of lettuce. Separate the leaves.
- Place the leaves, the stir-fried filling, and the toppings on your table, allowing guests to put together their own wraps.
- To assemble: Place 1–2 heaping tablespoons of the warm filling in the center of a lettuce leaf. Top with a sprinkling of fresh basil and peanuts, then wrap up and eat. Thai sweet chili sauce can be added as another topping for those who like it extra spicy.

TOM YUM GOONG

This world-famous Thai soup is both spicy and soothing.

Tom Yum Goong (Spicy Soup with Shrimp) has become known the world over as an intoxicating soup that both soothes the soul and stimulates the senses. Lemongrass is its most important ingredient, but other flavors that come into play include garlic, chili, lime, and lime leaf.

There are as many different versions of Tom Yum soup as there are Thai cooks, each one making it his or her own way; hence, there is some controversy over what constitutes authentic Tom Yum Goong. Some say it must never include coconut milk, while others insist a little coconut milk makes for a creamier, more satisfying soup. The following recipe treads a fine line between the two camps, with coconut milk being included as an optional ingredient.

Yield: Serves 4 as an appetizer

Ingredients

6 cups good-quality chicken stock

3 whole kaffir lime leaves

1 stalk lemongrass, minced, or 4 Tbsp. frozen prepared lemongrass

3 cloves garlic, minced

1–2 fresh red chilies, de-seeded and minced, OR 1–2 tsp. chili sauce

½ cup mushrooms, sliced

Juice of 1 lime (about ½ cup lime juice)

3 Tbsp. fish sauce

1–2 tsp. sugar, to taste

10–12 medium raw shrimp (thawed if using frozen), shells removed

Handful cherry tomatoes

Optional: ½–1 cup coconut milk

½ cup fresh basil

½ cup fresh coriander

Optional: Lime wedges for serving

Tom Yum Goong

- Place chicken stock in a large soup pot over high heat. Add the lime leaves and minced lemongrass.
- Boil the soup for 2–3 minutes to cook the lemongrass and release the fragrance of the lime leaf.
- Reduce heat to medium. Add the garlic, chili, mushrooms, lime juice, fish sauce and 1 tsp. sugar. Stir well and continue cooking 2–3 minutes, or until mushrooms are soft.

RECIPE VARIATION

This soup works well with a number of protein sources. Instead of adding only shrimp, try making this soup with mixed seafood. Include any or all of the following: mussels, scallops, squid, shrimp, clams, and/or chunks of filleted fish. Be sure to add ½–1 cup coconut milk as well. Coconut milk marries wonderfully with the flavors of seafood and will make this mixed seafood soup spectacular.

MAKE IT EASY

To prepare this soup ahead of time, boil the stock together with the lemongrass and lime leaf. Add the garlic, chili, mushrooms, lime juice, fish sauce, and sugar. Simmer, then cover and place in the refrigerator. When guests arrive, bring the soup to a boil and add the shrimp and tomatoes. Reduce heat and simmer until shrimp are cooked. Add the coconut milk and serve with the fresh herbs.

Simmering the Soup

- Add the shrimp and cherry tomatoes. Simmer 2–3 more minutes, or until the shrimp are pink and plump (avoid overcooking the shrimp, or they will lose their tenderness). Remove from heat.
- Taste test the soup, looking for a balance of these flavors: salty, sour, and spicy.
- If you prefer it saltier, add 1–2 more Tbsp. fish sauce. If it's too salty, add 1 Tbsp. more lime juice. If it's too sour, add 1 tsp. more sugar.

Adjusting the Flavors

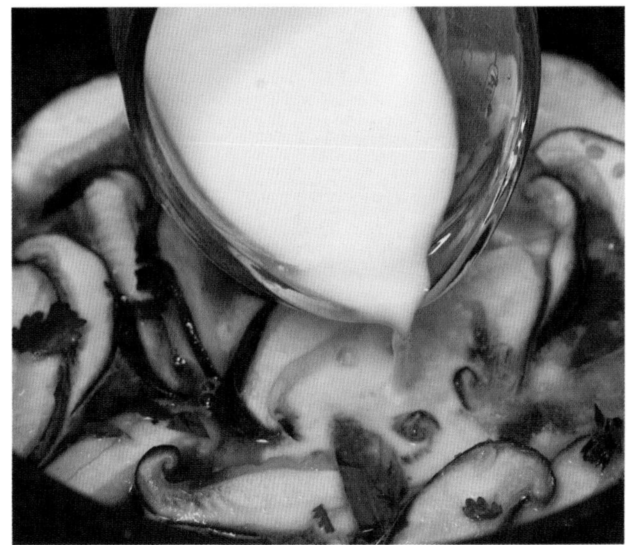

- If the soup is too spicy, or if the flavors are too pronounced—or if you simply prefer a creamier, richer tasting soup, add ½–1 cup coconut milk, stirring to dissolve over low heat.
- Avoid overheating the soup at this point, or you will lose the wonderful fresh taste of the coconut milk.
- To serve, ladle the soup into bowls and top with a little fresh basil and coriander. Lime wedges can also be served on the side.

TOM KHA GAI

This aromatic Thai version of chicken soup features lemongrass and creamy coconut milk.

Tom Kha Gai is yet another version of Tom Yum soup, this time made with chicken. But unlike Tom Yum Goong, everyone agrees that Tom Kha Gai is specifically made with coconut milk, so there is no question about the authenticity of this soup. Like many Western soups made with chicken, this Thai version is wonderfully soothing and nourishing, and is especially good if you happen to be suffering from a cold or the flu.

This soup recipe also makes an excellent way to use up leftover roast chicken or turkey. If you have leftover bones as well, throwing those into the soup pot will add even more flavor and nutrients to this splendid soup.

Yield: Serves 4 as an appetizer

Ingredients

6 cups good-quality chicken stock

2 fresh chicken breasts OR 1 1/2 cups leftover roasted chicken or turkey

1 lemongrass stalk, minced

3 whole kaffir lime leaves

3 cloves garlic, minced

1 Tbsp. grated galangal OR ginger

1 cup fresh shiitake mushrooms, sliced

1 red bell pepper, de-seeded and sliced

1 fresh red chili, minced, OR 1/2 tsp. cayenne pepper

1 can coconut milk

2 Tbsp. lime juice

3 Tbsp. fish sauce

1 tsp. sugar

1/2 cup fresh coriander leaves

Handful fresh basil leaves

2 green onions, sliced

Tom Kha Gai

- Place chicken stock in a large soup pot over high heat. While the stock is coming to a boil, cut the chicken (or turkey) into small pieces.
- Add the chicken plus the lemongrass, kaffir lime leaves, garlic, and galangal (or ginger) to the soup pot. Boil 5 minutes, or long enough to cook the fresh chicken.

ZOOM

Salty, spicy, sweet, and sour are sometimes known in Thai cooking as "the big four flavors." To be a good Thai cook, one must strive for the most delicious and tantalizing balance between these famous four. This is why taste testing and last-minute adjustments are so important. It can mean the difference between an excellent Thai dish and one that is merely mediocre.

MAKE IT EASY

If you are in a hurry, or if buying and preparing fresh lemongrass seems like too much work, there is a wonderful alternative. These days, it's easy to find frozen prepared lemongrass at most Asian food stores. It comes in a small tub already finely minced and of excellent quality. Keep the tub in your freezer; then, when you need it, simply scrape off 1-3 Tbsp. from the top with a tablespoon.

Adding the Vegetables

- Turn down the heat to medium. Slice the mushrooms and red bell pepper and add them to the soup. Also add the chili (or cayenne).
- Simmer 2–3 minutes, or until vegetables have softened but still retain much of their color and firmness.
- Reduce heat to low. Add the coconut milk, lime juice, fish sauce, and sugar, stirring well to incorporate.

Finding a Balance of Flavors

- Do a taste test, looking for a balance of salty, sour, sweet, and spicy. Add more fish sauce instead of salt to adjust the flavor and saltiness.
- If the soup is too spicy, add more coconut milk. If it's too sour, add a little more sugar. If it's too salty or too sweet, add more lime juice.
- Ladle the soup into bowls and top with sprinklings of fresh coriander, basil, and green onion.

EASY CRAB & CORN SOUP

A delicious soup that can be put together in just minutes.

We all have days when cooking a complicated recipe is the last thing we have the time or energy to do; yet, we would still prefer something healthy, hot, and tasty for dinner. On such days, this easy Thai soup is the perfect solution. With only a few items from your pantry, this soup can be put together in minutes; yet, it tastes like a gourmet treat. Creamy, nutritious, and Thai delicious, this soup both comforts and energizes.

The key ingredient in this dish is creamed corn, which is easy enough to find either at your local grocery store or in the back of your cupboard. Add some frozen, fresh, or canned crabmeat, and you have a soup that is truly satisfying. Even your kids will love it (just leave out the chili for them).
Yield: Serves 2 as a main entrée

Ingredients

4 cups good-quality chicken stock

3 kaffir lime leaves, left whole

1 shallot, minced

3 cloves garlic, minced

1 Tbsp. grated galangal OR ginger

1 fresh red chili, minced, OR 1/2 tsp. cayenne pepper OR 1 tsp. chili sauce

19 oz. can creamed corn

1 cup prepared cooked crab meat (drain if using frozen or canned crab)

2–3 Tbsp. fish sauce, to taste

1 Tbsp. lime juice

3/4 cup good-quality coconut milk

1 egg, lightly beaten

1/2 cup fresh coriander

Easy Crab & Corn Soup

- Place chicken stock in a large soup pot and place over high heat.
- Add the lime leaves, shallot, garlic, galangal (or ginger), and chili. Stir well to incorporate. Bring the soup to a rolling boil.
- Once the soup has reached a boil, reduce heat to medium.

• • • • RECIPE VARIATION • • • •

To make a Chinese-style version of this soup, use 1–1½ cups leftover roasted chicken or turkey instead of crab. Shred the meat by blitzing it in a food processor, or chop it up by hand, pulling the thickest pieces apart with your fingers to shred it. Add prepared meat to the soup and follow the recipe as written. If the soup turns out too thick, add a little more chicken stock and/or coconut milk.

ZOOM

Corn isn't usually thought of as a Thai food ingredient, but in fact, corn is an important crop in northern regions of the country and accounts for as much as 7 percent of the world market share. Most of the canned mini corncobs sold in North American supermarkets come from Thailand and are of excellent quality. These tiny cobs are great for adding to stir-fries, soups, and even curries.

Adding the Creamed Corn

- Add the creamed corn, stirring well to incorporate. Simmer 1–2 minutes.
- Reduce heat to low. Add the crab meat, fish sauce, lime juice, and coconut milk, stirring well after each addition.
- Simmer over low heat for 1-2 minutes, or until the crab meat is heated through.

Stirring the Egg into the Soup

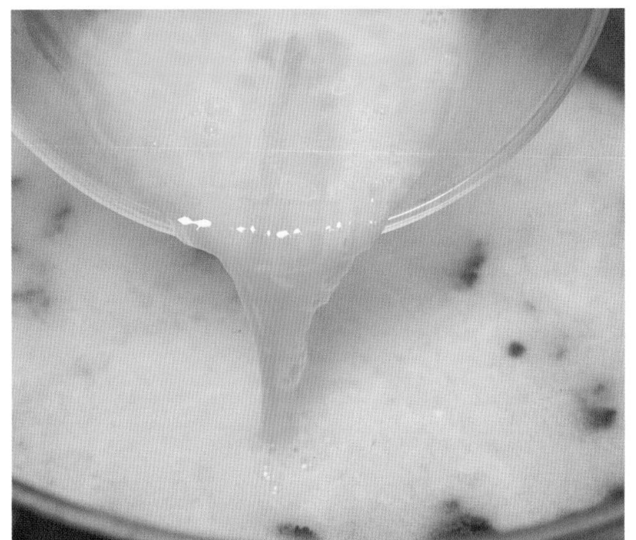

- Slowly add egg to the soup while stirring in wide circles: this will create attractive shreds of egg white. The heat of the soup will cook the egg almost instantly.
- Taste test the soup, adding more fish sauce until desired flavor and saltiness are reached. You can also add more fresh-cut chili or cayenne if you prefer it spicier or more coconut milk if too spicy for your taste.
- To serve, ladle the soup into serving bowls, top with a sprinkling of fresh coriander, and enjoy.

TOFU NOODLE SOUP

This noodle soup is Thai comfort food at its very best.

This soup features some of the same flavors as Tom Yum, yet it tastes vastly different. "Thai comfort food" probably best describes it, the flavors being much more mellow and with a creamier texture than Tom Yum. Also, this soup features rice noodles, an addition that makes it even more soothing and comforting—like your favorite noodle soup when you were a child. Hence, it makes a great dish to serve on a cold or rainy day, instantly soothing and brightening the spirits.

Be sure not to overcook the rice noodles for this dish. A good way to judge when to remove them from the water is to compare the taste with Italian pasta and the classic "al dente" texture—you want that same delightful chewiness in your rice noodles that you try to achieve in your best-made pasta.
Yield: Serves 2 as a main entrée

Ingredients

Thai rice noodles, linguini width, OR wheat noodles, enough for 2 portions

1 stalk lemongrass

5 cups chicken stock

3 kaffir lime leaves

1 Tbsp. grated galangal OR ginger

Handful of shiitake mushrooms, sliced

2 carrots, sliced

2 heads baby bok choy, leaves separated from stem and sliced in half if large

2 Tbsp. fish sauce, plus more to taste

2 Tbsp. soy sauce

½ can good-quality coconut milk

½ package soft tofu, sliced into cubes

Optional: 1 tsp. sugar

½ cup fresh coriander

Optional: Thai chili sauce (to serve)

Tofu Noodle Soup

- Bring a pot of water to boil and dunk in the rice noodles.
- Cover the pot and turn off the heat. Allow rice noodles to soak in the hot water until soft but still chewy ("al dente"). This may take anywhere from 5–12 minutes, depending on the type of rice noodle and how hot your water is.
- Drain and rinse with cold water to prevent sticking. Set aside.

RECIPE VARIATION

To make this recipe vegetarian or vegan, start with the best–tasting vegetarian stock you can find. Use soy sauce instead of fish sauce, or look for vegetarian fish sauce at your local Asian food store. To make this recipe gluten-free, use rice noodles and a soup stock that does not contain wheat. You will also need to use wheat-free soy sauce. Note that fish sauce is naturally wheat-free.

ZOOM

Unlike most Western noodle soups, in Asian cooking the noodles are normally kept separate from the soup until ready to eat. This is especially true with rice noodles, which would lose all their taste and texture if cooked in the soup pot. Although cooking the noodles separately might seem like more work, it makes for a better soup and guarantees that leftovers will be just as good.

Preparing the Lemongrass

- Cut off the lemongrass bulb and discard. Finely slice the lower ⅓ of the stalk. Then mince these slices well by hand, or with a food processor/chopper.
- Place stock in a soup pot together with the lemongrass, lime leaves, galangal, mushrooms, and carrots. Boil 5–6 minutes.
- Reduce heat to medium and add the bok choy. Simmer 2 more minutes.
- Reduce heat to low. Add fish sauce, soy sauce, coconut milk, and tofu, stirring very gently.

Putting the Dish Together

- Before putting the dish together, taste test the soup. Add more fish sauce if not salty or flavorful enough (note that the soup will taste less salty once the noodles are added).
- If too salty for your taste, add a squeeze of fresh lime juice. If too sour, add 1 tsp. sugar.
- To serve, place a generous mound of noodles in each bowl, then ladle over the soup. Add a sprinkling of fresh coriander and serve with Thai chili sauce on the side.

CHICKEN SOUP WITH LEMONGRASS

This Thai twist on chicken noodle soup nourishes, energizes, and chases chills away.

Remember the chicken noodle soup your grandmother used to make? Well, imagine that same soup but with Thai flavors like lemongrass and lime leaf, and with chewy-delicious rice noodles and delightfully crunchy Asian vegetables. Now you have a comforting bowl of chicken noodle soup that lives up to adult tastes and nutrient expectations.

Another addition that makes this soup different is coconut milk. When added to any clear broth, coconut milk adds depth of flavor as well as creaminess. And if you have leftover roasted chicken or turkey, use it in this dish.

Yield: Serves 2–3 as a main entrée

Ingredients

8–10 oz. Thai rice noodles, linguini width

6 cups good-quality chicken stock

2 chicken breasts OR 4 thighs, chopped

1 stalk lemongrass

4 kaffir lime leaves, left whole

1 large carrot, sliced

1 red chili, minced, OR 1 tsp. Thai chili sauce OR ½ tsp. cayenne pepper

1 Tbsp. grated galangal or ginger

3 cloves garlic, minced

2 heads baby bok choy, leaves separated and sliced in half if large

Juice of 1 large lime (about ¼ cup)

2 Tbsp. fish sauce, plus more to taste

¼–½ cup coconut milk

Optional: 1 tsp. sugar, to taste

White or black pepper, to taste

To serve: ½ cup fresh coriander

Chicken Noodle Soup with Lemongrass

- Bring a pot of water to a boil and remove from heat. Dunk the rice noodles into the water.
- Allow them to soak for 5–12 minutes (depending on the thickness of your noodles), until they are soft enough to eat, but still chewy ("al dente").
- Drain the noodles and rinse briefly with cold water to keep them from sticking. Set aside.

RECIPE VARIATION

Lemongrass Noodle Soup with Pork. For this variation, substitute pork for the chicken, slicing as thinly as you can. Then, in a cup, combine 3 Tbsp. soy sauce, ½ Tbsp. lime or lemon juice, and 1 tsp. cornstarch. Stir well to dissolve the cornstarch and pour over the pork. Set aside to marinate while you prepare the rice noodles. Add the marinated pork, and follow the remainder of the recipe.

ZOOM

Lemongrass has many health benefits and is therefore a wonderful addition to nearly any clear broth soup. In the West, we associate lemon with cold and flu remedies. But lemongrass is even more beneficial for the body. This herb has antibacterial and antifungal properties; it also helps digestion, increases blood circulation, reduces blood pressure, and is thought to be an excellent detoxifier.

Flavoring the Chicken Stock

- Bring chicken stock to a boil over high heat. Add chicken (or turkey) plus lemongrass, lime leaves, carrot, chili, galangal (or ginger), and garlic.
- Boil on high for 1 minute, then reduce heat to medium and cover with a lid. Allow soup to simmer for 5–8 more minutes, or until chicken is well cooked.
- Add the baby bok choy, plus the lime juice and fish sauce. Stir well and simmer 1 more minute.

Adding Coconut Milk

- Reduce heat to low and add the coconut milk, stirring to dissolve.
- Do a taste test, adding more fish sauce until desired saltiness is reached. If too salty for your taste, add a little more lime juice. If too sour, add 1 tsp. sugar.
- To serve, place a generous mound of noodles in each bowl and ladle over the hot soup. Add a sprinkling of pepper plus fresh coriander to each bowl. Serve with Thai chili sauce on the side.

CHICKEN DUMPLING SOUP

Similar to Chinese wonton soup, this Thai version boasts stronger and more varied flavors.

When visiting Thailand, you can easily see (and taste!) the influence of Chinese food and culture. Often the most delicious dishes are combinations of the two cuisines.

This chicken dumpling soup represents such a blending, with the wontons being a Chinese influence while the rest of the soup tastes decidedly Thai.

While dumplings are normally quite labor-intensive, the ones in this recipe are very simple. All you need is a package of wonton wrappers from your local supermarket, plus a few other basic ingredients. Leftover roasted chicken, turkey, or duck works well for this recipe.

Yield: Serves 2 as a main entrée

Ingredients

6 cups good-quality chicken broth
1 stalk lemongrass, sliced and minced
3 kaffir lime leaves, left whole
2 Tbsp. soy sauce
Handful fresh shiitake mushrooms, sliced
1/2 to 1 cup roasted chicken or turkey
1 Tbsp. grated galangal OR ginger
2 green onions, sliced
1 Tbsp. fish sauce
1 Tbsp. soy sauce
1 Tbsp. oyster sauce
1 pkg. square or round wonton wrappers
1 cup cherry tomatoes
1 red chili, minced, OR 1 tsp. Thai chili sauce OR 1/2 tsp. cayenne pepper
1 cucumber, sliced into matchsticks
1 Tbsp. lime juice
Optional: 1/2–1 tsp. sugar, to taste
1/2 cup fresh coriander

Chicken Dumpling Soup

- Place chicken stock in a soup pot over high heat. Add the lemongrass, lime leaves, soy sauce, and mushrooms. Bring to a boil, then reduce heat to medium-low. Allow soup to simmer while you prepare the dumplings.
- Place chicken, galangal (or ginger), green onions, fish sauce, soy sauce, and oyster sauce in a food processor. Process well to create a ground chicken or paste-like consistency.

RECIPE VARIATION

Shrimp Dumpling Soup. For this variation, use 1 cup of cooked or raw shrimp, which does not need long to cook: the boiling of the wontons is more than enough. Place shrimp meat in the food processor together with the ginger, green onion, 1 Tbsp. oyster sauce, 1 Tbsp. soy sauce, and ½ Tbsp. fish sauce. Blitz to create the filling and follow the recipe as written.

MAKE IT EASY

There are various ways to wrap dumplings. An easy way is to place 1 heaping tsp. of filling along the wrapper on the diagonal, from one corner to the other, then lift the wrapper and seal over the filling. Press down on the dumpling slightly, so that it will "sit" without falling over. Then pinch along the seal to create a decorative edge (like pinching a pie crust). Be sure to use plenty of water when sealing.

Making the Dumplings

- Peel off several wonton wrappers and lay them flat on a clean work surface. You will also need a little water for sealing.
- Place 1 tsp. or more of filling in the middle of each wrapper. Using your fingers or a baker's brush, wet the perimeter of the wrapper.
- Fold the wrapper in half and press to seal—this will give you triangular wontons. For more traditional-looking dumplings, bring all 4 corners up over the filling and press in the middle, twisting slightly to seal.

Adding the Dumplings & Cucumber

- Bring the soup back up to a boil and drop in the dumplings. Also add the tomatoes and chili. Cook 5–8 minutes, or until dumplings are floating around the top of the pot.
- Reduce heat to low and add the cucumber and the lime juice.
- Taste test for saltiness, adding more fish sauce (instead of salt) as needed. If the soup is too sour for your taste, add ½ to 1 tsp. sugar.
- Ladle the soup into bowls and add a sprinkling of fresh coriander.

CHICKEN STIR-FRY WITH LIME LEAF

This stir-fry is bursting with the quintessential flavors of Thai cooking.

If you're looking for authentic Thai flavor, try this special recipe. It's the lime leaf in combination with fresh basil and garlic that makes this dish sing.

Unlike most stir-fry sauces, the special sauce in this recipe is not meant to be cooked, but merely heated through, allowing the fresh flavors of the Thai herbs to remain in the dish.

Thai basil has a sharpness that is preferable in this particular dish (you'll recognize Thai basil by its purple stem). As for the lime leaf, there is no substitute—lime zest will not work in this recipe. Instead, look for fresh or frozen lime leaves at your local Asian food store.

Yield: Serves 3–4

Ingredients

2 Tbsp. oil

2 shallots, diced

4 chicken breasts or 8 thighs, sliced

2–3 Tbsp. white wine or sherry

2 bell peppers (1 red, 1 green), sliced

1/2 cup fresh basil (preferably Thai basil)

Special Fresh Lime Sauce:

8 kaffir lime leaves

1/2 cup fresh basil (preferably Thai basil)

3 green onions, sliced

1–2 tsp. Thai chili sauce, to taste

4 cloves garlic

3 Tbsp. fish sauce

2 Tbsp. lime juice

2 Tbsp. liquid coconut oil OR olive oil

2 Tbsp. soy sauce

1 tsp. dark soy sauce

2 tsp. brown sugar

Thai Chicken Stir-Fry with Lime Leaf

- Prepare the kaffir lime leaves by cutting them into thin strips with scissors. Discard the stem and central veins.
- Place these strips plus all the other Special Fresh Lime Sauce ingredients together in a mini chopper or a food processor (a mini chopper is perfect for this task). Blitz to create an aromatic Thai sauce.
- Cover and set aside until later.

• • • • RECIPE VARIATION • • • •

Thai Chicken & Lime Leaf Curry. In Thailand, the difference between a stir-fry and a curry is often minimal, since both are cooked in a wok. To make this stir-fry into a curry, after the chicken and peppers are cooked, instead of only adding the special sauce, also add ½ to ¾ cup coconut milk. Stir everything together and simmer on low heat for 1 minute, or until just heated through.

ZOOM

When making Thai stir-fries and curries, there is a choice between using chicken breast or thigh. In Thailand, people don't worry about the fat content, and therefore the darker, more flavorful cuts are preferred. However, because the flavors in Thai cooking are so intense, white chicken meat can be just as tasty. You can achieve more tenderness by cutting it thinly.

Stir-frying the Chicken and Peppers

- Warm a wok or large frying pan over medium-high heat. Add 2 Tbsp. oil and swirl around, then add the shallots and chicken.
- As you stir-fry, add a little white wine or sherry (1–2 Tbsp. at a time) whenever the wok becomes dry—just enough to keep ingredients frying nicely.
- Stir-fry 5–6 minutes, or until chicken is no longer translucent. Add the bell peppers and stir-fry another 2–3 minutes, until peppers have softened slightly but are still bright in color.

Adding the Fresh Lime Sauce

- Reduce heat to medium-low and add the sauce. Gently stir-fry, allowing the wok to remain on the burner for only 1 minute (just long enough to warm the sauce through).
- Remove from heat and taste test, adding more fish sauce if not salty enough. If too salty for your taste, add another squeeze of lime juice. If you'd prefer it spicier, add more chili sauce.
- Serve immediately with Thai jasmine-scented rice. Top with a generous sprinkling of fresh basil and enjoy.

CASHEW CHICKEN STIR-FRY

A popular dish in many Thai restaurants, this stir-fry is both delicious and nutritious.

This Thai stir-fry is a favorite as well as a "best-seller" at many Thai restaurants across North America. In Thailand, cashew trees are grown on the island of Phuket in the south, and in this region, cashews are thrown into various dishes, from salads to stir-fries and even possibly curries. Cashews may also be crushed up and substituted for ground peanuts as toppings for local noodle dishes, such as Pad Thai.

Texture is important in Thai cooking, and in this particular stir-fry, cashews offer that all-important crunch to an otherwise mainly soft-textured dish. They also provide flavor, plus added protein and nutrients.

Yield: Serves 4

Ingredients

4 tsp. cornstarch, divided
3 Tbsp. soy sauce
2 chicken breasts OR 4–6 thighs, sliced
2 Tbsp. oil
2 shallots, diced
3 cloves garlic, minced
1 red chili, minced
2 cups shiitake mushrooms, sliced
6 leaves Napa cabbage OR 3 heads baby bok choy, chopped
2/3 cup unsalted dry-roasted cashews
3 Tbsp. water

Stir-Fry Sauce:

1 cup good-quality chicken stock
3 Tbsp. white wine or sherry
3 Tbsp. soy sauce
2 Tbsp. rice vinegar
3 Tbsp. finely minced lemongrass
2 Tbsp. fish sauce
2 heaping Tbsp. brown sugar

Cashew Chicken Stir-Fry

- In a cup, stir together 1 tsp. cornstarch in soy sauce until the cornstarch dissolves. Pour this over the chicken and mix well to combine. Set aside to marinate.
- Combine all stir-fry sauce ingredients together in a bowl or measuring cup. Set this sauce near your stove.

RECIPE VARIATION

To make this dish vegetarian or vegan, substitute 1–1 ½ cups medium-firm tofu cut into matchstick-like pieces. Marinate the tofu in ¼ cup soy sauce combined with 1 tsp. cornstarch, allowing tofu to marinate up to several hours if possible. For the stir-fry sauce, use vegetable or simulated chicken stock and substitute 2½ Tbsp. soy sauce for the fish sauce. Follow the rest of the recipe as written.

MAKE IT EASY

When taste testing this dish, look for a balance of between spicy and salty, and with more sweet than sour tones ("tangy" would describe it). How salty your cashew chicken turns out depends on the sodium content of the chicken stock you're using. Adjust this by adding more fish sauce if not salty enough, or more lime juice if too salty. Add more sugar if you'd prefer it sweeter.

Stir-frying the Chicken and Mushrooms

- Warm a wok or large frying pan over medium-high heat. Add 2 Tbsp. oil and swirl around, then add the shallots, garlic, and fresh chili. Also add the chicken (along with its marinade), plus the mushrooms. Stir-fry until chicken is no longer translucent when sliced through (5–6 minutes).
- When the wok or pan becomes dry, add a little of the stir-fry sauce (1–2 Tbsp. at a time)—just enough to keep ingredients frying nicely.

Adding the Vegetables and Cornstarch

- Add the cabbage or bok choy and continue stir-frying 1–2 minutes.
- While the cabbage is cooking, dissolve remaining 2 tsp. cornstarch in 3 Tbsp. water.
- Add the rest of the stir-fry sauce, the cashews, plus the cornstarch-water you just made. Continue stirring until all ingredients are well combined and the sauce has thickened (1–2 minutes).
- Remove from heat and taste test for salt and spice.

ROASTED LEMONGRASS CHICKEN

This kid-friendly roasted chicken is extremely tender and juicy.

An oven is a rare sight in Thailand. Normally all dishes are prepared in a wok or over a grill. But here in North America, we do have ovens and like the convenience of cooking this way, which is how the following recipe came to be. Roasting a chicken inside a wok isn't easy, so unless you're a stickler for authenticity, follow the baking instructions presented here.

To ensure this dish is never dry or lacking in flavor, it comes paired with a sweet lime sauce that can either be poured over the entire chicken when served, or poured into a gravy boat and served in place of traditional gravy—it's wonderful whether drizzled over the chicken itself, over rice, or even over Western-style potatoes.

Yield: Serves 4–6

Ingredients

1 stalk lemongrass, sliced and minced
3 cloves garlic
1 Tbsp. grated galangal OR ginger
1/2 can coconut milk
2 Tbsp. fish sauce
3 tsp. dark soy sauce
2 kaffir lime leaves, torn in half
1 whole chicken, medium size
1/3 cup water

Sweet Lime Sauce:

2 cups water
2/3 cup liquid honey
Juice of 1 lime
3 Tbsp. white rice vinegar
1 Tbsp. grated galangal OR ginger
3 cloves garlic, minced
6 Tbsp. fish sauce
1 Tbsp. cornstarch dissolved in 1/4 cup water

Roasted Lemongrass Chicken

- Place lemongrass, garlic, galangal, coconut milk, fish sauce, dark soy sauce, and lime leaves together in a food processor or chopper. Blitz to create a fragrant marinade.
- Rinse and pat the chicken dry, then set it in a roasting pan.
- Pour the marinade over, and, using your hands, slather it across every surface of the chicken. Cover and leave to marinate at least 20 minutes.
- While chicken is marinating, preheat your oven to 325 degrees F.

ZOOM

In Asia, rice vinegar has been in use for millennia. There are three types: red, white, and black. The red and black are used as condiments, while white is used for cooking. In Thai cooking, there is a further option: coconut vinegar. If you can find it, use it in place of rice vinegar. Otherwise, a good Western substitute is apple cider vinegar, which offers many health benefits.

MAKE IT EASY

If you have children that like crispy skin on their roast chicken, or if you simply prefer a deep golden color to your chicken, take a moment to perform one last step. After chicken is finished roasting, turn the oven to the "broil" setting. Uncover and broil the chicken on high for 3–5 minutes, or until desired color and skin crispness are achieved.

Adding Water to the Pan

- Pour water into the bottom of the roasting pan (it can mix with any marinade that has dripped down).
- Cover and roast chicken slowly for 2½ to 3½ hours (2½ for a small chicken, and 3½ for a medium to large chicken).
- Check the pan every hour to make sure there is moisture in the bottom, and add more water as needed. Using a ladle, scoop up some of these juices and drizzle over the chicken. Cover and continue roasting.

Making the Lime Sauce

- While chicken is roasting, place all sauce ingredients (except cornstarch) in a saucepan over high heat. Bring to a boil, then reduce heat to medium-low.
- Taste test, adding more fish sauce instead of salt, or more honey.
- Now add the cornstarch-water, stirring until the sauce thickens.
- Serve the roasted chicken on a platter, either whole or chopped into pieces. Pour the sauce over, or serve it on the side and enjoy.

CHICKEN SATAY

This chicken satay recipe makes all others pale by comparison.

Satay is the perfect summer food and makes a wonderful meal for a family cookout. In Thailand, satay is a common street food and is very hard to pass up when seen (and smelled) simmering over a charcoal grill. It is an equally popular dish in the nearby countries of Indonesia, Burma, Laos, Malaysia, and Vietnam. As a result, there are many recipes and ways to make it. In Thailand, both chicken and pork satay are common, often served with a sauce for dipping.

Taste testing in Thai cooking is always important, but it's especially crucial in this dish. In order to achieve the best satay taste, the key here is to make the marinade predominantly salty and sweet. As long as these two flavors are at the forefront, your satay will be delicious.

Yield: Serves 4–5

Ingredients

1 package wooden skewers

8–10 skinless, boneless chicken thighs

Real Peanut Sauce for serving (see Chapter 19)

Marinade:

2 stalks lemongrass, minced, OR 1/2 cup frozen prepared lemongrass

1 shallot, diced

3 cloves garlic

1 Tbsp. grated galangal OR ginger

1/2 tsp. turmeric

2 Tbsp. ground coriander

2 tsp. cumin

3 Tbsp. dark soy sauce

4 Tbsp. fish sauce

5 Tbsp. brown sugar

1 Tbsp. fresh lime juice

Chicken Satay

- To prevent wooden skewers from burning on the grill, soak them in water while you prepare the meat. The kitchen sink works well for this—just put in the plug and fill with an inch of water, then dunk in the satay sticks.
- Cut the chicken into thin strips or pieces, preferably ½ to ¾ inch wide. For satay, the thinner the meat is sliced, the more tender it turns out; however, you also want it wide enough that it doesn't fall off the stick.

GREEN LIGHT

If you're planning on doing a lot of grilling, it's worth investing in a set of permanent satay sticks rather than using the wooden variety. In everyday North American usage, they are known as "skewers" or "kebab skewers." Look for a set made of stainless steel that are dishwasher safe, with good-sized handles for turning. Prices range between $12 and $30, depending on the quality.

MAKE IT EASY

It's a good idea to fill only the upper half of the satay stick with meat (up to the tip), leaving the lower half empty. This way, you have a handle for turning. In Thailand, the "satay man" can turn 20–30 satay sticks at once by grasping all the handles and turning. Another tip is to position only the upper half of the stick (where the meat is) over the grilling surface—this way the handles remain cool.

Marinating the Chicken

- Place all marinade ingredients in a food processor and blitz to create a thick marinade of paste-like consistency.
- Taste test the marinade. Note that it needs to taste predominately salty and sweet. If necessary, add more sugar or more fish sauce (instead of salt) to ensure these two flavors are more pronounced than the spicy and sour tones.
- Place chicken strips in a bowl and add the marinade, mixing well to coat. Marinate for at least 1 hour, or up to 24 hours.

Skewering the Meat

- Weave the strips of marinated chicken onto the skewers. Note: As you skewer the meat, you may notice what appear to be short pieces of hair—this is simply the lemongrass fiber, and is healthy to eat.
- Grill the satay 10–20 minutes depending on the thickness of the meat and the heat of your grill. As you turn the sticks the first time, brush with the leftover marinade.
- Serve with rice and the suggested peanut sauce on the side, and enjoy.

MANGO CHICKEN STIR-FRY

Fresh mango combines with chicken and vegetables for a tangy-tasting stir-fry.

Mango is one of the world's favorite tropical fruits, and in Thailand, numerous different varieties of mango are grown and sold both domestically and on the international market. Because of the ready abundance of this luscious fruit, mango has found its way into many Thai dishes, from salads to stir-fries to desserts.

Here, fresh mango is used to create a tangy-tasting stir-fry sauce whose flavors marry beautifully with chicken. To get the best flavor and sweetness, use fresh, ripe mangos. While frozen or canned mango can be used, neither will give you the wonderful results of fresh fruit.

Yield: Serves 4

Ingredients

2 chicken breasts OR 5–6 chicken thighs
3 Tbsp. soy sauce
1 tsp. cornstarch
2 Tbsp. oil
1 shallot, diced
1 red bell pepper, sliced
1½ cups snow peas
½ cup dry-roasted unsalted cashews
Mango Sauce:
Fruit of 2 ripe mangoes
1 red chili, minced, OR 1 tsp. chili sauce
1 Tbsp. rice vinegar (or other type)
3 Tbsp. soy sauce
3 Tbsp. fish sauce
Juice of ½ lime
1 Tbsp. brown sugar
1 Tbsp. grated galangal OR ginger
3 cloves garlic, minced
½ cup coriander leaves and stems
2 kaffir lime leaves, snipped into strips

Mango Chicken Stir-Fry

- Chop the chicken into bite-size pieces or strips and place in a bowl.
- Combine the cornstarch and soy sauce together in a cup, stirring to dissolve the cornstarch.
- Pour the soy sauce-cornstarch mixture over the chicken and stir well. Set in the refrigerator to marinate while you make the stir-fry sauce.

ZOOM

There are many types of mango being grown in the world today. Most of our mangoes in North America hail from Mexico and the Caribbean, and while these work for most Thai dishes, if you happen to live near an Asian food store or market, look for imported Asian mangoes. Look for a flatter, tapered shape (sometimes pointy on one end), with yellow skin when ripe.

GREEN LIGHT

These days, it seems everyone in North America is cooking with olive oil; however, this is not always the best choice. At high temperatures, olive oil breaks down and smokes, which can be toxic. Though olive is one of the healthiest oils, it should be consumed at room temperature or merely warmed through; otherwise, it loses all of its wonderful health benefits. The best oil for frying is coconut oil. Other types include canola, peanut, and sunflower.

Making the Mango Stir-Fry Sauce

- Place all mango sauce ingredients together in a food processor, chopper, or blender. Blitz to form a smooth orange-colored sauce.
- Taste test the sauce, looking for a balance of sweet, sour, spicy, and salty. Depending on the sweetness and ripeness of your mangoes, you may have to add more sugar if the sauce tastes sour; if too sweet or too salty, add a little more lime juice. If not spicy enough, add more chili. If not salty enough, add more fish sauce.

Adding the Sauce to the Chicken

- Warm a wok over medium-high heat. Add 1–2 Tbsp. oil, then add the shallot. Stir-fry 30 seconds. Add marinated chicken and stir-fry 2–3 minutes.
- Add the stir-fry sauce along with red pepper and snow peas. Reduce heat to medium and simmer 3–5 minutes, until chicken is cooked and vegetables have softened. Finally, add the cashews.
- Remove from heat and taste test, adding a little more fish sauce if not salty enough. Serve with rice and enjoy.

CLASSIC THAI GRILLED CHICKEN

This recipe will fast become your favorite barbecued chicken.

Few cuisines manage to build as much flavor into grilled chicken as Thai, and when you taste this classic grilled chicken dish, you'll agree there is little that can top it. The special black pepper and garlic marinade is the key, while the dipping sauce ensures this chicken is never dry or lacking in taste. If you can, prepare the chicken ahead of time and allow it to marinate as many hours as possible (up to 24).

Before Portuguese traders brought the chili pepper to Thailand, Thai cooks spiced up their food with peppercorns, and this recipe is a good example of this kind of ancient Thai flavoring. If possible, it's best to use whole black peppercorns that you grind yourself—preferably in a coffee grinder or with pestle and mortar in order to get a coarse, more rustic grind. *Yield: Serves 2–3*

Ingredients

1/2 chicken, chopped into parts, OR 6–8 fresh chicken thighs

Marinade:

8–10 cloves garlic, minced

2 Tbsp. soy sauce

1 tsp. dark soy sauce

2 Tbsp. fish sauce

3 Tbsp. sherry (or cooking sherry)

2 Tbsp. brown sugar

1 Tbsp. black peppercorns, lightly ground

Dipping Sauce:

1/2 cup rice vinegar

1/3 cup brown sugar, lightly packed

3–4 cloves garlic, minced

1 Tbsp. soy sauce

1 Tbsp. fish sauce, plus more to taste

1 red chili, minced, OR 1 tsp. Thai chili sauce OR 1/2 tsp. cayenne

Classic Thai Grilled Chicken

- Combine marinade ingredients together in cup or small bowl, stirring well to dissolve the sugar. Place chicken in a large bowl. If using chicken thighs, slice them in half for easier grilling.
- Pour the marinade over the chicken and stir well, ensuring the chicken is covered with marinade.
- Cover and place in the refrigerator to marinate while you heat up the grill and prepare the dipping sauce (or marinate chicken up to 24 hours ahead of time).

ZOOM

Grilling is part of everyday life in Thailand, with grilled foods being sold on the streets and beaches, or along roadsides. Charcoal braziers are a common sight, their owners selling everything from satay to whole fish. Many are portable; Thais are, in fact, known for their portable kitchens that can be set up in a moment's notice and then taken down at the end of the day.

MAKE IT EASY

This recipe can also be made in your oven. Just marinate the chicken as instructed, then place on a foil-lined baking sheet. Turn up the edges of the foil to prevent spilling. Bake at 350 degrees F for 45 minutes to 1 hour. Then move baking sheet up to the second-highest rung of your oven and set to "broil." Cook chicken 5–7 minutes, or until lightly browned. Serve with the dipping sauce.

Making the Dipping Sauce

- Place all the dipping sauce ingredients together in a saucepan. Stir and bring to a boil.
- Once sauce has reached a bubbling boil, reduce heat to medium-low. Allow the sauce to simmer 10–15 minutes, stirring occasionally.
- The sauce will gradually thicken as it cooks and become tangy: a mixture of sweet, sour, salty, and spicy.
- Note that the smell of the vinegar may be quite strong as you boil it—this is normal and will diminish once the sauce is cooked.

Grilling the Chicken

- Grill chicken over a hot grill. When turning the first time, brush the pieces with the leftover marinade. Grill until chicken is well cooked.
- Before serving, taste test the sauce, adding more fish sauce if not salty enough, or more sugar if you'd prefer it sweeter. If too sweet or salty, add a squeeze of lime juice.
- Serve the chicken hot from the grill with the warm dipping sauce on the side.

GREEN CURRY BEEF

Simmered with eggplant and red pepper, this beef curry is both aromatic and sumptuous.

Green curry is one of Thailand's signature dishes. Whether made with chicken or beef, Thai green curry has become known the world over for its spicy taste and fresh, aromatic qualities. In order to cook up a good green curry, start with the best possible curry paste you can find. These days, it's fairly easy to buy packaged Thai green curry paste, but for the freshest taste, it's better to make your own from scratch.

This Thai green curry recipe includes a fresh green curry paste recipe that is simple enough to whip up in your food processor or chopper. You might even want to make extra and keep it in the refrigerator.

Yield: Serves 4–6

Ingredients

1 can good-quality coconut milk, divided

8 kaffir lime leaves, cut into thin strips

2 Tbsp. oil

1 lb. beef tenderloin or sirloin steak, cut into thin, bite-size pieces

1 Chinese eggplant, chopped into chunks

1/2–1 cup fresh basil

Green Curry Paste:

3–4 small green chilies

1 shallot, diced

4 cloves garlic, minced

1 Tbsp. grated galangal OR ginger, grated

1 stalk minced lemongrass

2 tsp. ground coriander

1 tsp. shrimp paste

1/2 cup chopped coriander leaves and stems

1 tsp. ground white pepper

1 Tbsp. soy sauce

2 Tbsp. fish sauce

Green Beef Curry

- Place all the green curry paste ingredients together in a food processor. Add 2–3 Tbsp. of the coconut milk and blitz to create a fragrant green paste. Set aside.
- Prepare the lime leaves by cutting them into thin strips. Discard the stem and central vein of the leaf. Set the lime leaf strips aside until later.

RECIPE VARIATION

Green Curry with Pork, Bell Pepper, and Tomato. Substitute pork for the beef, slicing it thinly. Chop 1–2 bell peppers into bite-size pieces. Use either 1 cup cherry tomatoes, or 1–2 regular field tomatoes, chopped. Add the vegetables when you add the lime leaf. Simmer until the pork is well done (the tomato will be quite soft, its juices contributing to the taste of the dish). Top with fresh basil.

ZOOM

The predominant taste of a Thai curry depends on personal preferences. While some people prefer a sweeter, richer-tasting curry (wherein sugar is added and sometimes also a sweetened coconut cream), others prefer it sour or spicy. There are certain Thai dishes that depend on sugar as a key ingredient, but curry isn't one of them. So feel free to reduce the sugar or even omit it.

Stir-frying the Paste with the Beef & Eggplant

- Heat up a wok or large frying pan over medium-high heat. Add 1–2 Tbsp. oil and swirl around, then add the curry paste. Stir-fry briefly to release the fragrance (30–60 seconds), then add the rest of the coconut milk, stirring to dissolve any lumps.
- Add the beef and the eggplant. When the curry sauce reaches a boil, reduce heat to medium. Cover and simmer 2–3 minutes, stirring occasionally.

Adding the Lime Leaf

- Add the strips of lime leaf, stirring well to incorporate. Continue simmering the curry 8-10 more minutes, or until the beef is well done and the eggplant is soft.
- Do a taste test, adding 1–2 Tbsp. fish sauce if not salty or flavorful enough. If you'd prefer a sweeter curry, add a little more sugar. If too spicy, add more coconut milk.
- Serve the curry in bowls with rice on the side. Top each portion with a generous sprinkling of fresh basil and enjoy.

BROILED SIRLOIN WITH THAI SAUCE

This easy broiled steak recipe is based on the classic Thai dish Weeping Tiger Beef.

Because the weather in Thailand is always warm, this dish is normally grilled outdoors rather than broiled inside. So if you're lucky enough to be enjoying barbecue weather where you live, feel free to grill instead of broiling the steaks.

One of the more curious ingredients in this recipe is the addition of ground toasted rice in the dipping sauce. Varying textures are an important feature of Thai cuisine, and this ingredient is a good example, adding more texture than taste. It may seem like a strange and superfluous ingredient until you try it for yourself. Then you may start to find that bit of grittiness appealing—perhaps even slightly addictive.

Yield: Serves 2

Ingredients

2 sirloin steaks

Marinade:

1 Tbsp. oyster sauce

1 Tbsp. soy sauce

3 Tbsp. fish sauce

1 Tbsp. brown sugar

3 cloves garlic, minced

1/4 tsp. ground coriander

1/4 tsp. ground black pepper

Sauce:

6 Tbsp. fish sauce

5 Tbsp. lemon juice

2 tsp. sugar

2–3 Tbsp. ground toasted rice OR substitute ground peanuts

1 tsp. dried chili flakes

1/4 cup finely chopped tomato

1/4 cup coriander leaves and stems

Broiled Sirloin with Thai Sauce

- Combine marinade ingredients together in a cup, stirring until the sugar dissolves.
- Pour this mixture over the meat. Turn the steaks several times in the marinade and set in the refrigerator for at least 30 minutes (or up to 24 hours).

ZOOM

There are several stories behind the name "Weeping Tiger Beef." One is that a man with a gun came into the forest one day where a tiger was hunting. The man ended up killing and taking away the cow that the tiger had been stalking, and so the tiger cried. The other explanation is that a tiger tried to steal a taste of this dish, but that the chilies were so hot, they made him cry.

MAKE IT EASY

For the ground rice, use sticky rice if you have it (if not, use Thai jasmine-scented rice). Place uncooked sticky rice in a wok. Stirring constantly, "dry-fry" it over medium-high heat. The rice will turn slightly golden and will begin to pop (like popcorn). Remove the toasted rice from the wok; otherwise, it will keep on toasting. Tip it into a bowl to cool, then grind up and add it to your sauce.

Making the Sauce

- Combine all sauce ingredients together in a bowl.
- For the ground toasted rice, place 1 Tbsp. uncooked sticky rice in a frying pan or wok. Stirring constantly, "dry-fry" it over medium-high heat, then grind it to a powder using a coffee grinder or pestle and mortar. Stir it into the sauce.
- Taste test the sauce, adding more fish sauce if you'd like it saltier, or more sugar for a sweeter sauce. Add more chili flakes or fresh-cut chili for a spicier sauce.

Broiling the Beef

- Set oven to "broil" and place oven rack on the second-to-highest rung.
- Place marinated steaks either in a broiling pan, or on a regular baking sheet lined with foil. Broil 6–8 minutes, then turn and broil the other side. Note that for this dish the steak should remain pink in the middle.
- Slice the steak as thinly as you can and place on a platter together with the sauce. If desired, garnish the platter with cucumber and tomato slices.

BEEF & BROCCOLI STIR-FRY

This popular stir-fry reveals Chinese influence on Thai cuisine.

The combination of beef and broccoli is well known in Chinese cuisine, and, indeed, this recipe is actually a Thai version of that same basic dish. The Thai influences can be found in the addition of fish sauce, galangal, and chili, which makes for a more lively taste combination. Other vegetables may be used in place of broccoli, such as Chinese broccoli (gai lan) or baby bok choy.

While in Western cooking the beef would normally be chopped into thick chunks (as in chunky beef stews), in Thai cuisine red meats are nearly always sliced thinly because meat is expensive and therefore one or two steaks are shared by many people. Also, thinly sliced meat turns out more tender, especially when stir-fried.

Yield: Serves 2-3

Ingredients

4 Tbsp. soy sauce

1 heaping tsp. brown sugar

1 lb. sirloin steak, sliced thinly

2 Tbsp. oil for stir-frying

2 shallots, diced

2 Tbsp. grated galangal OR ginger

1 head broccoli, chopped

2 tsp. sesame oil

Stir-Fry Sauce:

2 Tbsp. fish sauce

1/2 tsp. cornstarch

3 Tbsp. sherry (or cooking sherry)

2 Tbsp. oyster sauce

3 Tbsp. lime juice

2 tsp. sugar

3 cloves garlic, minced

1 tsp. Thai chili sauce

2 Tbsp. coriander leaves and stems

Beef & Broccoli Stir-Fry

- Combine together in a cup the soy sauce and sugar, stirring well to dissolve the sugar. Pour this mixture over the strips of beef and mix well. Set aside to marinate while you prepare the other ingredients.
- To make the stir-fry sauce, place the fish sauce in a cup or small bowl. Add the cornstarch, stirring to dissolve. Now add all the other stir-fry sauce ingredients. Mix well to combine and then set near the stove.

RECIPE VARIATION

Stir-Fried Pork with Bok Choy. Substitute pork loin for the beef, slicing it thinly. Use the same marinade as you would for the beef, but instead of broccoli, substitute baby bok choy or green beans. Slice any larger leaves into halves or thirds. If using green beans, stir-fry 2–3 minutes. If using baby bok choy, wait until after the stir-fry sauce has been added, since bok choy needs only 1–2 minutes.

ZOOM

Because Thailand was never colonized, the Thai people have retained much of their original culture. However, foreign traders and workers did come and go over the centuries, including the Chinese. The influence of Chinese cooking can easily be seen in Thai cuisine, from the use of the wok to Chinese sauces such as oyster sauce, soy sauce, sesame oil, and rice vinegar.

Stir-Frying the Beef

- Warm a wok or large frying pan over medium-high heat. Add the oil and swirl around, then add the shallots and galangal or ginger. Stir-fry briefly to release the fragrance (about 1 minute).
- Now add the beef (together with the soy sauce marinade). Stir-fry 5 minutes, or until beef is lightly cooked. If your wok becomes dry, add a little water, 1 Tbsp. at a time—just enough to keep ingredients frying nicely.

Adding Stir-Fry Sauce

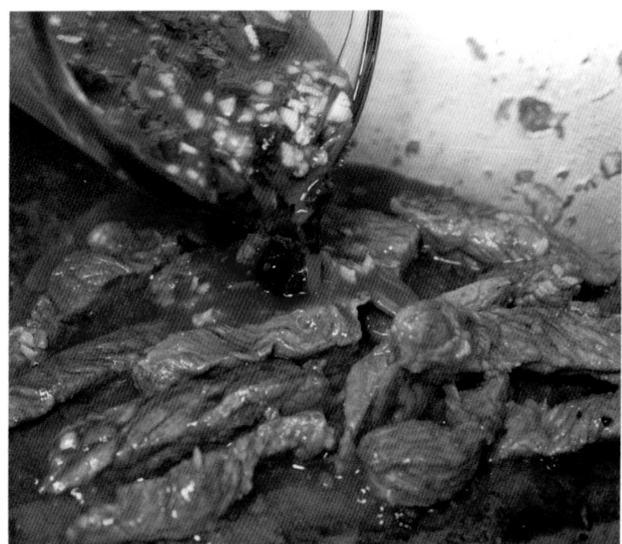

- Give the stir-fry sauce a quick stir and add it to the wok. Also add the broccoli plus ¼ cup of water. Stir-fry until broccoli turns bright green and has softened slightly (2–3 minutes). The sauce will gradually thicken.
- Remove from heat and taste test for salt and spice. Add a little fish sauce (instead of salt), or a little chili sauce to increase the flavors, as desired.
- Drizzle the sesame oil over and serve immediately with Thai jasmine rice.

THAI WATERFALL GRILLED BEEF SALAD

This special salad offers a glorious mixture of flavors and textures with every bite.

The name of this dish is very evocative, bringing to mind a beautiful waterfall in one of the more natural jungle areas that still exist in Thailand. However, some say the name is merely representative of the sound of beef juices splashing onto a hot grill. In any case, this salad really is special and as beautiful to serve as its name suggests.

If it happens to be cold where you live, or if the weather doesn't cooperate with your grilling plans, note that the beef can also be made indoors in your oven. Just follow the broiling instructions provided in the recipe for results that are equally tantalizing.

Yield: Serves 2 as a main entrée

Ingredients

2 sirloin steaks

Enough salad greens for 2 servings

1 cup bean sprouts

1 cup fresh papaya, sliced or cubed

1/2 cup fresh mint or basil

1 cup fresh coriander

1 cup cherry tomatoes

Marinade:

2 Tbsp. soy sauce

2 Tbsp. oyster sauce

1 Tbsp. lemon juice

2 Tbsp. brown sugar

Salad Dressing:

4 Tbsp. lime juice

2 Tbsp. fish sauce

2 Tbsp. soy sauce

1/2 tsp. cayenne pepper

1 Tbsp. brown sugar

2 Tbsp. toasted and ground sticky rice

Thai Waterfall Grilled Beef Salad

- Combine marinade ingredients together in a cup, stirring to dissolve the sugar. Pour this mixture over the steaks, ensuring the meat is well coated. Set in the refrigerator to marinate while you prepare the salad and dressing.
- Place all salad dressing ingredients together in a cup or small bowl and stir until sugar dissolves.
- In a large salad bowl, combine salad greens plus the bean sprouts, fresh papaya, fresh herbs, and cherry tomatoes.

RECIPE VARIATION

Waterfall Beef Salad with Fresh Mango. Prepare and cook the beef as instructed. For the salad, substitute 1 fresh mango for the papaya. Make sure the mango is ripe and sweet. Slice it open and scoop out the fruit, then cut it into cubes and add to the salad. For the herbs, use basil rather than mint, and instead of cherry tomatoes, add slices of fresh cucumber. Follow remaining recipe as written.

MAKE IT EASY

To make the ground rice, place 2 Tbsp. uncooked sticky rice (or jasmine-scented rice) in a dry frying pan over medium-high heat. Stir continuously, "dry-frying" the rice until it turns golden and begins to pop. Tip the toasted rice into a bowl to cool, then use a coffee grinder or pestle and mortar to grind it into a powder. In place of ground toasted rice, ground roasted peanuts may be used.

Cooking the Sirloin

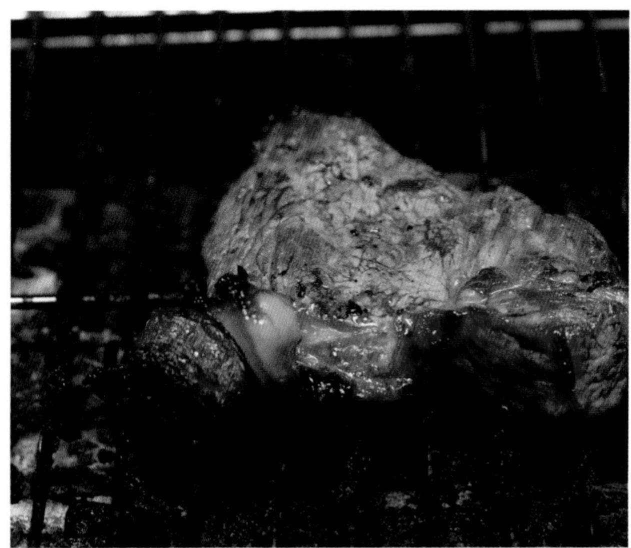

- Grill the steaks over a hot grill, turning as few times as possible to retain the juices. Steaks are done when well cooked on the outside but still pink in the center.
- For indoor cooking: Set your oven to "broil" setting. Place steak on a foil-lined baking sheet (turn up the edges of the foil to prevent juices from spilling). Place in oven on second-to-highest rung below heating element. Broil 5–7 minutes per side, or until steak is well done on the outside, but still pink at the center.

Slicing the Sirloin

- Cutting against the grain, slice the grilled or broiled steak as thinly as you can. A sharp serrated knife is best for this, or use an electric meat cutter.
- Toss the salad with the dressing, then taste test it, looking for a balance of salty, spicy, sweet, and sour. Add more fish sauce if you'd prefer it saltier or more flavorful. Add a squeeze of lime juice if it's too salty or too sweet for your taste.
- Portion out the salad and top with the sliced waterfall beef.

JUNGLE CURRY

This simple curry hails from jungle regions of northern Thailand.

In the north of Thailand lies the city of Chiang Mai, rich in traditional atmosphere and charm. The city is surrounded by mountains, forest, and jungle and is cooler than other areas of Thailand. Because of the lack of access to the sea (and the fresh seafood that can be found so readily in the south), the cuisine in this region is more red meat–based. Also, because of the cooler climate, coconut trees and coconut milk are not normally part of the local diet.

One of the most popular dishes from this region is Jungle Curry, a dish that is often made with wild red meats, such a boar. The following recipe is an adaptation of traditional jungle curry, calling for sirloin instead of wild game, plus it includes the addition of coconut milk for creamier, slightly richer results.
Yield: Serves 2–3

Ingredients

1 lb. beef tenderloin
1 Chinese eggplant
1 cup cherry tomatoes
1/2 cup fresh coriander for garnish
Curry Sauce:
3 Tbsp. fish sauce
2 shallots, diced
2 Tbsp. grated galangal or ginger
1 Tbsp. bottled green peppercorns
1 stalk lemongrass, minced
6 cloves garlic
8 kaffir lime leaves, cut into thin strips
1 Tbsp. chili powder
1 red chili, minced, OR 3/4 tsp. cayenne
Juice of 1/2 lime
1 tsp. shrimp paste
1 can coconut milk
1 tsp. brown sugar

Jungle Curry

- Preheat oven to 350 degrees F.
- Prepare the beef by slicing it against the grain into thin pieces—this will help keep it tender.
- Place all curry sauce ingredients in a food processor. Process well to create a rich red curry sauce.
- Place the sliced beef in a casserole dish and pour the sauce over. Mix together, cover, and set in the oven to bake for 45 minutes.

RECIPE VARIATION

For a more authentic jungle curry, substitute chicken or beef stock for the coconut milk—this will give you a thinner sauce similar to those in the Chiang Mai region. If you wish, add extra fresh-cut chili; plenty of spicy "heat" is an intrinsic part of this dish. For the meat, instead of beef use bison or any other type of wild meat. In Thailand, this dish is also sometimes made with wild catfish.

ZOOM

Oftentimes when people look at a jungle curry recipe, they are surprised because there are no traditional curry spices in it at all—no curry powder, turmeric, coriander, or cumin. This is because, in remote jungle areas of Thailand, such spices were not traditionally available. In this case, jungle curry gains most of its flavor from chili, lemongrass, and green peppercorns.

Chopping and Adding the Vegetables

- To prepare the eggplant, cut it down the middle into two parts. Now slice each part in half again lengthwise, or until you have several long 1–2-inch-thick pieces. Chop these up into chunks. Add these to the curry, and also add the cherry tomatoes, stirring them in.
- Cover and return the curry to the oven for 15–20 minutes. After this time the beef should be well cooked and the eggplant tender when pierced with a fork.
- If needed, bake another 5–10 minutes.

Adjusting the Flavors

- Before serving, stir the curry well and taste test for salt, adding more fish sauce if not salty or flavorful enough.
- If you would like your curry spicier, add more fresh-cut chili, chili sauce, or cayenne pepper. If it's too spicy, add a little more coconut milk; if too sour for your taste, add a little more sugar.
- Scoop the curry into serving bowls or onto individual plates. Top with fresh coriander and accompany with plenty of Thai jasmine-scented rice.

THAI RIVER NOODLES WITH BEEF

Also known as Pad See Ew, this noodle dish is both comforting and flavorful.

In Thailand, the flat rice noodles used in this dish are known as "river noodles," a name that evokes a broad, slow-moving river. They are nearly always made and sold fresh rather than as dried noodles so you will need to shop for them at an Asian food store, or a mainstream grocery store that has a good Asian deli section.

Pad See Ew simply means "fried with soy sauce." As its name suggests, the dish can be made with a number of different ingredients so long as the sauce and stir-fry method remain the same. This dish can be cooked up a variety of ways, with beef, chicken or even seafood.

Yield: Serves 4–5

Ingredients

1 Tbsp. oyster sauce
2 Tbsp. soy sauce
2 tsp. brown sugar
1–2 sirloin steaks, sliced thinly
2 Tbsp. oil for stir-frying
3 cloves garlic, minced
1–2 heads broccoli, chopped into florets
1 egg
1/4 cup sherry or cooking sherry
1 1/2–2 lbs. fresh broad flat rice noodles
1/2 cup fresh coriander for garnish

Stir-Fry Sauce:
1 Tbsp. dark soy sauce
2 Tbsp. regular soy sauce
3 Tbsp. fish sauce
2 tsp. brown sugar
1/2 tsp. white pepper
1/2 tsp. cayenne pepper

Beef Fried with Thai River Noodles

- Combine the oyster sauce, soy sauce, and brown sugar, stirring to dissolve sugar. Pour this marinade over the strips of beef and mix well. Set in the refrigerator while you prepare the other ingredients.
- Combine all stir-fry sauce ingredients together in a cup, stirring to dissolve the sugar. Set aside until needed.

RECIPE VARIATION

This dish is also delicious made with chicken. Simply substitute 2 boneless chicken breasts, slicing them up into bite-size pieces. Instead of an oyster sauce marinade, use 1 tsp. cornstarch dissolved in 3–4 Tbsp. soy sauce. Pour this over the chicken and set aside to marinate while you prepare the other ingredients as listed. Instead of sherry use ¼ cup chicken stock or broth.

MAKE IT EASY

Because most fresh river noodles come pressed together in a package, you will need to separate them before cooking. To make the task of separating them easier, get yourself a kitchen hand: children are especially good at this task. Note that when separated, you will have two or three huge mounds of noodles; once cooked, however, you'll find they quickly reduce in bulk.

Stir-frying the Beef, Broccoli, and Egg

- Warm a wok over medium-high heat. Add oil and garlic. Stir-fry until fragrant (30 seconds).
- Add the marinated beef and stir-fry 2–3 minutes. Add a little sherry, 1 Tbsp. at a time, whenever your wok becomes dry.
- Add the broccoli and continue stir-frying in the same way 1–2 minutes. Push ingredients aside and drizzle a little more oil into the center of your wok. Break the egg into this space and quickly stir to cook it (like making scrambled eggs).

Stir-Frying the Noodles

- Add the noodles and pour the stir-fry sauce over. Using two utensils, gently lift and turn the noodles to mix them with the other ingredients and sauce. The noodles will gradually soften (about 2 minutes). Note that they break easily, so be sure to lift and turn them gently.
- When noodles have softened and are of a consistent color, remove from heat. Taste test for salt, adding more fish sauce until desired taste is achieved. Sprinkle the fresh coriander over and serve.

DEEP-FRIED SPARERIBS

These tasty ribs are common street fare in Thailand and make a wonderful finger food.

Not all deep-fried ribs are created equal, and you'll definitely find this Thai version a cut above average. It's the marinade that makes it—a combination of fresh coriander, fish sauce, and garlic. These three simple ingredients come together in a paste-like consistency to coat the ribs in an abundance of flavor that few recipes can match. It may sound involved, but this dish is actually easy to make, especially because there is no messy egg mixture to dip into. Just marinate the ribs, roll them in flour, and then fry.

Yield: Serves 2–3

Ingredients

8 cloves garlic

3/4 cup chopped fresh coriander leaves and stems

2 Tbsp. fish sauce

1 Tbsp. sherry (or cooking sherry)

1–2 lbs. short pork ribs, chopped into 2–3-inch-wide segments

1/2 cup all-purpose flour

1/2 tsp. salt

1/2 tsp. white pepper

1–1 1/2 cups high heat oil for deep-frying, such as coconut or canola oil

Thai sweet chili sauce for dipping

Deep-Fried Spareribs

- Place the garlic, coriander, fish sauce, and sherry in a food processor or mini chopper. Blitz to create a fragrant green paste. Mix this paste with the pork ribs, stirring well to coat. Cover and leave in the refrigerator to marinate at least 30 minutes, or up to 24 hours.

ZOOM

In Thai cooking, both regular wheat and rice flours are used. For gluten-free diets, you can easily substitute rice flour for all-purpose (wheat) flour in most recipes. However, just keep in mind that rice flour isn't as thick in texture, which means you will need more of it to achieve the same results. If the recipe calls for 1 cup regular all-purpose flour, substitute up to 1½ cups rice flour.

GREEN LIGHT

When working with hot oil, it pays to follow a few cooking rules. Never leave hot oil (or oil that is heating up) unattended: it gets hot very fast and can easily cause a fire. As the oil is heating up, test it by dipping a corner of a rib into it—if the oil sizzles and begins to cook the meat, it is ready. Once you've started frying the ribs, reduce the heat slightly or it will overheat and begin to smoke.

Coating the Ribs with Flour

- Measure the flour into a mixing bowl. Add the salt and white pepper, stirring well to combine.
- Gently roll the ribs in this flour mixture to coat, allowing the coriander-garlic paste to remain on the ribs as much as possible (it will become part of the batter and give the ribs their wonderful flavor).
- Set coated ribs on a plate near the stove. Heat oil in a wok or skillet (make sure oil is at least 1 inch deep).

Deep-Frying the Ribs

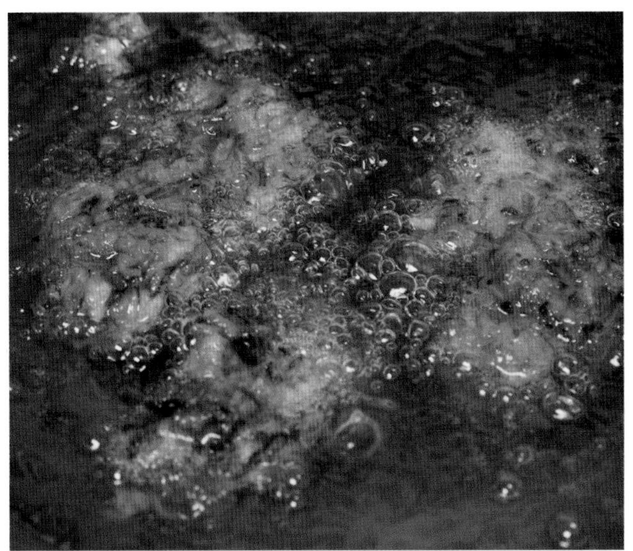

- Using tongs, carefully place ribs in the hot oil.
- Turn them often, until all sides are dark golden-brown. To check whether ribs are cooked, remove one from the oil and slice it open near the bone (at its thickest part): the meat should be light pink or white.
- Drain the fried ribs on paper towels or a clean tea towel.
- Serve these delicious ribs with Thai sweet chili sauce on the side for dipping, and enjoy.

THAI SWEET & SOUR PORK

This tangy-delicious dish is quick and easy to make.

Sweet and sour dishes conjure up images and reminiscences of Chinese cooking, and, of course, this is where the following dish has its roots. As with other Chinese-inspired Thai recipes, the sauce in this version has been adapted to suit Thai tastes: unlike Chinese sweet and sour dishes, it includes chili for a spicier, more flavorful rendition.

In Thailand, tomato paste would likely be used in this recipe, but for ease of preparation, here tomato ketchup makes a wonderful (and even more delicious) substitution. Be sure to add the required amount of sugar in this recipe, as you will need to balance out the sour tones of the vinegar to achieve the most delicious taste.

Yield: Serves 4

Ingredients

¼ cup soy sauce
3½ tsp. cornstarch, divided
1–2 lbs. pork ribs, chopped into segments
3–4 heads of baby bok choy
2 Tbsp. oil
2 shallots, diced
3 cloves garlic, minced
1 Tbsp. grated galangal or ginger
1 red and 1 green bell pepper, chopped
1–2 cups snow peas
3–4 Tbsp. water
To serve: handful fresh coriander
Sweet and Sour Sauce:
¾ cup chicken stock
¼ cup tomato ketchup
4 Tbsp. fish sauce
¼ cup brown sugar (loose, not packed)
1–3 tsp. Thai chili sauce
1 Tbsp. vinegar
2 Tbsp. soy sauce
1 Tbsp. lemon juice

Thai Sweet & Sour Pork

- Stir the soy sauce and 2 tsp. cornstarch together until cornstarch dissolves. Pour this mixture over the meat and set in the refrigerator to marinate while you prepare the other ingredients.
- Prepare the bok choy by separating the heads into individual leaves. Chop the larger of these leaves in half; the smaller ones can be left whole.
- Combine all sweet and sour sauce ingredients in a small mixing bowl. Stir well to dissolve sugar, and set near the stove.

RECIPE VARIATION

Sweet & Sour Chicken. Use 1 pound chicken breast or thigh meat, chopped. Marinate using the same marinade as written. When stir-frying, instead of adding water use chicken stock. Otherwise, follow the same ingredients list and instructions. A final optional ingredient is 1 small can pineapple chunks (drained). Add this at the end of the recipe, stirring it into the dish to combine.

ZOOM

In Thailand, refined sugars are rarely used. Instead, palm sugar is the norm. Palm sugar comes from date palms, and is sold in various forms, from hard round "cakes" to blocks, pastes, or in cans. Another type of sweetener commonly used is coconut sugar from the coconut palm. If you have a good Asian store near you, check out these Thai sugar options, or simply substitute brown sugar.

Stir-Frying the Pork

- Warm a wok over medium-high heat. Add 1–2 Tbsp. oil and briefly stir-fry the shallots, garlic, and galangal or ginger (30 seconds). Add the pork (including the marinade). Stir-fry 2–3 minutes, adding 1–2 Tbsp. water when the wok or pan becomes dry.
- Add the sweet and sour sauce and bring it to a boil. Reduce heat to medium, cover, and simmer 8–10 minutes. Add the bell peppers and snow peas and simmer another 2 minutes. Finally, add the bok choy and simmer 1 more minute.

Thickening the Sauce

- In a cup, stir together remaining cornstarch with water, until cornstarch dissolves. Add this to the wok, stirring continually to mix it in.
- Reduce heat to low. As the sauce thickens, taste test it for salt and sweetness. If not salty or flavorful enough, add more fish sauce. If not sweet enough, add more sugar.
- If desired, sprinkle with a little fresh coriander. Serve with plenty of Thai jasmine-scented rice and enjoy.

SAVORY STICKY RICE WITH PORK

This wonderful sticky rice is a complete meal unto itself.

If you're a Chinese dim sum fan, you'll be sure to enjoy the following recipe. Adapted from the classic Chinese sticky rice dish, this savory Thai version of sticky rice is Asian comfort food at its best. The sticky rice is pleasantly chewy and full of flavor, and because it is steamed together with pork, mushrooms, shallots, and green onion, it makes for a complete meal unto itself.

This dish also provides for wonderful leftovers. To re-heat, simply steam 5–6 minutes, or use the banana or bamboo leaves to create individual sticky rice "packets," which can easily be taken to work and heated up in a microwave (just follow the instructions provided in the sidebar).

Yield: Serves 2–3 as a main entrée

Ingredients

2 cups Thai sweet rice

6 strips bacon

2 shallots, diced

3 cloves garlic, minced

1 cup shiitake mushroom, chopped into small pieces

Optional: 1 red chili, minced

2 Tbsp. fish sauce

1 Tbsp. regular soy sauce

1½ tsp. dark soy sauce

3 green onions, sliced, divided

1 package banana leaves OR bamboo leaves, thawed if frozen

Steamed Sticky Rice with Pork & Mushrooms

- Soak the sweet rice in water for at least 30 minutes. Drain and set aside.
- While rice is soaking, fry the bacon in a wok or large frying pan over medium-high heat, adding a little water if the wok becomes dry. Fry until chewy rather than crisp.
- Remove bacon, but reserve all or half the residual fat in the wok. Cut bacon into small pieces and return to the wok. Also add the shallots, garlic, mushrooms, and chili (if using), and stir-fry 2–3 minutes.

MAKE IT EASY

You needn't own an electric steamer to make this dish. Simply line a bamboo steamer or stainless steel colander with a double layer of banana leaf. These leaves are available at most Asian or Chinese food stores. Cut the leaf to cover the inside of your steamer. The leaf is better too large than too small as you can fold any excess over the rice before putting on the lid and steaming.

GREEN LIGHT

Banana and bamboo leaves are a wonderful natural resource (both grow abundantly and rapidly). The leaves enhance the flavor of the rice, and also make for wonderful presentation. For dim sum style, wrap the sticky rice inside the leaf and secure with a satay stick or with baker's twine. After you're done eating, the leftover leaves can be added to your compost bin for recycling.

Combining Sticky Rice with Other Ingredients

- When the shallots and mushrooms have softened, reduce heat to low and add the drained sticky rice. Also add the fish sauce, both soy sauces, and half the green onion.
- Gently stir over low heat until the color of the rice is consistent and ingredients are well incorporated. Remove from heat.

Steaming the Sticky Rice

- Transfer rice to a banana or bamboo leaf–lined steamer. Cover and steam 30 minutes over high heat, checking your steamer occasionally to ensure it doesn't boil dry.
- Turn off heat, but leave the lid on, allowing rice to sit 5 more minutes. Rice is done when soft and translucent.
- Taste test the rice, sprinkling over a little more fish sauce until desired taste is achieved. Gently fluff with a fork or chopsticks to mix in the fish sauce.
- Top with remaining green onion and serve.

BARBECUED PORK WITH SAUCE

This grilled pork is simple to make and very flavorful.

Barbecued pork is a common dish across China and many Southeast Asian countries, including Thailand. The pork may be the star player of the meal, as it is here, or it may be cooled and sliced up for use in other dishes such as fried rice, soups, or noodles.

In the following Thai dish, the pork is first marinated for a good length of time, then barbecued over a hot grill. It is sliced very thinly and served hot with rice. The accompanying sauce is salty, spicy, and sweet—flavors that marry well with the taste of the grilled pork. To put the dish together, simply place the sliced pork on a mound of rice with the accompanying sauce drizzled over. Fresh cucumber and tomato slices can be added to this dish or used as a garnish.

Yield: Serves 2–3

Ingredients

1 lb. pork tenderloin or pork belly
1/3 cup fresh coriander
Marinade:
1/4 cup tomato ketchup
2 Tbsp. fish sauce
2 Tbsp. soy sauce
1 Tbsp. oyster sauce
5 Tbsp. palm sugar or brown sugar
1 tsp. chili sauce
1 Tbsp. sherry (or cooking sherry)
Sauce:
1/4 cup good-quality chicken or pork stock
1 Tbsp. fish sauce
2 green onions, finely sliced
1/2 tsp. cayenne pepper, to taste
1 Tbsp. lime juice
2 Tbsp. palm or brown sugar
1/2 tsp. cornstarch
2 Tbsp. soy sauce

Barbecued Pork with Sauce

- Place unsliced pork in a bowl for marinating. Be sure to leave any fat on the pork, as this will help flavor the meat.
- Make the marinade by combining all marinade ingredients, stirring well to dissolve the sugar. Pour this marinade over the pork, turning the meat several times to coat.
- Cover and leave in the refrigerator to marinate at least 1 hour, or up to 24 hours (the longer the better).

ZOOM

In Thailand, unless you eat in 5-star hotels, you'll find the food laced with moderate to great amounts of chili. Chili sauce and chili powder (also known as "gun powder") are also served on the side. If you like your Thai food hot, feel free to add more chili. In fact, most Thai chefs won't tell you how much to add in recipes; rather, they will only say: "Chili: as much as you like."

GREEN LIGHT

Thais are very respectful of food, especially meat. In Thailand, a whole steak or cut of pork is never consumed by just one person, but is always shared. This is why traditional Thai recipes give instructions for slicing up the meat. Aside from being more economical, reducing red meat intake eases environmental stress and is considered healthier as well.

Making the Accompanying Sauce

- Place all sauce ingredients—except the cornstarch and soy sauce—in a pot or saucepan. Stir well and bring to a boil.
- Reduce heat to medium. Stir the cornstarch into the soy sauce until dissolved, then add to the sauce. Stir continually until the sauce thickens (1–2 minutes).
- Remove from heat and taste test for a sauce that is salty, sweet, and spicy. Add more fish sauce if it needs more salt, or more sugar if too sour. Cover to keep warm.

Barbecuing the Pork

- When pork is done marinating, cook over a hot grill, brushing the surface areas with leftover marinade during the first couple of turns. Pork is done when white or light pink inside.
- Slice the barbecued pork as thinly as you can. Give each person a mound of hot rice and top with the slices of barbecued pork. Drizzle over several tablespoons of the warm sauce, and top with a generous sprinkling of fresh coriander. In Thailand, this dish is also served with slices of fresh cucumber. Enjoy.

THAI PORK FRIED RICE

The most popular fried rice in Thailand, and also one of the easiest to make.

Fried rice is one of the world's favorite foods, and luckily it's an easy dish to make once you've learned a few cooking tips.

The first (and probably most important) tip is to use cooked rice that is several days old. The second tip is to keep your wok hot and dry during the cooking process, using as little liquid as possible.

There is a delicate balance to be achieved here: the wok must be hot enough to fry the rice evenly, but not so hot that the ingredients burn. Also, you want to add sauces for flavoring while at the same time being careful not to add too much moisture.

Yield: Serves 2 as a main entrée

Ingredients

4–5 cups cooked rice, several days old

3 Tbsp. oil, divided

3 cloves garlic, minced

1 1/2 cups raw or cooked baby shrimp

1 cup Chinese or regular breakfast sausage, cut into very small pieces

Optional: 1/2 cup roasted chicken

1 egg

2/3 cup fresh or frozen peas

3 spring (green) onions, sliced

1/8 tsp. white pepper

Stir-Fry Sauce:

2 Tbsp. fish sauce

1 Tbsp. oyster sauce

1 Tbsp. soy sauce

1 Tbsp. lime juice

2 tsp. sugar

1/2 tsp. cayenne pepper

Thai Pork Fried Rice

- If using rice that is several days old, drizzle over 1 Tbsp. oil and gently work it through with your fingers, separating any lumps back into individual rice grains. Set aside.
- Mix all stir-fry sauce ingredients together in a cup and set aside.
- Warm a wok or large frying pan over medium-high heat. Add remaining 2 Tbsp. oil and swirl around. Add the garlic and stir-fry to release the fragrance (about 30 seconds).

MAKE IT EASY

If using freshly cooked rice for this recipe, lay it out in one or two large bowls (a salad-type bowl works well) and place uncovered in the refrigerator for a few hours (or overnight). This will help dry it out for frying. Note that if the grains haven't yet formed into lumps, you can skip the first step of this recipe.

GREEN LIGHT

Leftover rice can be a challenge to heat up, as it dries quickly and loses its taste when refrigerated. Fortunately, this kind of dry, "old" rice is exactly what is needed to make the best-tasting fried rice. Other leftovers that can be used for fried rice include leftover roasted chicken or turkey, leftover chicken stock or broth, leftover breakfast sausage, and leftover peas or green onion.

Stir-Frying the Shrimp, Sausage, and Egg

- Add the shrimp, sausage, and chicken (if using) and stir-fry until the shrimp and sausage are cooked (if using pre-cooked shrimp and sausage, this will only take a moment).
- Using a wooden spoon or other cooking utensil, push ingredients to the side and add a little oil to the space cleared in the middle of the wok. Crack the egg into this space and quickly stir-fry to cook it (like making scrambled eggs).

Stir-Frying the Rice

- Add the rice, peas, and stir-fry sauce. Using 2 utensils and a tossing motion (like tossing a salad), stir-fry everything together for 3–4 minutes.
- Keep the wok hot and dry at this point, but not so hot that the rice burns. Add the green onion and continue stir-frying another 1–2 minutes until rice is hot and light.
- Remove from heat and taste test, adding more fish sauce until desired taste is achieved. Finish with a sprinkling of white pepper and serve with Thai chili sauce.

PORK SATAY

Pork satay grilled over a hot brazier is a common sight on the streets of Thailand.

While satay probably originated in Indonesia, today it is a popular dish in most Southeast Asian countries. It is one of the most popular street foods in Thailand, and can be found anywhere street food hawkers gather to sell their delicious wares.

Satay can be made with a variety of meats: chicken, pork, beef, mutton, and even shrimp and fish. By far the most popular types of satay in Thailand are those made with chicken and pork.

If the weather doesn't cooperate for outdoor cooking, or if grilling season is still out of reach where you live, this dish can also be broiled in your oven with delicious results.

Yield: Serves 2–4

Ingredients

Stainless steel or wooden skewers

1–2 lbs. pork tenderloin cut into thin strips approximately 1 inch wide

Marinade:

1 shallot, minced

4 cloves garlic, minced

1 tsp. ground coriander

1/2 tsp. cumin

1/2 tsp. turmeric

1/2 tsp. cayenne pepper

4 Tbsp. fish sauce

1 Tbsp. lime juice

2 tsp. dark soy sauce

1/3 cup liquid honey

1/2 cup coconut milk

Pork Satay

- If using wooden satay sticks, soak them in water to prevent burning (the kitchen sink works well for this).
- Combine all marinade ingredients together in a bowl, stirring well to dissolve the honey. Pour marinade over the pork strips and mix well.
- Cover and set in the refrigerator to marinate at least 30 minutes (or up to 24 hours).

ZOOM

Satay can be enjoyed a number of ways. The first is simply to serve it as a finger food along with a sauce for dipping. Satay can also be served with plain rice, coconut rice, or sticky rice. The latter is quite common in Thailand, with the sticky rice being pressed into balls with one's fingers and then dipped into the sauce. To complete the meal, serve with slices of fresh cucumber.

MAKE IT EASY

To make this dish in your oven, follow the marinating and skewering instructions (be sure to soak wooden satay sticks in water). Turn your oven to the "broil" setting. Line a baking sheet with foil, turning up the edges to prevent spilling. Lay the satay on the sheet and place under the broiler for 5 minutes, or until pork is sizzling and lightly browned. Turn over and broil until done.

Skewering the Pork

- Remove the pork from the refrigerator, and have ready a plate or platter for the finished satay.
- To skewer the meat, weave the strips of pork lengthwise along the stick.
- It's a good idea to fill the sticks like they do in Thailand: with only the upper half (up to the tip) filled, leaving the lower half empty. This gives the cook a ready handle for turning the satay (and the eater a handle for eating it!).

Grilling the Satay

- Warm up your barbecue or grill and lightly grease the cooking surface by brushing on a little oil.
- Place the satay sticks on the hot grill, allowing the handles to remain off the grilling surface (to keep them cool for turning). Brush with the leftover marinade the first time you turn them.
- Grill until the meat is browned and sizzling but still tender. Serve with Real Peanut Sauce (see Chapter 19) and enjoy.

VEGETARIAN TOM YUM SOUP

This vegetarian version of Tom Yum Goong is just as delicious as the original classic.

The term "Tom Yum Goong" refers to the now world-famous classic Thai soup made with shrimp in a spicy lemongrass broth. Although the shrimp is left out of the following recipe, the soup itself remains the same and is wonderfully delicious.

The health benefits of Tom Yum soup have been coming to light in recent years, with several scientific studies still under way. The soup is reportedly adept at chasing away cold and flu viruses, as well as boosting one's overall immune system. *Yield: Serves 2–4*

Ingredients

4–5 cups good-quality simulated "chicken" or vegetable stock

1 stalk lemongrass, minced, OR 3 Tbsp. frozen prepared lemongrass

4 kaffir lime leaves, left whole

3 cloves garlic, minced

1 red chili, minced, OR 1/2 tsp. cayenne pepper

2/3–1 cup fresh shiitake mushrooms

3 heads baby bok choy

1 cup cherry tomatoes

1 can coconut milk

1/2 Tbsp. fresh lime juice

1 tsp. sugar

2 Tbsp. vegetarian fish sauce OR 3 Tbsp. soy sauce

1 cup soft tofu

1/2 cup fresh coriander

Vegetarian Tom Yum Soup

- Place stock in a soup pot and bring to a boil over high heat. Add the lemongrass and lime leaves and boil hard for 1 minute.
- Reduce heat to medium and add the garlic and chili. Simmer for 5 more minutes.

ZOOM

Tofu is also known as soybean curd. Like cheese curd, tofu is made by curdling soy milk. Although still relatively new to the West, tofu has been around for millennia in Asia. Today there are various types of tofu, including firm, medium-firm, soft, and silken, the latter being used mainly for desserts. When buying tofu, look for brands made with organic soybeans wherever possible.

MAKE IT EASY

This soup can be made with a variety of vegetables depending on what is fresh in your region, or what you happen to have on hand. Instead of cherry tomatoes, regular tomatoes can be used. Any type of mushroom can be substituted for shiitake, including dried—just be sure to soak them thoroughly first. Instead of bok choy, try using broccoli or even asparagus.

Preparing and Adding the Vegetables

- Thinly slice the mushrooms and add to the soup. Simmer for 3–5 minutes, or until mushrooms have softened.
- Prepare the bok choy by breaking off the leaves from the stem. Slice the larger leaves in half, while any smaller leaves can be left whole.
- Add the bok choy plus the cherry tomatoes and simmer another 2–3 minutes.
- Reduce heat to low. Add the coconut milk, lime, sugar, and vegetarian fish sauce or soy sauce. Stir well to incorporate.

Preparing and Adding the Tofu

- Slice the tofu into cubes and add to the soup, stirring gently to keep it from breaking. Simmer for 1 minute over low heat.
- Taste test the soup, adding more vegetarian fish sauce or soy sauce (instead of salt) until desired taste is achieved. If too salty for your taste, add another squeeze of lime juice. For even more flavor and spice, add a dollop of Thai nam prik pao chili sauce.
- Ladle into bowls, sprinkle the fresh coriander over, and enjoy.

THAI FRESH ROLLS WITH DIP

These fresh rolls are healthier than spring rolls and are just as scrumptious.

There are various types of rolls in Thai cuisine, but mainly they can be divided into two groups: spring/egg rolls and fresh rolls. Unlike the former type, which are deep-fried, fresh rolls are exactly as the name suggests: fresh and light. Of the two types, fresh rolls are much healthier, not only because there is no hot oil involved, but also because they are made with rice wrappers instead of wheat; this means they are easier to digest, lighter in calories, and naturally gluten-free.

The other health benefit of fresh rolls is the fact that the vegetables remain crisp and uncooked, which means more nutrients per bite.

Yield: Serves 3–4

Ingredients

1½ cups cooked rice vermicelli noodles
1 cup baked flavored tofu
1 cup bean sprouts
½ cup fresh basil
½ cup fresh coriander
1 large carrot, shredded or grated
3 green onions, sliced into matchsticks
3 Tbsp. soy sauce
1 Tbsp. rice vinegar
1 pkg. small, round rice wrappers (dried)

Dipping Sauce:

½ cup water
½ tsp. tamarind paste
2 heaping tsp. brown sugar
3 Tbsp. soy sauce
2 cloves garlic, minced
1 chili, minced OR 1 tsp. chili sauce
1 heaping tsp. cornstarch
3 Tbsp. water

Thai Fresh Rolls with Dip

- Gently boil the rice vermicelli noodles until cooked, or simply soak them in a pot of hot water for 5–10 minutes (until soft enough to eat). Rinse with cold water to keep from sticking. Set aside.
- Using a large salad or mixing bowl, combine the tofu, bean sprouts, basil, coriander, carrot, green onion, soy sauce, and vinegar. Toss as you would a salad—this is your fresh filling. Set aside.

ZOOM

Rice wrappers might be considered one of the many wonders of Asian cooking. From their appearance, one would hardly think these round, thin "disks" could turn into beautiful clear wrappers just by immersing them in water! Rice wrappers are also known as rice paper, because they are paper-thin and are transparent as traditional rice paper once soaked.

MAKE IT EASY

The dipping sauce that accompanies these fresh rolls is a good example of Thai flavors: a mixture of spicy, salty, sweet, and sour. In order to achieve the best balance, the sauce must be taste tested and adjusted. If you prefer a saltier, more flavorful sauce, add more fish sauce. If you'd like it sweeter, add more sugar; and if you'd like it spicier, add more chili or chili sauce.

Softening the Rice Wrappers

- Fill a large bowl with hot (but not scalding) water. Slide a rice wrapper into the water. It will soften in 20–30 seconds. Remove the softened wrapper and place on a clean working surface (it will remain damp—this is normal).
- Position some of the cooked noodles across the lower half of the wrapper. Add a heaping tablespoon of tossed filling over the noodles, spreading ingredients out horizontally in the shape of a roll.

Rolling the Rice Wrappers

- Fold over the sides of the wrapper, then lift up the bottom and tuck it around the filling. Roll to the end of the wrapper and seal by wetting it with a little water and pressing firmly.
- Mix dipping sauce ingredients—except the cornstarch and water—together in a saucepan. Bring to a boil, then reduce heat to medium.
- Dissolve the cornstarch in 3 Tbsp. water and add to the sauce. Stir until sauce is thickened.
- Serve the fresh rolls with the warm sauce and enjoy.

VEGETARIAN STEAMED DUMPLINGS

This delicious dumpling recipe gives vegetarians a hearty dim sum offering.

Like other Chinese dim sum offerings, dumplings can be found in Thailand, especially in areas where Chinese immigrants have settled.

In North America, dim sum has become very popular in recent years. However, normally dumplings are filled with pork or shrimp, and are therefore off-limits for vegetarians. Fortunately, there are alternatives, as in the following vegetarian dumpling recipe, which, by the way, is just as delicious as most meat-filled dumplings. Made with a combination of shiitake mushrooms and tofu plus ginger, these dumplings are a complete meal unto themselves.

Yield: Serves 5–6

Ingredients

1 package fresh or frozen banana leaves

1 package dumpling or wonton wrappers

Filling:

3 cups fresh shiitake mushrooms

1 cup medium-firm tofu

1/4 cup vegetable stock or simulated "chicken" broth

1 Tbsp. grated galangal or ginger

3 cloves garlic

3 Tbsp. soy sauce

1 Tbsp. dark soy sauce

2 Tbsp. sesame oil

2 green onions, sliced

1/2 cup fresh coriander leaves and stems

1/4 tsp. white pepper

1 tsp. Thai chili sauce

Vegetarian Steamed Dumplings

- Prepare a bamboo steamer or Western-style stainless steel colander by lining it with banana leaves. The leaves will keep the dumplings from sticking (they are available in the freezer section of most Asian food stores).
- Place all filling ingredients together in a food processor. Process well to create a filling with the consistency of ground meat.

RECIPE VARIATION

There are two ways to make these dumplings into pan-fried goyzas or pot-stickers. In the first method, steam the dumplings as instructed, then briefly fry them until lightly browned. A second way is to omit the steaming and simply pan-fry them until lightly browned. Then add ½ cup broth to the frying pan and cover with a lid. Cook 10 minutes over medium-high heat, or until broth is gone.

ZOOM

There are many different types of Asian-style wrappers to choose from. Wonton wrappers are available everywhere; however, for the best possible dumplings, look for frozen round dumpling wrappers at your local Asian store. Dumpling wrappers make for the best-tasting dumplings and are also the prettiest to serve, as they do not turn dark in color.

Making the Dumplings

- Lay 6 wrappers out on a clean working surface. Also have ready a small dish of water.
- Place 1 heaping tsp. of the dumpling filling in the center of each wrap. Then generously moisten the periphery of each wrapper (using your fingers or a brush).
- Draw up the two sides of the wrapper and press together to form either a half-circle (round wrapper) or a triangle (square wrapper). Pinch to create a decorative edge.
- Set completed dumplings on a plate dusted with flour or cornstarch.

Steaming the Dumplings

- Place the dumplings in the prepared steamer (note that they can be touching, so long as they are not piled on top of one another). If you have stackable bamboo steamers, you can steam more than one batch at a time.
- Steam over high heat for 15–20 minutes, checking steamer occasionally to ensure it doesn't boil dry.
- Serve steamed dumplings with a dipping sauce made of equal parts soy sauce and plum sauce, or with one of the savory sauces in Chapter 19.

VEGETARIAN THAI GREEN CURRY

Served with rice, this healthy and aromatic curry makes a complete vegetarian meal.

Because of its incredible mingling of flavors, Thai green curry pastes and sauces work exceedingly well with vegetables as well as meat substitutes like tofu and wheat gluten. In fact, if you are vegetarian or vegan (or know someone who is), it's helpful to know that Thai cuisine offers a wide array of vegetarian dishes.

One of the advantages of Thai cuisine for vegetarians is the fact that most vegetarian recipes also happen to be vegan. While eggs appear occasionally (as in fried rice recipes), there are no cheese, milk, or other dairy products used in Thai cooking.

Yield: Serves 3–4

Ingredients

1 can good-quality coconut milk, divided

4 kaffir lime leaves

2 Tbsp. oil

1 pkg. medium-firm tofu OR wheat gluten "chicken" cutlets, sliced

1 small yam or sweet potato, cubed

1 cup cauliflower, cut into florets

1 red bell pepper

1 cup snow peas

Optional: 1/2 cup fresh basil for serving

Green Curry Paste:

1 stalk lemongrass, minced

2 tsp. freshly ground coriander

3 Tbsp. vegetarian fish sauce OR 4 Tbsp. soy sauce

1–3 green chilies, to taste

1 shallot, diced

2 cloves garlic

1 Tbsp. grated galangal or ginger

1 cup chopped coriander leaves and stems

1 1/2 tsp. dark soy sauce

Vegetarian Thai Green Curry

- Place all curry paste ingredients together in a food processor or chopper. Add a few Tbsp. of the coconut milk, enough to help blend ingredients and keep the blades moving smoothly. Process well to create a fragrant green curry paste.
- Prepare the lime leaves by snipping them into thin strips with scissors. Be sure to discard the stem and central vein of each leaf.

ZOOM

Most Thai dishes are not considered ready to be served without some kind of fresh topping. Usually a Thai herb such as coriander is added, while other times only something crunchy will do: ground peanuts or crispy fried noodles, for example. Still other dishes are served with a sauce poured over, inundating the dish with an abundance of Thai taste. For curries, the best topping is always basil.

GREEN LIGHT

Either tofu or wheat gluten can be used to make a delicious vegetarian curry. Here in the West, wheat gluten is only beginning to turn up in supermarkets, but in Asia, Buddhist monks have been using it for centuries to make all types of vegetarian fare. Wheat gluten is considered an environmentally friendly and cruelty-free source of protein, and safe for all diets (except those with celiac disease).

Stir-Frying the Green Curry Paste

- Warm a wok over medium-high heat. Add 1–2 Tbsp. oil and swirl around, then add the curry paste. Stir-fry until fragrant (about 1 minute), then add the rest of the coconut milk, stirring to mix in.
- Add the tofu or wheat gluten, plus the yam and cauliflower. Bring to a gentle boil, then reduce heat to medium. Cover and simmer 5–6 minutes.
- Add the red bell pepper, snow peas, and prepared lime leaf, stirring well to incorporate. Cover and simmer another 5 minutes.

Adjusting the Flavors

- Remove curry from heat and taste test it. Add up to 2 Tbsp. vegetarian fish sauce or soy sauce for more salt or flavor; if too salty, add a little lime juice. If too spicy, add a little more coconut milk. Sugar can be added for a sweeter curry, or fresh chili or chili sauce if you prefer it spicier.
- Serve immediately with plenty of Thai jasmine-scented rice or coconut rice. If desired, top with a sprinkling of fresh basil, and enjoy.

PUMPKIN CURRY WITH CITRUS NOTES

A delightful curry that is both nutritionally complete and beautiful to serve.

This curry is not a common dish in Thailand, but is based on some of the vegetarian Buddhist dishes one can find there. Pumpkin (or squash) is a common Thai ingredient, often found in curries, soups, and even desserts. Instead of tofu or wheat gluten, the following recipe also features chickpeas, which performs as the main protein source along with roasted pumpkin seeds as a topping.

Because of the beautiful colors in this curry, the dish makes a wonderful autumn recipe and is well suited as the main dish for a vegetarian or vegan Thanksgiving dinner and a Thai dessert to finish off the meal.

Yield: Serves 4

Ingredients

½ small pumpkin (3–4 cups) OR squash
½ large yam OR 1 sweet potato
1–1½ cups cherry tomatoes
1 cup chickpeas
2 Tbsp. freshly grated orange zest

Curry Sauce:
1 shallot
4 cloves garlic, sliced
1–2 red chilies OR 1–2 tsp. chili sauce
1 can coconut milk
1 tsp. tamarind paste
3 Tbsp. soy sauce
2 tsp. brown sugar
Juice of ½ lime
Juice of 1 orange
½ tsp. turmeric
1 Tbsp. rice vinegar
1 Tbsp. coriander seeds, ground
1 Tbsp. cumin seeds, ground
1 tsp. fennel seeds, ground

Pumpkin Curry with Citrus Notes

- For the curry sauce, prepare all curry sauce ingredients and place them in a food processor or blender. Note: use a coffee grinder (or spice grinder) to grind up the coriander, cumin, and fennel (or substitute ground coriander and cumin, and leave the fennel seeds whole).
- Blitz to create a fragrant Thai curry sauce.

ZOOM

There is a growing vegetarian movement in Thailand with vegetarian restaurants popping up in every major Thai city. If you are vegetarian or vegan, the best time to visit Thailand is during the vegetarian festival in Phuket, held in September or October. The festival lasts 9 days and features fascinating religious and cultural customs and an enormous array of vegetarian food.

MAKE IT EASY

Finish off this dish with one of the following toppings. Reserve the pumpkin seeds and roast them with a little oil and salt in your oven until crisp (or buy roasted pumpkin seeds). Sprinkle over the curry. Another topping is a few nasturtium flowers—or choose another type of edible flower depending on what is available in your garden. Violas, pansies, and rose petals can all be used.

Preparing and Simmering the Vegetables

- Peel the pumpkin (or squash) and yam (or sweet potato). Chop both into cubes or bite-size chunks.
- Warm a wok or large frying pan over medium-high heat. Add the curry sauce plus the pumpkin (or squash) and yam (or sweet potato). Stir well.
- When the curry begins to boil, reduce heat to medium. Simmer 6–8 minutes, stirring occasionally until vegetables have softened.
- Now add the cherry tomatoes, chickpeas, and orange zest. Stir and simmer for 3–4 more minutes.

Taste Testing and Adjusting the Flavors

- Taste test the curry for salt and spice. Add a little more soy sauce or a few shakes of sea salt if not salty enough. If not spicy enough for your taste, add more chili or chili sauce; if too spicy, add a little more coconut milk.
- To serve, scoop the curry into a large serving bowl, or portion out onto individual plates. Accompany with plenty of Thai jasmine rice or coconut rice, and enjoy this colorful and fragrant dish.

VEGETARIAN PAD THAI NOODLES

A true vegetarian pad Thai that doesn't disappoint.

Pad Thai is one of those wonderful noodle dishes no one should have to live without. Luckily, the dish can easily be made without meat or fish, so there is no need for vegetarians or vegans to go without. In fact, this vegetarian Pad Thai is so good, you'll want to make it for your non-vegetarian friends, if for no other reason than to demonstrate how wonderful vegetarian food can really be!

If you can, look for vegetarian fish sauce for this recipe, or substitute soy sauce. Most brands of vegetarian fish sauce are actually manufactured in Vietnam, so you will have more luck finding it in a Vietnamese food store rather than a Chinese one.

Yield: Serves 3–4

Ingredients

4 Tbsp. oil for stir-frying, divided

4 cloves garlic, minced

3–4 heads baby bok choy, chopped

2 eggs, lightly beaten

7–8 oz. Thai rice noodles (linguini width), soaked in hot water until "al dente"

2 cups bean sprouts

2 green onions, sliced

1/2 cup fresh coriander

1/4 cup unsalted dry-roasted peanuts, ground

Sauce:

2 Tbsp. vegetarian fish sauce OR 2 1/2 Tbsp. soy sauce

1/2 Tbsp. tamarind paste

3 Tbsp. water

1–2 tsp. Thai chili sauce

2 Tbsp. brown sugar

Vegetarian Pad Thai Noodles

- Combine the sauce ingredients together in a saucepan. Bring to a boil, then reduce heat, simmering 2–3 minutes until sauce thickens slightly.
- Taste test for a balance of flavors: spicy, sweet, salty, and sour, with an emphasis on sweet and salty. If too sour, add more sugar.
- Warm a wok over medium-high heat. Add 2 Tbsp. oil plus the garlic and bok choy. Stir-fry 1 minute or until bok choy has softened. Push ingredients aside, crack the eggs into the wok, and stir-fry to scramble them.

• • • • RECIPE VARIATION • • • •

To make this recipe vegan, instead of using eggs, substitute ¼ cup soft tofu. Add the tofu to the wok when the noodles are added and continue the recipe as is. The other option is to add ¼ cup cashews at the end of the recipe (when bean sprouts are added). Both methods provide adequate protein, and will taste wonderful too.

MAKE IT EASY

Soaking rice noodles is key to making Pad Thai. Start with a large pot of boiling water that has been removed from the burner. Dunk in the noodles, stirring to prevent sticking. Leave to soak 5 minutes. When noodles are soft enough to eat but still a little "crunchy," drain and rinse with cold water. The noodles will finish cooking when you fry them, turning wonderfully chewy-sticky in your wok.

Stir-Frying the Rice Noodles

- Add the drained noodles plus ⅓ of the sauce. Stir-fry everything together for 1 minute using 2 utensils and a gentle tossing motion (like tossing a salad).
- Add a little more sauce and continue stir-frying in the same way 1–2 more minutes, or until the noodles soften and become sticky.
- Depending on how many noodles you're using, you may need to add all the remaining sauce, or just a little more to achieve your desired flavor. Taste test as you go, adding more sauce as needed.

Stir-Frying the Noodles with Bean Sprouts & Egg

- Add bean sprouts and continue to gently toss the noodles 1 more minute. Noodles are done when they are chewy and a little sticky.
- Remove from heat and taste test, adding another sprinkling of vegetarian fish sauce or soy sauce (instead of salt) if needed. Add more chili or chili sauce if you prefer it spicier. Lime juice can be added if noodles are too sweet or too salty.
- Scoop noodles onto a serving platter. Sprinkle with green onion, coriander, and ground nuts, and enjoy.

STEAMED FISH WITH GINGER

This classic steamed fish turns out moist and melt-in-your-mouth tender.

This dish was first served to me in the Krabi Bay region at a restaurant located at the very edge of the sea. The place was, in fact, held aloft over the water by a set of rather precarious-looking stilts. The fish was very fresh (probably caught that very morning), and the steaming method used was the best way to cook it, preserving and enhancing that fresh fish tenderness and taste.

All of this is to say that, for this recipe at least, try to use fresh fish instead of frozen. Nearly any type of white-fleshed fish will work, including sole, snapper, halibut, tilapia, and many others.

Yield: Serves 2–4

Ingredients

2-4 white-fleshed fish fillets or steaks
Salt to taste
1 Tbsp. galangal or ginger, sliced thinly into strips
3 green onions, cut into matchsticks
2 Tbsp. coconut or canola oil
1/3 cup fresh coriander

Sauce:
1/2 cup chicken broth
1 stalk lemongrass, minced
3 Tbsp. white wine
2 Tbsp. fish sauce, plus more to taste
1 Tbsp. rice vinegar
2 tsp. brown sugar
1 Tbsp. soy sauce
1 red chili, minced, OR 1 tsp. chili sauce
1 tsp. cornstarch dissolved in 3 Tbsp. water

Steamed Fish with Ginger

- Prepare a steamer for the fish, ensuring you have a baking dish small enough to fit inside the steamer.
- The baking dish should be small or narrow enough to allow some steam to rise from the pot beneath and surround the fish.
- Rinse and pat dry the fish. Sprinkle salt on both sides of each piece and set aside.

• • • • RECIPE VARIATION • • • •

If you don't have a steamer, you can bake this dish. Preheat oven to 350 degrees F. Place the salted fish in a casserole-type baking dish. Prepare the sauce as instructed and pour half over fish. Top with ginger and green onion, then cover and bake 20 minutes. When fish is cooked, warm up the oil and drizzle over. Serve with remaining sauce. Add a sprinkling of fresh coriander and enjoy.

ZOOM

Steaming isn't a common cooking method in North America, yet it's one of the best ways to cook fish. If you own an electric steamer, this gadget will do a great job. In Thailand, a traditional Chinese-style bamboo steamer is placed over a pot of boiling water. A heatproof glass plate (or one made of stainless steel) is then set inside the steamer to hold the fish and its juices.

Making the Sauce

- Combine sauce ingredients (except cornstarch mixture) together in a saucepan and bring to a boil. Reduce heat to medium and simmer 5 minutes to cook the lemongrass.
- Add the cornstarch dissolved in water, stirring constantly until the sauce has thickened slightly. Remove from heat.

Steaming the Fish

- Set fish in the baking dish and pour ⅓–½ of the lemongrass sauce over. Cover remaining sauce and set aside.
- Sprinkle the galangal or ginger and green onions over the fish, then cover and steam 8–10 minutes. Fish is done when inner flesh is no longer translucent (thicker steaks may take longer).
- Remove fish from heat. Warm up the oil and pour it over the fish, then surround with the remaining sauce.
- Sprinkle the fresh coriander over and serve with rice.

BAKED SALMON IN CURRY SAUCE

The rich taste of salmon marries well with the intense flavors of Thai cuisine.

Although salmon is not a fish normally eaten in Thailand, you'll find that Thai flavors work well with the rich taste of the fish. Thai curry sauces are especially effective, as is the case here where fillets or steaks of fresh or frozen salmon are baked in a rich red curry sauce.

Although you can easily use a packaged Thai curry paste or sauce from the store for this recipe, you will nearly always get better results by making your own from scratch. The red curry sauce featured here is quick and easy to whip up, plus you get to choose your own level of chili spiciness.

Yield: Serves 2–4

Ingredients

2–4 salmon steaks or fillets

Optional: 1 banana leaf

1/2 cup fresh coriander

Sauce:

1 cup good-quality coconut milk

1 shallot, diced

3 cloves garlic

1 red chili, minced, OR 1–2 tsp. Thai chili sauce OR 1/2–3/4 tsp. cayenne pepper

1 Tbsp. grated galangal OR ginger

4 kaffir lime leaves, cut into thin strips

2 Tbsp. fish sauce

1/4 tsp. ground coriander

1/2 tsp. ground cumin

2 tsp. chili powder

1 Tbsp. palm sugar OR brown sugar

1/4 cup fresh coriander leaves and stems

1 Tbsp. freshly squeezed lime juice

Baked Salmon in a Rich Red Curry Sauce

- Place all sauce ingredients together in a food processor, chopper, or blender. Blitz to create a fragrant red curry sauce. Set aside.
- If you have banana leaf, use it to line a baking dish for the salmon (a casserole-type baking dish works well).
- The leaf may extend beyond the boundaries of the dish—this is fine. The salmon can also be made without banana leaf—simply grease the bottom of the dish with a little oil.

• • • • RECIPE VARIATION • • • •

To make banana leaf packets, cut 1 banana leaf (about 1 foot square) for each portion. Spoon 2 Tbsp. sauce onto the middle of the leaf, then place a portion of salmon on top. Drizzle over another 2 Tbsp. more sauce and fold the leaf over the salmon to create a packet. Secure with a satay stick or baker's twine. Place packets on a foil-lined baking sheet and bake 20-30 minutes. Serve with extra sauce.

ZOOM

The chili powder in this recipe is North American (which is the one found at any supermarket). This chili powder first came to us from Mexico and is not the same as Thai or Indian chili powder, which is far hotter. If you bought your chili powder in an Asian store, start by adding just half the indicated amount—you may find this more than enough to make your curry red hot!

Preparing the Fish for Baking

- Rinse and pat dry the salmon. Pour about ¼ of the sauce into the bottom of your lined or unlined baking dish.
- Add the salmon steaks, turning them over several times in the sauce. Finally, drizzle a little more sauce over each steak. If using banana leaf, gently fold the sides of the leaf over the fish to cover it.
- Cover the baking dish with a lid or foil and bake at 350 degrees F for 20–30 minutes, depending on the thickness of your fish.

Testing the Baked Fish

- Remove salmon from oven and check it by inserting a fork at the thickest part and gently pulling back. Salmon is cooked when inner flesh is no longer translucent.
- Before serving, taste test the fish and sauce, adding a little more fish sauce (instead of salt) until desired flavor is achieved.
- Briefly heat up the leftover sauce and serve on the side along with Thai jasmine-scented rice. Top the dish with a generous sprinkling of fresh coriander and enjoy.

FISH BAKED IN BANANA LEAF

This fish recipe is easy, exotic, and exquisitely flavorful.

Banana leaf is used extensively in Thai cooking and in myriad ways. In this recipe, fish fillets or steaks are marinated in a rich curry sauce, then wrapped up in banana leaves to make individual packets. While in Thailand these packets would then be steamed, in this recipe, for ease of preparation, they are oven-baked.

If you're game, eat this dish as you would if you were on a Thai beach: using the banana leaf as a plate. Simply open the packet, add a scoop or two of rice onto the side of the leaf (beside the fish), and enjoy!

Aside from plain rice, coconut rice goes incredibly well with this recipe.

Yield: Serves 2

Ingredients

2–3 white-fleshed fillets such as sole, tilapia, or halibut

1 pkg. banana leaves (thawed if frozen)

Handful fresh coriander for garnish

Curry Sauce:

1 shallot, diced

3 cloves garlic

1/2 can good-quality coconut milk

1 Tbsp. grated galangal OR ginger

2 tsp. ground coriander

1/2 cup coriander leaves and stems

2 Tbsp. fish sauce

3 kaffir lime leaves, cut into thin strips

1 fresh red chili, minced, OR 1 tsp. Thai chili sauce OR 1/2 tsp. cayenne pepper

1 tsp. chili powder

Juice of 1/2 lime

Fillet of Fish Baked in Banana Leaf

- Preheat oven to 350 degrees F.
- Place all curry sauce ingredients in a food processor or blender. Blitz until smooth.
- Place fish in a large bowl and add ½ the curry sauce, turning several times to coat. Set remaining sauce aside.
- Cover fish and place in the refrigerator to marinate for at least 10 minutes (or up to 30 minutes).

ZOOM

Banana leaf can be purchased at your local Asian store (if not fresh, look for frozen). The leaves come folded together. Unravel one and rinse it under hot water. Using scissors, cut the leaf to the size you need. Banana leaves won't last long in the refrigerator, so store them in your freezer (note that banana leaves need ½ hour to thaw before they can be separated).

MAKE IT EASY

Even if you haven't managed to find banana leaf, you can still make this recipe using foil or parchment paper. Simply tear off a sheet large enough to wrap each portion of fish, then follow the instructions in the recipe, marinating the fish and then wrapping each piece in foil or parchment paper (to keep paper from opening, turn the packet seam-side down).

Wrapping the Fish in Banana Leaf

- Cut 1 banana leaf (approximately 1 foot square) for each of the fish fillets or steaks. Lay the first banana leaf out on a clean working surface.
- Place a fillet in the center of the leaf, then fold the sides of the leaf over the fish. Fold the bottom and top over to create a square packet.
- Secure by weaving the end of a wooden satay stick through the leaf, or binding with baker's twine. Or, simply rest the packet seam-side down.

Baking the Fish

- Banana leaves are porous, so place the fish packets in a casserole dish or pie plate. Bake 20 minutes (or longer depending on the thickness of the fish). Fish is cooked when inner flesh is opaque and flakes easily.
- Warm up the reserved curry sauce. To serve, open the packets and scoop some rice onto the leaf (beside the fish). Drizzle the warm curry sauce over both fish and rice, and add a final sprinkling of fresh coriander.

EASY GRILLED HALIBUT

You'll have this delicious fish marinated and on the grill in no time.

For a quick and easy meal any night of the week, try this simple grilled halibut. Other types of white-fleshed fish can also be used including sole, tilapia, or trout (for fish that doesn't fall apart on the grill, look for thicker cuts).

The marinade for this dish is very simple to put together. One of its key ingredients is Thai sweet chili sauce, available at most supermarkets these days (look for it in the Asian section). The fish is then marinated briefly, or for several hours if preparing ahead of time.

If you like this marinade, experiment with using it for other types of meat or seafood, such as shrimp, scallops, chicken, or pork. You'll find the sweet, garlicky flavor goes well with nearly anything you might happen to be grilling up.

Yield: Serves 2–4

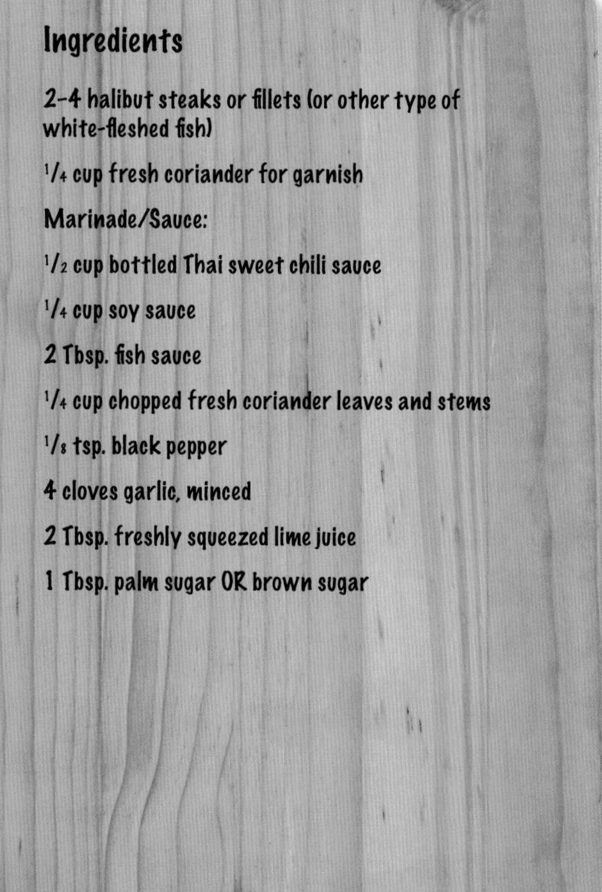

Ingredients

2-4 halibut steaks or fillets (or other type of white-fleshed fish)

1/4 cup fresh coriander for garnish

Marinade/Sauce:

1/2 cup bottled Thai sweet chili sauce

1/4 cup soy sauce

2 Tbsp. fish sauce

1/4 cup chopped fresh coriander leaves and stems

1/8 tsp. black pepper

4 cloves garlic, minced

2 Tbsp. freshly squeezed lime juice

1 Tbsp. palm sugar OR brown sugar

Easy Grilled Halibut

- Rinse the halibut steaks or fillets and pat them dry. Place in a flat-bottomed dish for marinating.
- Combine all marinade/sauce ingredients together in a small bowl, stirring well to dissolve the sugar. Pour ⅓ over the fish. Set the rest aside until later (this will be served as a side sauce).
- Turn the steaks several times in the marinade, ensuring all surfaces are well coated. Cover and place in the refrigerator to marinate at least 20 minutes (or up to 24 hours).

ZOOM

Grilling fish can be a challenge, as the more tender cuts or types of fish tend to fall apart on the grill. In Thailand, this problem is avoided by grilling whole small to medium-size fish rather than individual pieces. Rainbow trout works well for this method. Otherwise, consider using a fish cage, which can be easily turned without losing part of your fish between the bars of the grill.

MAKE IT EASY

Knowing when to take fish off the grill is one of the keys to making perfect melt-in-your-mouth grilled fish. To check whether fish is cooked, insert a fork into the thickest part and gently pull back. If inner flesh is soft and no longer translucent, the fish is cooked. As you grill, test the fish often to avoid overcooking, or you will lose the wonderfully moist tenderness of the halibut.

Grilling the Halibut

- While the fish is marinating, heat up your grill and brush the cooking surface with a little oil to prevent fish from sticking.
- When ready to cook, place fish on the oiled grill, leaving it to cook undisturbed (without moving or turning) for at least 5 minutes.
- Brush fish with some of the marinade (from the bottom of marinating dish) the first time you turn it.

Warming the Sauce

- While fish is grilling, place the reserved sauce in a saucepan and warm it up over medium heat (avoid boiling, or you will lose the fresh taste of the sauce).
- Serve the steaks with the extra sauce on the side, or plate up the halibut and spoon the sauce over each portion (this sauce is also excellent over rice or potatoes).
- Finish the dish with a sprinkling of fresh coriander and serve with your choice of Thai jasmine rice or Western-style roasted or grilled potatoes.

THAI WHOLE FISH

A classic dish that is popular in coastal regions of Thailand.

Some travelers to Thailand are horrified when, after ordering what sounds like a wonderful fish meal, they are served a whole fish complete with eyes and tail. The Thais are nothing if not frugal with food, and, thus, cooking the whole fish—rather than just parts of it—makes perfect sense. Not only is there less waste with this cooking method, there is also more taste and flavor, as the natural oils of the fish aren't allowed to escape as tends to happen when a fish is cut open and divided.

If you're game, try making this traditional Thai recipe for whole fish. Or, if you prefer, consider purchasing rainbow trout that already has the head and tail removed (available at most large supermarkets).

Yield: Serves 2

Ingredients

2 small to medium whole cleaned rainbow trout OR other type of white-fleshed fish

2 Tbsp. lime or lemon juice

1/2 tsp. salt

1/2 cup flour

1–1 1/2 cups oil for deep-frying

Optional: Slices of cucumber and tomato for garnish

Coriander-Chili Sauce:

3 cloves garlic, minced

3 Tbsp. sherry

1/2 cup coriander stems and leaves

2 Tbsp. soy sauce

2 Tbsp. fish sauce

1 Tbsp. lime juice

1 red chili, minced, OR 1–2 tsp. chili sauce

1/2 tsp. tamarind paste

2 Tbsp. palm sugar OR brown sugar

3 tsp. cornstarch dissolved in 1/4 cup water

Thai Whole Fish

- Make the coriander-chili sauce by stirring all sauce ingredients together in a small pot or saucepan.
- Place over medium-high heat, stirring until the sauce simmers and thickens.
- Remove from heat and taste test, looking for a balance of flavors: sweet, sour, salty, and spicy. Add more sugar if too sour, or more fish sauce if not salty enough. If too salty or sweet, add another squeeze of lime juice.
- Cover to keep warm and set aside.

MAKE IT EASY

Deep-frying fish is easy enough if you keep a few tips in mind. First, test the heat of the oil before plunging the fish into it. Drop in a cube of bread; if the bread sizzles and begins to cook within a second or two, the oil is ready. Second, once you have placed your fish in the hot oil, do not disturb it for at least 1 minute, or the flesh will tear.

GREEN LIGHT

To reduce the amount of waste involved with deep-frying, instead of paper towels, use a clean tea towel for draining. Also, when deep-frying only 1 or 2 items, check your oil—you may be able to reuse if it is still fairly clear and light in color. Never discard oil down the drain. Whenever possible, used oil or grease should be discarded at your local household hazardous-waste collection facility.

Preparing the Fish

- Place cleaned fish on a cutting board. Using a sharp, serrated knife, make 3–4 vertical cuts on each side of the fish. Cut about ½ inch deep, until you feel your knife reach the bone. These cuts allow the sauce to penetrate, and also make the fish easier to eat.
- Drizzle over the lime or lemon juice, then season with salt. Dredge fish with flour to coat.
- Pour the oil into a wok or large frying pan (oil should be at least 1 inch deep) and set over medium-high heat.

Frying the Fish

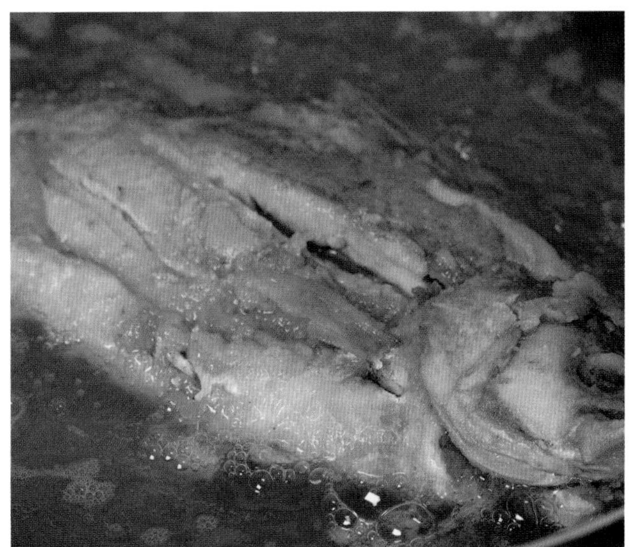

- Carefully place fish in the hot oil and fry 3–5 minutes per side (depending upon thickness). Fish is done when it is golden-brown on the outside and the flesh inside the cuts has turned opaque.
- Remove fish from oil and drain on paper towels or a clean tea towel.
- Place fish on a platter and pour the warm coriander-chili sauce over. Top with a sprinkling of fresh coriander and accompany with rice. If desired, garnish the platter with slices of fresh cucumber and tomato.

GRILLED FISH IN GARLIC SAUCE

This simple recipe works well with both mild and strongly flavored fish.

Because this fish recipe is lightly spiced, it tends to appeals to everyone at the dinner table. It also makes a quick and easy meal when you're in a hurry, as it can be put together in as little as 30 minutes. In addition, this dish is very adaptable: either fresh or frozen fillets or steaks can be used, and nearly any type of fish works with the mild flavors of the garlic-pepper sauce, from salmon to sole.

Finally, this fish tastes delicious any way you might want to serve it, whether with rice or Western-style potatoes—or even over a plate of salad greens if you happen to be watching your carbs.

Yield: Serves 3–4

Ingredients

3–4 fish fillets or steaks

1/8 tsp. freshly ground black pepper (for seasoning the fish as you grill)

1 1/2 tsp. cornstarch dissolved in 4 Tbsp. water

Handful of fresh coriander for garnish

Garlic-Pepper Sauce:

1/4 cup sherry (or cooking sherry)

1/4 cup soy sauce

3 Tbsp. fish sauce

2 Tbsp. palm sugar OR brown sugar

6 cloves garlic, minced

1/8 tsp. freshly ground black pepper

1/2 Tbsp. freshly squeezed lime juice

Grilled Fish in Garlic Sauce

- Rinse the fish fillets or steaks and pat dry. Place in a flat-bottomed dish for marinating.
- Combine all garlic-pepper sauce ingredients together in a small bowl, stirring well to dissolve the sugar. Pour ½ of this sauce over the fish, reserving the rest for later.
- Turn the fish several times, ensuring all sides are saturated with sauce.
- Place fish in the refrigerator to marinate for at least 10 minutes (or up to 24 hours).

• • • • RECIPE VARIATION • • • •

This recipe can also be made in your oven. Simply marinate the fish in a casserole-type dish, then bake at 350 degrees F for 20 minutes, or until inner flesh is no longer translucent. Serve as is, or transfer fish to a foil-lined baking sheet. Set oven to "broil." Spoon over some of the sauce and juices from the casserole dish and broil the fish until lightly browned. Serve with the warm garlic sauce.

GREEN ● LIGHT

In Thailand banana leaf is used for grilling all sorts of foods. If you're worried about losing some of your precious fish through the grill, cut a banana leaf (large enough for your fish) and place it over your grill. Cook your fish right on the leaf (as you would with foil). The leaf will become fragrant and gradually turn brown. Afterward, the used banana leaf can be added to your compost bin.

Grilling the Fish

- Preheat your grill and lightly brush it with a little vegetable oil to prevent fish from sticking.
- Grill fish 10–20 minutes, depending on the heat of your grill and the thickness of your fish.
- Upon turning the fish for the first time, brush it with a little of the leftover marinade, then lightly season it with freshly ground black pepper.
- Fish is cooked when inner flesh is opaque, soft, and flakes easily.

Thickening the Sauce

- Warm the reserved sauce over medium-high heat. When it starts to bubble, reduce heat to medium and add the cornstarch dissolved in water. The sauce will thicken in 30 seconds to 1 minute.
- Remove sauce from heat and taste test. If not salty or flavorful enough, add a little more fish sauce. If too salty, add another squeeze of lime juice. If too sour, add a little more sugar.
- Spoon the warm garlic sauce over both fish and rice, top with fresh coriander, and enjoy.

MUSSELS WITH THAI HERBS & SPICES

These aromatic mussels make for a beautiful appetizer or main course dish.

Mussels are a common seafood treat in Thailand, whether used in combination with other foods (as in a seafood soup or pancake), or on their own as in the following recipe.

The exquisite taste of this mussel dish comes from the various Thai herbs and spices used to flavor it. Fresh lemongrass is key, as are the kaffir lime leaf and fresh herbs. When it's finished, this dish might remind you of a beautiful mussel entree from the menu of your favorite gourmet restaurant. While it can be served with rice, in order to best soak up all those wonderful juices, I've found a crusty loaf of French bread makes the perfect accompaniment.

Yield: Serves 4–5 as an appetizer, 2 as a main entrée

Ingredients

1/2 cup good-quality chicken stock

1 stalk lemongrass, minced

4 kaffir lime leaves, torn in half

1/4 cup white wine

1 Tbsp. rice vinegar

1 fresh red chili, minced, OR 1/2 to 1 tsp. cayenne pepper

2 1/2 Tbsp. fish sauce

1 Tbsp. palm sugar OR brown sugar

1/2 cup coriander leaves and stems, plus extra for garnish

1 lb. fresh mussels, cleaned and rinsed

4 cloves garlic, minced

1 1/2 tsp. cornstarch dissolved in 3 Tbsp. water

1/4 cup fresh basil

To serve: Lemon or lime wedges

Mussels with Thai Herbs & Spices

- Warm a wok or large frying pan over high heat. Add the chicken stock plus the minced lemongrass and torn lime leaves.
- Bring the stock and herbs to a boil, then reduce heat to medium. Add the wine, vinegar, chili, fish sauce, sugar, and coriander, stirring well to incorporate.

ZOOM

Mussels come in all stages of preparedness. Wild mussels especially require some attention. First, dunk them in a large bowl of cold water. Then lightly scrub them with a small brush to remove any sand or grit. Remove any beards by giving them a firm tug. If not cooking mussels right away, store them in a fresh bowl of water in your refrigerator.

MAKE IT EASY

To prepare lemongrass, remove any dry outer leaves. Slice off the lower bulb and discard. Now thinly slice the lower ⅓ of the stalk (the softest part). Finely mince these slices or process them in a mini food chopper (or pound with pestle and mortar). Finally, cut the remaining (upper) stalk into 3–4-inch-long segments and add these to your stock as well, removing them just before serving.

Steaming the Mussels

- Add the mussels, gently stirring them into the flavored stock. Cover with a tight-fitting lid and simmer 2–3 minutes.
- Remove lid and gently stir the mussels. If some still haven't opened, put the lid back on and allow to steam 1 more minute.
- At this point, remove any unopened mussels from the wok and discard.
- Reduce heat to low and add the garlic, stirring it in.

Thickening the Sauce

- Push mussels aside to reveal the sauce. Add cornstarch (dissolved in water), stirring well to incorporate. As the sauce thickens, gently stir to combine it with the mussels.
- Remove from heat and taste test the sauce, adding more fish sauce if not salty or flavorful enough.
- Use a ladle to scoop mussels into a large serving bowl. Pour any remaining sauce from the pan over mussels and finish with a topping of fresh coriander and basil. Garnish with wedges of fresh lime or lemon.

EASY CHILI-GARLIC SHRIMP

These spicy shrimp make a quick and succulent finger food.

There are few world cuisines that really do justice to fresh shrimp, and Thai is one of them. The following recipe is a good example of just how flavorful and delicious Thai shrimp can be. Medium to large shrimp are best for this dish, and if you can find fresh, so much the better.

While these spicy shrimp can be served as a wonderful dinner entrée, they also make a perfect finger food for a party. You can easily prepare the marinade ahead of time, then just toss them in the marinade and broil them up (this only takes 10 minutes). Serve your chili-garlic shrimp on a platter with toothpicks pierced in each one for an easy and delightful eating experience.

Yield: Serves 4–6 as an appetizer, 2–3 as a main entrée

Ingredients

2 Tbsp. fish sauce

2 Tbsp. vegetable oil

2 Tbsp. coconut milk

½–1½ tsp. cayenne pepper

1½ heaping Tbsp. brown sugar

½ tsp. shrimp paste

3 cloves garlic, minced

Optional: 2 kaffir lime leaves, torn (stem and central vein removed)

Optional: 1 red chili, minced, OR
½ tsp. dried chili flakes (for extra-hot shrimp)

18–20 medium to large raw shrimp (thawed if frozen)

To serve: Lemon or lime wedges and fresh coriander

Easy Chili-Garlic Shrimp

- Place the fish sauce, oil, coconut milk, cayenne pepper, brown sugar, shrimp paste, garlic, and lime leaves (if using) in a mini chopper or food processor. Process well to create to a fragrant chili-garlic marinade.
- When adding the cayenne, adjust the amount according to how spicy you want your shrimp (½ tsp. will give you mild shrimp, while 1½ will give you hot shrimp).

ZOOM

When buying shrimp, it's always worth spending a little more and purchasing shrimp that are caught wild (as opposed to farmed shrimp). The health benefits of wild shrimp far outweigh that of farmed shrimp—and you'll also be ingesting far fewer toxins. Another option is to buy organic shrimp (either fresh or frozen), which are grown very cleanly and with respect to environmental concerns.

MAKE IT EASY

When broiling shrimp, you'll know they're ready to be turned when they are sizzling and steaming under the broiler; they may also be lightly browned, as when grilled. Turn the shrimp and wait for the same effect on the other side (about 3 minutes). Shrimp are well done when they turn plump and pink, and the inner flesh is no longer translucent but pinkish-white.

Preparing the Shrimp

- To prepare the shrimp, remove shells except for the tails (this makes for easier eating). Butterfly the shrimp by making a cut down the length of the back. Avoid cutting too deeply: ¼–⅓ inch is deep enough. Remove any veins that you find and rinse under cold water.
- Place prepared shrimp in a bowl and pour the marinade over, tossing to coat. Marinate 5 minutes while your oven heats up (avoid over-marinating shellfish: 10 minutes maximum).

Broiling the Marinated Shrimp

- Turn oven to "broil" and set an oven rack on the second-to-highest rung.
- Lay shrimp on their sides on a baking sheet (if desired, line the baking sheet with foil or parchment paper). For even more spice, sprinkle over the optional chili.
- Broil the shrimp 3 minutes per side. When turning, spoon over any leftover marinade from the bottom of the bowl.
- Plate up the broiled shrimp and garnish with wedges of lemon or lime, plus a sprinkling of fresh coriander.

PAN-SEARED SCALLOPS

These scallops offer melt-in-your-mouth taste and texture.

This scallop dish is a good example of what I would call "gourmet Thai food"; that is, it's not a classic Thai dish you would find regularly on the streets of Thailand. However, the ingredients and overall taste are decidedly Thai. If you like fresh seafood prepared in an easy gourmet style, you'll love this recipe.

While bay scallops are wonderful for mixed Thai seafood dishes, for this recipe it's better to use the larger sea scallops, mainly because they are pan-seared (which is tricky to accomplish adequately when using small scallops). The dish makes a delightful main entrée for two people, but because it's so beautiful to serve, this dish would also make a wonderful appetizer the next time you find yourself cooking for guests.

Yield: Serves 2

Ingredients

5–7 medium to large sea scallops

2 Tbsp. oil for pan-frying

Salt and freshly ground black pepper

Thai Sauce:

Juice of 1/2 lime

2 Tbsp. coconut oil OR light olive oil

1 Tbsp. coconut milk

2 Tbsp. fish sauce

1 tsp. minced garlic

3 Tbsp. chopped fresh coriander

1 fresh red chili, de-seeded, OR 1 tsp. Thai chili sauce

pinch white pepper

To Serve:

A bed of mixed salad greens

1/4 cup fresh coriander

1/4 cup fresh basil

Wedges of fresh-cut lime

Pan-Seared Scallops

- Prepare your serving plate by lining it with lettuce leaves or mixed salad greens. Sprinkle over half of the fresh coriander and basil and set the plate aside.
- Rinse the scallops and pat them dry. Set aside.

ZOOM

In Thailand, scallops are served in a variety of ways. Sometimes they are simply grilled on the half-shell, but often they are just one ingredient among many types of seafood within the same dish. Small bay scallops can be found in mixed seafood salads, seafood stir-fries, or in soups or curries; some of the larger and pricier hotels might present larger sea scallops in gourmet entrees.

MAKE IT EASY

To get a good sear on your scallops, make sure they are dry—use a clean tea towel or paper towels to wick away any moisture. When placing them in the pan, leave enough room between for easy turning. Then, don't move them or they will tear. Wait 1½–2 minutes, allowing scallops to develop a natural sear on the bottom. Scallops are done when both sides have a crispy-looking sear.

Preparing the Thai Sauce

- Combine all sauce ingredients together in a saucepan.
- Warm up the sauce over medium heat (avoid "cooking" the sauce, or you will lose its fresh flavor).
- When hot, remove sauce from heat and taste test for salt and spice. Add more fish sauce if not salty or flavorful enough, or more lime juice if too salty for your taste. If too spicy, add a little more coconut milk; if too sour, add a little sugar.
- Cover to keep warm and set aside.

Searing the Scallops

- Warm a wok over medium-high heat. Add 2 Tbsp. oil.
- Place the dry scallops in the hot, oiled wok. Season with salt and pepper. Allow at least 1½ minutes before attempting to turn them.
- After 3–4 minutes, gently turn the scallops. Season with salt and pepper, and continue frying 3–4 minutes.
- Place seared scallops on your prepared serving plate. Pour the warm sauce over and garnish with remaining coriander and basil.

BAKED THAI OYSTERS

These oysters are perfect for a party or special dinner for two.

For most North Americans, oysters are considered a delicacy and too expensive to eat on a regular basis. This isn't necessarily the case in coastal areas of Thailand where all manner of seafood can be found at affordable prices. In fact, one of the most common ways of cooking oysters in Thailand is in an egg-based pancake fried up together with vegetables and several Thai sauces (called "hoi tod," also sometimes made with fresh mussels instead of oysters).

For the following recipe, it's best to use fresh shucked oysters. Ask your fishmonger for oysters that are already shucked, plus some leftover shells that you can use for cooking and serving. This is much easier than shucking your own, which requires not only a good tool but also an experienced hand.
Yield: Serves 2–4

Ingredients

1 container rock salt

16–20 shucked oysters with cleaned, reserved half-shells

To serve: Fresh coriander and lime wedges

Sauce:

1/3 can good-quality coconut milk

1 shallot, sliced

4 cloves garlic

2 Tbsp. fish sauce

1 tsp. ground coriander

4 kaffir lime leaves, snipped into thin strips with scissors, stems discarded

1/4–1/2 tsp. cayenne pepper, to taste

1 tsp. chili powder

Juice of 1/2 lime

1 tsp. sugar

1/2 tsp. shrimp paste

Baked Thai Oysters

- Pour some rock salt out onto a baking sheet (preferably one with sides to prevent salt from spilling). Make the bed of salt thick enough to hold the oyster shells securely.
- Now position the half-shells in rows over the salt bed. Set aside.

ZOOM

In Western culture, oysters are associated with expensive champagne and celebrations of all kinds. But if you're more interested in the food than the champagne, consider a less expensive option. Oysters can be paired with nearly any dry white wine, but are especially wonderful with a crisp Riesling or chardonnay, or a sauvignon blanc. Or, look for a dry, sparkling white wine.

MAKE IT EASY

If serving this dish to guests, here are a few make-ahead tips. Prepare the baking sheet in advance, laying out the salt and shells so they are ready to be filled. The Thai sauce can also be made up to 1 day ahead of time. When guests arrive, simply fill the prepared shells with the oysters, spoon over the sauce, and broil. The Thai sauce will thicken when refrigerated, so take it out 30 minutes before.

Making the Thai Sauce

- Place all sauce ingredients together in a food processor, chopper, or blender. Adjust the amount of cayenne pepper added according to how spicy you'd like your oysters. Process well to create a fragrant Thai sauce.
- Taste test the sauce, adding more fish sauce if you'd prefer it saltier or more flavorful. Add more cayenne or more chili powder if you'd like it spicier. If too salty, add another squeeze of lime juice. If too spicy, add a little more coconut milk. Set aside.

Spooning Sauce Over Oysters

- Turn oven to the "broil" setting.
- Scoop the oysters out of their container and place in the shells you prepared earlier.
- Spoon some of the Thai sauce you just made over each oyster, filling close to the brim of each shell.
- Broil 2–3 minutes directly under the heating element, or until oysters are lightly cooked and piping hot.
- Sprinkle fresh coriander over the oysters, and add lime wedges on the side. Serve immediately.

COCONUT SHRIMP

These coconut-battered shrimp are wonderful to serve company.

Battered, deep-fried shrimp exist across many cuisines and cultures, and are no stranger to Thai cooking. Coconut and shrimp is an exotic combination, and just one bite of these shrimp can conjure up the feeling of being on a hot Thai beach, enjoying the sunset. These shrimp are especially wonderful when paired with my Fresh Mango Sauce for dipping.

For this recipe, either fresh or frozen shrimp will work, but be sure to use raw rather than pre-cooked shrimp (which won't give you the tender results you're looking for). The shrimp are easier to serve and eat if they are first "butterflied" according to the instructions, with some of the shell left on the tail.
Yield: Serves 2–4

Ingredients

12-16 medium to large raw shrimp

3/4 cup all-purpose flour

1 1/2 tsp. baking powder

1/2 tsp. salt

1/4 tsp. cayenne pepper

1 egg

1/2 cup ice water

3/4 cup dry shredded unsweetened coconut (baking type)

1-2 cups coconut, canola, or other high-temperature oil for deep-frying

Coconut Shrimp

- Remove shells from shrimp, but leave on the tails for easier eating.
- "Butterfly" the shrimp by making a shallow cut (1/4 inch deep) along the length of the back of each shrimp. Remove any veins that you find.
- Rinse and set shrimp aside.

RECIPE VARIATION

Coconut Battered Scallops. For this variation, use medium-size scallops. Rinse and pat them dry, then follow the same instructions as indicated for the shrimp, dipping them first in the batter, then rolling in the coconut. Scallops are done when their battered coating turns light to medium golden-brown, and the inner flesh is opaque rather than translucent. Serve with the dipping sauce.

MAKE IT EASY

For this recipe, fry the shrimp as quickly as possible, preferably in one or two batches; otherwise any dropped bits of coconut will start to burn in the oil. Use tongs to place and remove the shrimp, doing so gently so as not to lose any of that precious batter. Drain the fried shrimp on a clean tea towel or paper towels. If not serving right away, keep them hot on a baking sheet in a warm oven.

Coating Shrimp with Batter and Coconut

- Make the batter by stirring together the dry ingredients: flour, baking powder, salt, and cayenne pepper.
- Crack the egg into the flour mixture, then add the ice water, stirring quickly to create a fairly smooth batter (don't worry if there are a few small lumps).
- Spread the dry shredded coconut over a plate and set beside the batter.
- Holding shrimp by the tail, dip them into the batter, then roll in the coconut to coat. Place on a dry plate near the stove.

Frying the Shrimp

- Pour oil into your wok (it should be 1 inch deep) and set over medium-high heat. To test if oil is hot enough, drop in a tiny bit of batter; if it sizzles and cooks, the oil is ready.
- Carefully drop shrimp in the oil. Fry about 20 seconds per side, or until shrimp are light golden-brown.
- Remove from oil and serve while still hot and crisp with Thai sweet chili sauce for dipping, or with my Fresh Mango Sauce (see Chapter 19).

THAI CALAMARI

This delicious deep-fried squid is surprisingly easy to make.

Squid can be found in many Thai mixed seafood dishes, such as soups, stir-fries, and even salads. It is fried, steamed, or even grilled, and of course deep-fried as in this recipe. Here the squid is cut into rings and fried up like Western-style calamari.

For ease of preparation, look for fresh or frozen calamari (squid) tubes that are already cleaned and ready for cooking. All you need to do then is slice them up, dip in my batter mixture, and fry to golden-brown perfection. Serve the deep-fried calamari together with either Thai sweet chili sauce for dipping, or my own Easy Coconut Dip, and this dish makes for a true seafood treat.

Yield: Serves 2

Ingredients

2 large (or 3–4 medium) fresh or frozen squid tubes

½ cup semolina flour

½ tsp. salt

¼ tsp. cayenne pepper

¼ tsp. white pepper

1–2 cups coconut, canola, or other oil for deep-frying

Optional: Bed of lettuce for serving

To serve: Thai sweet chili sauce OR Easy Coconut Dip (see Chapter 19)

Thai Calamari

- Place thawed squid tubes in front of you on a cutting board. Using a sharp knife, cut slices about ½ inch wide. Because the calamari is actually a long tube, slicing it will create rings. Open up the calamari rings and set aside. Note that the calamari should remain moist (no need to pat it dry).
- Mix together the semolina flour with the salt, cayenne pepper, and white pepper. Spread this mixture out over a plate or in a mixing bowl.

ZOOM

Semolina flour can be purchased at most health or organic food stores. Other types of flour won't give you the much-desired crunchy coating. Semolina is a granular type of flour made from the bran that flakes off during the processing of wheat. Note that the type you want to buy is the harder, more granular type as opposed to the softer kind used to make cream of wheat cereal.

MAKE IT EASY

Well-seasoned chefs will tell you that squid is best either very lightly cooked, or cooked for very long periods: anywhere in between results in a rubber-like texture that has no taste. For the following recipe, you will want to deep-fry your calamari briefly—just long enough to achieve a light golden-brown coating. This only takes a minute or two, depending on how hot your oil is.

Coating the Calamari with Batter

- Roll the calamari rings one by one in the flour mixture until they are covered. Place floured rings on a clean plate near the stove.
- Pour the oil into a wok or frying pan (it should be at least 1 inch deep) and place over medium-high heat.
- To test if oil is hot enough, dip just the tip of one of the battered rings into the oil. If it starts to sizzle and cook, the oil is ready.

Frying the Calamari

- Using tongs, place as many rings into the oil as can comfortably fit at one time. Reduce heat to medium and stand back as you fry, as sometimes the calamari can pop as it releases its juices.
- Fry about 1 minute per side. Calamari is cooked when batter has turned light golden-brown.
- Drain calamari on a tea towel or paper towels. If desired, serve on a bed of lettuce with Thai sweet chili sauce or my Easy Coconut Dip (see Chapter 19).

STIR-FRIED BOK CHOY WITH SHRIMP

A delicious bok choy recipe that can be served as a side dish or main entrée.

Whether you're looking to make a side vegetable dish or a well-rounded meal, this Thai stir-fry more than satisfies. Bok choy is one of the most popular of Asian vegetables, and for good reason. Its delicious flavor and natural crunchiness are perfectly suited to a stir-fry.

In this recipe, baby shrimp provide the main protein source, but feel free to substitute thin strips of chicken or pork.

Either baby bok choy or regular bok choy works with this recipe, depending on what is fresh and available where you live.

Yield: Serves 2 as a main entrée

Ingredients

5–6 heads of baby bok choy OR 4–5 cups chopped regular bok choy

2 Tbsp. oil for stir-frying

1 cup cooked baby shrimp, thawed if frozen

Stir-Fry Sauce:

2 Tbsp. oyster sauce

2 Tbsp. soy sauce

2 Tbsp. fish sauce

2 Tbsp. Thai sweet chili sauce

2 Tbsp. brown sugar

2 tsp. freshly squeezed lime juice

7–8 cloves garlic, minced

Easy Stir-Fried Bok Choy with Baby Shrimp

- Prepare the bok choy. If using baby bok choy, separate the heads into individual leaves and discard the stem. If the white sections of these leaves are very wide or large, you can slice them in half lengthwise.
- If using regular (large) bok choy, chop each leaf into square, bite-size pieces.

RECIPE VARIATION

Vegetarian/Vegan Bok Choy with Tofu. Instead of shrimp, add 1 cup soft tofu sliced into small cubes. Add tofu at the end (when you add the remaining stir-fry sauce). Stir gently to incorporate, cooking just long enough to heat it through. Instead of regular oyster sauce, look for vegetarian oyster sauce (available at most Asian stores). Instead of the fish sauce, substitute soy sauce.

ZOOM

Bok choy is a member of the cabbage family, and offers many of the same health benefits. These days, bok choy is available in most supermarkets, though it is often fresher if purchased at an Asian market. Bok choy is also easily grown in your garden, with seeds now being readily available. Bok choy makes a perfect stir-fried vegetable, as it cooks in just minutes.

VEGETABLES

Making the Stir-Fry Sauce

- Combine all the stir-fry sauce ingredients together in a bowl or cup, stirring well to dissolve the sugar.
- Heat a wok or large frying pan over medium-high heat for 30 seconds. Add oil and swirl around, then add the bok choy plus 2–3 Tbsp. of the stir-fry sauce.
- Stir-fry 1–2 minutes, or until wok starts to become dry.

Adding the Stir-Fry Sauce and Shrimp

- Add another 2–3 Tbsp. sauce plus the baby shrimp, and continue stir-frying another 2–3 minutes.
- Add all the remaining sauce. This dish is done when bok choy has softened, but the green leaves are still bright and colorful.
- Do a taste test, adding more sugar if you prefer it sweeter, or more lime juice if it's too salty.
- Transfer to a serving platter, pouring any remaining sauce from the bottom of the wok over the stir-fry. Serve with rice and enjoy.

THAI GREEN BEANS WITH PORK

This Chinese-inspired dish is so spicy and deliciously salty, it can be addictive.

This dish is yet another example of the strong influence of Chinese food and cooking practices on Thai cooking. Based on the famous Chinese dish of the same name, this Thai version is even more delicious, made with lots of red chili (or chili sauce) and fish sauce for a salty-spicy combination that is simply wonderful if you enjoy spicy food. Pair with a generous portion of plain rice to balance out the zinging assault on your taste buds. Finally, a cold lager finishes the taste experience perfectly, cooling the palate so you're ready for more.

This dish is traditionally made with ground pork, but ground chicken or turkey could easily be substituted.

Yield: Serves 2

Ingredients

4 cups Asian long beans or regular green beans

3 Tbsp. very small dried shrimp

3–4 Tbsp. hot water

2–3 Tbsp. oil for stir-frying

2 shallots, diced or finely chopped

1 cup ground pork

Paste:

2 Tbsp. fish sauce

1 Tbsp. soy sauce

2 tsp. sesame oil

3 cloves garlic, minced

1 Tbsp. grated galangal or ginger

1 tsp. shrimp paste

1 tsp. palm sugar or brown sugar

1–2 red chilies, minced, or 1–3 tsp. Thai chili sauce

Thai Green Beans with Pork

- To prepare the beans, rinse well under cool water and cut or snip off the tails. Chop the beans into 2-inch lengths. Set aside.
- Prepare the shrimp by soaking them in hot water.

ZOOM

The dried shrimp featured in this recipe are used across much of China and Southeast Asia. They are the basis of what is used to make shrimp paste. If you can't find them at your local Asian store (check the shelves and refrigerated sections), look for them in Chinatown or at any Asian store where dried fish and herbs are sold in bulk by weight.

MAKE IT EASY

There is a definite advantage to preparing long beans. Instead of cutting off the tails of each individual bean and then slicing them into sections, with long beans all you have to do is line them up and chop the whole lot at once. Though they are easier to chop, they take slightly longer to cook, being denser than the Western green bean. Also note that they remain chewy in texture.

Making the Paste

- Place all paste ingredients in a food processor or chopper. Process well. Set this paste next to the stove.
- Warm a wok or large frying pan over medium-high heat. Add the oil and swirl around, then add the shallots plus the ground pork.
- Stir-fry 2–3 minutes. When the wok becomes dry, add some of the shrimp along with the shrimp's soaking water, 1 Tbsp. at a time.

Adding the Shrimp and Water

- Add the rest of the shrimp and soaking water, plus the paste and beans. Stir-fry 5–8 minutes, until beans have softened and the pork is cooked.
- Remove from heat and taste test for salt and spice. Note that this dish is meant to be both salty and spicy. If too salty for your taste, add a squeeze of lime juice. If not salty or flavorful enough, add 1–2 Tbsp. more fish sauce; if not spicy enough, add more chili.
- Serve with rice and enjoy.

CURRIED CHICKPEAS

This wonderful recipe reveals one of Thai food's many influences: Indian cuisine.

Indian cooking has always been an important influence in Thai cuisine, and, indeed, the two cultures share many of the same spices and herbs. Curry is popular across both nations, and though Thai curries are decidedly different from Indian ones, many of the same ingredients come into play.

There are various types of curried dishes in Thailand, and often they are made with Indian-style curry powders. The following dish does not rely on a curry powder, but uses traditional curry ingredients instead, such as turmeric, coriander, and cumin.

Yield: Serves 2 as a main entrée, 4 as a side dish

Ingredients

2 Tbsp. oil for stir-frying

1 shallot, diced

3–4 cloves garlic, minced

12–14 oz. can chickpeas, drained

3 tsp. ground cumin

1/2 tsp. ground coriander

1/2 tsp. turmeric

1/4–1/2 tsp. cayenne pepper

2 Tbsp. fish sauce (OR 2 1/2 Tbsp. soy sauce if vegetarian)

1/4 cup freshly squeezed lemon or lime juice

1/8 tsp. black pepper

3/4 cup fresh coriander, lightly chopped

Curried Chickpeas

- Warm a wok or large frying pan over medium-high heat.
- Add 2 Tbsp. oil and swirl around. Now add the shallots and garlic.
- Stir-fry 1 minute to release the fragrance of the garlic.
- Add the chickpeas plus the cumin, coriander, turmeric, and cayenne pepper.

ZOOM

Chickpeas are an incredibly healthy food, and because of their high protein content, they make the perfect meat substitute for vegetarians. Also known as garbanzo beans, chickpeas are high in folate as well as iron and various trace minerals. Chickpeas are good for your heart, naturally lowering your cholesterol. Also, their high fiber content helps stabilize blood sugar levels.

MAKE IT EASY

To make your own dried chickpeas instead of buying canned, rinse 1 cup dried chickpeas, removing any dark or stone-like peas. Place in your slow cooker together with 4 cups water and ½ tsp. salt. Set on "high" and cook 2–3 hours, or until chickpeas have absorbed most of the water and are soft enough to eat. Any extra chickpeas will keep in the refrigerator for up to 3 days.

Stir-Frying the Chickpeas

- Stir-fry the chickpeas with other ingredients for 1–2 minutes. Add 2–3 Tbsp. water when the wok or pan becomes dry.
- Add the fish sauce (or soy sauce) and continue stir-frying 5 more minutes, or until the chickpeas are covered with the spice mixture and are piping hot.

Adding the Lemon or Lime Juice

- Remove chickpeas from heat. Stir in the lemon or lime juice, black pepper, and most of the fresh coriander, reserving a handful for the garnish.
- Taste test the chickpeas. If not salty or flavorful enough, add a little more fish sauce (or soy sauce). If too salty for your taste, add another squeeze of lemon or lime juice.
- Top with remaining coriander and serve with plenty of Thai jasmine-scented rice.

STIR-FRIED VEGETABLES WITH TOFU

Choose your own combination of vegetables for this tangy-delicious stir-fry.

Watching a Thai chef at work over a hot wok makes the process of creating a stir-fry look easy. But when you do it yourself, you may well find your stir-fry lacking in taste. Unless you're very experienced in Asian cooking practices, getting a stir-fry sauce to taste just right is a challenge.

For this reason, it's sometimes helpful to make the stir-fry sauce before you start frying. This way you can taste test it and get the flavors exactly as you like them. Because the following recipe does exactly this, it's pretty much foolproof, even for beginners.

Yield: Serves 2-3

Ingredients

1 thumb-size piece of galangal or ginger
3 heads of baby bok choy
1 medium carrot, sliced
5–6 shiitake mushrooms, sliced
1 red bell pepper, sliced
1 orange or yellow bell pepper, sliced
1 small head broccoli, cut into florets
3 green onions, cut into matchsticks
1 cup soft or medium tofu
2 Tbsp. oil
3-4 Tbsp. white wine

Stir-Fry Sauce:

1/3 cup good-quality chicken stock
2 Tbsp. fish sauce
1 Tbsp. lime juice
1 tsp. liquid honey, plus more to taste
1 red chili, minced, OR 1 tsp. chili sauce
2 tsp. cornstarch
4 Tbsp. water
5–7 cloves of garlic, minced

Stir-Fried Mixed Vegetables with Tofu

- To prepare the galangal or ginger, cut it into thin slices, then into thin strips. If you rinse it well, you can leave on the skin for extra fiber and nutrients.
- To prepare the baby bok choy, separate the leaves from the stem. Slice any of the larger leaves in half for easier eating.
- Cut up all other vegetables as well, and have them ready for stir-frying.
- Prepare the tofu by slicing it into cubes.

RECIPE VARIATION

If you are vegetarian, instead of the chicken stock, substitute vegetable stock or simulated chicken stock. Instead of fish sauce, use vegetarian fish sauce, or substitute 2½ Tbsp. soy sauce. For even more protein, add ½ cup dry roasted cashews at the end of the recipe (when you add the last of the stir-fry sauce), or finish the dish with a topping of ground peanuts.

MAKE IT EASY

For this stir-fry to taste its best, be sure to taste test it, looking for a balance of salty, spicy, sweet, and sour. A final test can be done before serving, as the flavors will change slightly with the addition of the vegetables and tofu. If you prefer more salt, add more fish sauce; if too salty or sweet for your taste, add more lime juice. If you'd prefer it spicier, add more chili. More honey can also be added.

Making the Stir-Fry Sauce

- Place all the sauce ingredients—except cornstarch, water, and garlic—in a saucepan. Set over medium-high heat.
- When the sauce begins to bubble, reduce heat to medium-low. Stir together the cornstarch and water until cornstarch dissolves. Add this mixture plus the garlic, stirring well. The sauce will thicken in about 1 minute.
- Remove from heat and taste test the sauce, adjusting the sweet, sour, and salty flavors to suit your taste.

Stir-Frying the Vegetables

- Warm a wok over medium-high heat. Add oil plus the galangal, carrots, and mushrooms. Stir-fry 2–3 minutes. When wok becomes dry, add a little wine.
- Add remaining vegetables plus ⅓ of the stir-fry sauce. Stir-fry another 1–2 minutes, or until broccoli has softened.
- Add remaining stir-fry sauce plus the tofu. Gently stir until everything is hot (soft tofu may break up a little—this is normal).
- Serve hot from the wok with plenty of Thai jasmine-scented rice.

GRILLED SHRIMP & PINEAPPLE SALAD

This dish is fun to make and beautiful enough to serve company.

This is the perfect summer dish, as the shrimp can be grilled on your barbecue and there is no call at all for a stove. While grilled shrimp are always delicious, when they're paired up with a little grilled pineapple and served with fresh greens as well as a cool coconut salad dressing, they're simply spectacular.

While either fresh or canned pineapple can be used for this recipe, fresh always tastes better, and has a firmer texture which works well for grilling. The same holds true for the shrimp, although frozen could be substituted in a pinch.

Pair this delightfully tropical salad with a glass of your favorite white wine, or, alternatively, a fresh fruit spritzer, and enjoy a taste of summer.

Yield: Serves 2 as a main entrée

Ingredients

12–14 fresh medium to large shrimp

1 cup pineapple chunks

1 package wooden skewers

Salad greens, enough for 2 large portions

1 red bell pepper, diced

½ English cucumber, sliced

⅓ cup fresh coriander

Marinade:

4 Tbsp. oyster sauce

1 Tbsp. brown sugar

4 cloves garlic, minced

Dressing:

1 cup coconut milk

2 Tbsp. oil

2½ Tbsp. fish sauce

2 Tbsp. lime juice

½ red chili, minced, OR ½ tsp. cayenne

1–3 tsp. palm sugar OR brown sugar

Grilled Shrimp & Pineapple Salad

- Combine marinade ingredients together in a small bowl or cup, stirring to dissolve the sugar.
- Place both shrimp and pineapple in a mixing bowl and pour the marinade over. Gently turn the pineapple and shrimp in the marinade, ensuring all surfaces are saturated.
- Set in the refrigerator to marinate 5–10 minutes, or until you're ready to cook (no longer than 15 minutes for the shrimp).

ZOOM

Coconut oil and milk are similar to butter in that they become solid at cooler temperatures. You can use this to your advantage. If, for example, you find your coconut milk salad dressing too thin in consistency—or if you'd like a richer coconut taste—place it in the refrigerator until you're ready to eat. The cold will thicken the coconut milk, making for a creamier dressing.

MAKE IT EASY

If using wooden skewers, dunk them in water to prevent them from catching fire and burning on the grill. Leave them to soak while you prepare the shrimp and pineapple, as well as the salad and dressing. The kitchen sink works well for this task: just fill it with an inch of water and dunk in the skewers. Alternatively, buy a set of stainless steel skewers, which can be reused for other grilled recipes.

Making the Salad Dressing

- Prepare the salad dressing by stirring all dressing ingredients together in a small bowl. If there are any lumps in your coconut milk, they will dissolve soon enough with the stirring action and the warmth of your kitchen.
- Taste test the dressing for spiciness and sweetness, adding more chili or more sugar as desired. If too sweet or too salty for your taste, add more lime juice.
- Place greens in a salad bowl together with the red pepper and cucumber.

Grilling the Shrimp & Pineapple

- Heat up your grill and lightly brush the cooking surface with a little oil.
- Weave the shrimp and pineapple onto the sticks and grill for 10 minutes, or until shrimp are pink and plump and pineapple is bright yellow. Baste with a little leftover marinade the first time you turn them.
- Serve the skewers on the salad, or use a fork to slide shrimp and pineapple off the sticks and onto the salad. Drizzle the dressing over and top with fresh coriander.

GRILLED CHICKEN SALAD

This dinner salad offers multiple layers of Thai flavor and texture.

There are lots of grilled chicken salads around, but few can match the multiple flavors that burst forth with a single bite of this Thai salad. The dish starts with strips of chicken, which are soaked in a tangy marinade featuring freshly ground black pepper. Add to this already flavorful chicken a lemon-lime flavored salad dressing, plus a topping of Thai herbs, and you have a grilled chicken salad that is naturally low in fat but incredibly high in flavor and taste satisfaction.

If the weather doesn't cooperate, or if you'd like to make this salad during the winter months, the chicken can also be cooked under the broiler for the same delicious results.

Yield: Serves 2–4

Ingredients

1/4 cup fish sauce
5 cloves garlic, minced
2 Tbsp. lime or lemon juice
2–4 boneless chicken breasts OR 4–8 chicken thighs, cut into strips
1 Tbsp. coarsely ground black pepper
Enough salad greens for 2-4 portions
1/4 cup fresh coriander
1/4 cup fresh basil

Dressing:

1/4 cup water
1 Tbsp. finely minced lemongrass
2 kaffir lime leaves, cut into thin strips
2 Tbsp. fish sauce
2 Tbsp. soy sauce
2 Tbsp. freshly squeezed lime juice
1 clove garlic, minced
1 Tbsp. palm sugar OR brown sugar
1/4 cup finely chopped fresh coriander
1 tsp. Thai chili sauce

Grilled Chicken Salad

- Combine the fish sauce, garlic, and lime or lemon juice together in a cup. Pour this mixture over the chicken strips, ensuring all parts are saturated.
- Next, rub the freshly ground black pepper over all sides of the chicken.
- Set in the refrigerator to marinate for at least 15 minutes (while you warm up the grill and prepare the dressing), or up to 24 hours.

ZOOM

Packaged ground pepper does not taste the same as freshly ground. Whenever possible, use whole black peppercorns for this dish and grind them yourself to achieve a coarser grind and the freshest taste. This can be done easily using a coffee grinder (or a spice grinder). A pestle and mortar also do a great job. Alternatively, use a peppermill set to grind coarsely.

MAKE IT EASY

This recipe can also be made in your oven. Marinate the chicken as indicated, then lay the strips on a foil-lined baking sheet. Set oven to "broil," and place an oven rack on the second-to-highest rung of your oven. Turn up the edges of foil to prevent spilling. Turn the strips every 3–4 minutes until meat is nicely browned and well done. Serve as instructed.

Making the Salad Dressing

- To make the dressing, place water, lemongrass, and lime leaf strips in a saucepan and bring to a boil. Boil for 1 minute to soften lemongrass and bring out the flavor of the lime leaf.
- Remove from heat and add the rest of the dressing ingredients, stirring well to dissolve the sugar.
- Taste test the dressing, adjusting the flavors to your taste by adding more fish sauce if not salty enough, or more lime juice if too salty or sweet. Set aside.

Grilling the Chicken

- Grill chicken over a hot grill until well cooked. Use any leftover marinade from the bottom of the bowl to baste chicken the first time you turn it. Discard thereafter.
- When chicken is ready to eat, toss the salad with the dressing and portion it out into individual bowls or plates. Top with the strips of grilled chicken, plus a generous sprinkling of both fresh coriander and basil. Enjoy.

COCONUT RICE

This simple dish is a great standby, making any Thai or Asian meal extra special.

Coconut rice can be found across many cultures, from India to Indonesia and even South and Central America.

At most Thai restaurants these days, coconut rice is offered as an alternative to plain jasmine-scented rice. It marries particularly well with any type of seafood or curry dish.

The following recipe is very simple to make and turns out wonderfully fluffy, even though it is boiled in a pot on your stove. Serve it next time you're planning a Thai meal and see how it makes nearly any accompanying dish taste even better.

Yield: Serves 2–4

Ingredients

1 tsp. coconut oil, or other vegetable oil

2 cups white Thai jasmine-scented rice

2 cups good-quality coconut milk (canned, not from a powder)

1 3/4 cups water

1/2 tsp. salt

Coconut Rice

- For this recipe you will need a fairly deep pot with a tight-fitting lid (make sure the pot has enough room to accommodate the expanding rice).
- Rub the oil over the bottom of the pot to keep rice from sticking and burning.

ZOOM

Although brown jasmine-scented rice is now readily available in North America, brown rice isn't the best choice for making coconut rice. This is because brown rice has a strong flavor that tends to overpower the subtle taste of the coconut milk. The best way to make brown rice taste more delicious is to cook it in chicken stock, or a good-tasting vegetable stock.

MAKE IT EASY

To make an easy topping for your coconut rice, "dry-fry" (fry without oil) 2 Tbsp. dry shredded coconut in a wok or frying pan over medium-high heat. Stir continuously until the coconut turns light golden-brown and is fragrant (3–5 minutes). Use toasted coconut as a tasty topping for the coconut rice, or other dishes with coconut milk, such as curries, salads, or desserts.

Combining Ingredients

- Place rice in the pot. Add the coconut milk, water, and salt, and stir well.
- Set over medium-high heat. Stir at least twice every minute until the coconut-water comes to a gentle bubbling boil. (Note: stirring prevents the thick coconut-water and rice mixture from burning.)

Simmering the Rice

- Reduce heat to medium-low and place lid askew on the pot, allowing ⅓ of the steam to escape.
- Simmer in this way 15–20 minutes, or until the rice has absorbed the coconut water.
- Switch off the heat, but leave the pot on the burner. Cover tightly with the lid and let rice sit 5 more minutes, or until you are ready to eat.
- To serve, fluff the rice with chopsticks or a fork, and enjoy.

STEAMED STICKY RICE

In Thailand, steamed sticky rice is served with both sweet and savory dishes.

Sticky rice is also known as sweet or glutinous rice. Most North Americans tend to associate this type of rice with Asian-style desserts. Although it's true that sticky rice is a common ingredient in many Thai desserts, in Thailand sticky rice is also eaten as an accompaniment to stir-fries, curries, and even salad (green papaya salad). It is especially popular in northern regions of the country, where the rice in often packed into balls and dipped into curry sauces or whatever main course dishes are being offered. In Thailand, sticky rice is normally steamed in a funnel-shaped woven basket. We'll use a colander and banana leaf.

Yield: Serves 2–4

Ingredients

2 cups Thai sweet rice (also known as glutinous rice or sticky rice)

4 cups water

1–2 banana leaves

1/2 tsp. sea salt

Steamed Sticky Rice

- Have ready an electric steamer, a traditional Chinese-style bamboo steamer, or a Western-style steel or metal colander.
- Place the sweet rice in a bowl and cover with water. Soak for at least 30 minutes or up to 4 hours.
- Sticky rice has a tough outer coating that needs to be softened before cooking; otherwise it will turn out hard and inedible.
- Drain the water off the rice.

ZOOM

There are various types of sticky rice (usually labeled as "sweet rice"). The difference between Thai sticky rice and the Chinese or Japanese variety is mainly in the shape of the grain, with Thai sticky rice being longer and thinner, while Japanese or Chinese sweet rice is short-grained. Brown sweet rice can also be found in health food stores.

MAKE IT EASY

To boil sticky rice, soak rice as indicated, then drain and transfer to a pot. Add 3½ cups water plus ½ tsp. salt. Bring to a gentle boil. Reduce heat to medium-low and set a lid askew over the pot, allowing some steam to escape. Simmer 20 minutes, or until water has been absorbed. Switch off heat but leave the pot on the burner. Cover with the lid and allow to sit 5–10 more minutes.

Lining Steamer with Banana Leaf

- Cut the banana leaf into 1-foot-square sheets, or large enough to fit your steamer or colander (plus a little extra).
- Use the leaves to double-line your steaming device.
- Place the drained rice in the banana leaf–lined steamer. Sprinkle the sea salt over and gently stir with chopsticks or a fork to mix in.

Steaming the Sweet Rice

- Cover with a tight-fitting lid and steam on high heat (or over a pot of rapidly boiling water) for 30 minutes, or until rice has turned translucent and is completely soft.
- To test whether rice is cooked, slide chopsticks or a fork down into the center of the sticky rice and remove a little to taste. If it is still hard or crunchy, steam 5–10 more minutes.
- Serve steamed sticky rice with "saucy" Thai dishes, such as richly flavored curries or stir-fries.

HEAVENLY PINEAPPLE FRIED RICE

One of Thailand's signature dishes, this fried rice is beautiful to serve.

If you travel to Thailand, this might be one of the first dishes you are served. It's a special Thai fried rice dish that is proudly presented in a carved-out pineapple. The dish makes a very tropical impression, especially when jeweled with fresh shrimp and chunks of just-cut pineapple.

This fried rice is curry-flavored and also features raisins or currants as well as crunchy cashews. Definitely one of the world's best fried rice dishes, it is sure to please even the most discerning of tastes.

If you are vegetarian or vegan, note that this recipe can easily be made without seafood, with the resulting dish tasting just as wonderful as the original recipe.

Yield: Serves 2 as a main entrée, 4 as a side dish

Ingredients

4–5 cups cooked rice, preferably several days old

4–5 Tbsp. oil, divided

3 Tbsp. fish sauce

2 tsp. curry powder (Madras works well)

1 tsp. palm sugar OR brown sugar

2 shallots, finely chopped

3 cloves garlic, minced

1 red chili, de-seeded and minced

1 cup baby shrimp, raw or cooked

2 Tbsp. chicken or vegetable stock

1 egg

1/2 cup frozen peas

1/2 cup roasted unsalted cashews

1 cup pineapple tidbits, fresh or canned

1/4 cup currants OR raisins

3 green onions, sliced

1/3 cup fresh coriander

Classic Thai Heavenly Pineapple Fried Rice

- For this recipe, it's best to use rice that is several days old (firm and dry in texture). If using freshly cooked rice, spread it out in a large bowl and refrigerate for a few hours.
- Drizzle 1 Tbsp. oil over the cold rice. Using your fingers, gently work the oil into the rice while separating any chunks or lumps back into individual grains. Set aside.
- Combine fish sauce with the curry powder and sugar in a cup, stirring well to dissolve the sugar. Set aside.

RECIPE VARIATION

Vegetarian Heavenly Pineapple Fried Rice. To make this recipe vegetarian or vegan, instead of using fish sauce, substitute 3½ Tbsp. soy sauce. Omit the shrimp; instead, increase the amount of cashews to 1 cup. Vegans can omit the egg without any loss of flavor to the dish, OR substitute ½ cup deep-fried tofu, cut into very small pieces. Add the deep-fried tofu when you add the rice.

MAKE IT EASY

To serve this dish in a carved-out pineapple: Slice the pineapple in half, or simply cut off one side of it, leaving the stem and ¾ of the skin intact. Use a sharp knife to cut around the perimeter of the pineapple, as you would a grapefruit. Then use your knife to cut up the fruit into cubes. Take a tablespoon and dig out the fruit until you have a hollowed-out pineapple. Fill with fried rice.

Stir-Frying the Shrimp

- Warm a wok over medium-high heat. Add 1–2 Tbsp. oil plus the shallots, garlic, chili, and shrimp. Stir-fry 1–3 minutes (2–3 minutes if using raw shrimp). When the wok becomes dry, add 1–2 Tbsp. of the stock.
- Make a space in the center of the wok and add another ½–1 Tbsp. oil. Crack the egg into this space and quickly stir-fry to scramble.
- When egg is cooked, add the peas and cashews, plus the fish sauce mixture, and stir everything together.

Stir-Frying Rice with Other Ingredients

- Add the rice, pineapple, and currants. Quickly stir-fry everything together by using a flat-bottom utensil (like a spatula) and a scooping motion (lifting the rice up from the bottom of the wok). Stir-fry in this way 2–3 minutes, or until rice is hot and light in texture.
- Remove from heat. Do a taste test, adding 1–2 Tbsp. fish sauce if more salt or flavor is needed.
- Serve with the green onion and coriander sprinkled over, and Thai chili sauce on the side.

CHICKEN FRIED RICE WITH LIME LEAF

A wonderfully aromatic Thai version of Chicken Fried Rice.

Thai cuisine offers some of the best fried rice dishes in the world, and the following recipe has to be one of them. Aromatic and tantalizing in flavor, this fried rice turns out light and airy in texture, especially if the rice is at least several days old.

Old rice always makes for the best fried rice. This is because refrigeration dries it out, making it lighter and firmer, which is more conducive to frying (whereas freshly cooked rice is soft and can easily turn mushy once oil is added to it). For this reason, fried rice is a good way to ensure that leftover rice never goes to waste (note that leftover roasted chicken or turkey can also be used for fried rice).

Yield: Serves 3–4 as a main entrée

Ingredients

4 Tbsp. oil, divided

6 cups cooked rice, several days old

1 shallot, minced

3 cloves garlic, minced

1 chicken breast, sliced into small pieces

3 Tbsp. chicken stock for stir-frying

4–5 kaffir lime leaves, cut into thin strips

1 egg

3 green onions, finely sliced

1/4 tsp. white pepper

1/3 cup fresh basil

Optional: Fresh red chili, sliced thinly

Stir-Fry Sauce:

4 Tbsp. chicken stock

3 Tbsp. fish sauce, plus more to taste

1 Tbsp. soy sauce

1 tsp. Thai chili sauce

1/2 tsp. sugar

Chicken Fried Rice with Basil & Lime Leaf

- Drizzle 1 Tbsp. oil over the rice and work through with your fingers, separating any clumps back into grains. Set aside.
- Combine the stir-fry sauce ingredients in a cup, stirring well to dissolve the sugar. Set aside.
- Warm your wok over medium-high heat. Add 2 Tbsp. oil and swirl around, then stir-fry the chopped shallot and garlic until fragrant (1 minute).
- Add the chicken and 2 Tbsp. of the chicken stock. Stir-fry 2–3 minutes, or until chicken turns opaque.

ZOOM

For stir-frying rice, use a flat-bottom utensil (like an "egg flipper") and a scooping motion, lifting the rice from the bottom of the wok. Or, use 2 utensils and a tossing motion, like tossing a salad. Thai cooks often use a kind of "shovel," usually made of wood or steel. Be sure to keep the wok hot and dry, and listen for the sound of it the rice popping (often referred to as "dancing" rice).

MAKE IT EASY

Lime leaf is a key ingredient in this dish, so don't be tempted to leave it out or try substitutions. Lime leaf can be purchased fresh or frozen at Asian or Chinese food stores. To store leftover leaves, wrap them in a plastic bag and freeze, only taking out as many as needed. Briefly rinse the leaves under hot water, then use a pair of clean scissors to cut them into thin strips. Discard the stems.

Stir-Frying the Lime with the Chicken

- Add the lime leaf strips and continue stir-frying another 2–3 minutes, until chicken is cooked. As you stir-fry, add a little more stock if the wok becomes dry—just enough to keep ingredients frying nicely.
- Push ingredients aside to make a space in the center of the wok. Add another ½ to 1 Tbsp. oil, then crack in the egg. Stir-fry the egg quickly to scramble it.
- When egg is cooked, mix it in with the other ingredients.

Stir-Frying the Rice with Other Ingredients

- Add the rice and stir-fry sauce. Stir-fry 2–3 minutes, or until rice is hot and consistent in color.
- Add the green onion and white pepper, briefly stir-frying to mix in.
- Remove from heat and do a taste test. For saltier, more flavorful rice, add more fish sauce.
- Place the basil leaves on top of one another, roll them up, and then thinly slice to create shreds of basil. Sprinkle some over each portion of fried rice. If desired, also add a little fresh chili.

SHRIMP FRIED RICE

This shrimp fried rice makes a wonderful main course entrée.

Shrimp and rice go so well together that even in other types of fried rice—such as pork, chicken, or pineapple—shrimp is usually also present. In this recipe, however, shrimp remains the star player, with the rice flavored to enhance it (with shrimp paste, fish sauce, and several other ingredients).

Small to medium shrimp are recommended for fried rice, and while normally frozen or cooked is fine to use, because shrimp are the main feature of this dish, I recommend using only fresh, uncooked shrimp if you can find it (preferably organic or wild for even better quality). Remove all of the shells, or, if using medium to larger shrimp, leave the tails on for easier eating.

Yield: Serves 2 as a main entrée, 4 as a side dish

Ingredients

4 Tbsp. oil, divided

4–5 cups cooked rice, preferably 2–3 days old

2 shallots, finely chopped

3 cloves garlic, minced

2–4 Tbsp. white wine

15–20 small or 12–15 medium shrimp, shells removed (tails removed or left on)

2 eggs, yolks broken

2/3 cup frozen peas

Optional: 1/2 cup dry-roasted cashews

2–3 green onions, sliced

Stir-Fry Sauce:

2 Tbsp. soy sauce

2 Tbsp. fish sauce

1/2 tsp. shrimp paste

1 tsp. white sugar

1/8 tsp. white pepper

1 tsp. Thai chili sauce

Shrimp Fried Rice

- Drizzle 1 Tbsp. oil over the rice and gently work it through with your fingers, separating any clumps until rice has returned to individual grains. Set aside.
- Mix the stir-fry sauce ingredients together in a cup, stirring well to dissolve sugar. Set aside.
- Warm your wok over medium-high heat. Add 2 Tbsp. oil and swirl around, then add the shallot and garlic. Stir-fry 30 seconds, until fragrant.
- Add 1–2 Tbsp. wine and continue stir-frying another 2 minutes, or until shallots have softened.

ZOOM

Though white pepper has been around for centuries in Asia, in North America it is still somewhat of a novelty. That said, it is gaining popularity and can now be found in many supermarkets. White pepper has a mild, sweet flavor and is suited to Thai dishes like fried rice or rice porridge (congee). White pepper can be purchased already ground or in whole peppercorns.

GREEN LIGHT

Thais consider food a precious gift, so normally either every morsel is consumed in one sitting, or leftovers are re-fried the following day (as in fried rice). Traditionally it was believed that discarding food might anger the Thai God of Rice, a female deity who watches over the people, ensuring everyone has enough to eat. It was thought that bad luck or even widespread famine would ensue if food was needlessly wasted.

Stir-Frying the Shrimp

- Add the shrimp and stir-fry another 2–3 minutes. If wok becomes dry, add a little more white wine, 1 Tbsp. at a time—just enough to keep ingredients frying nicely. Stir-fry until shrimp are pink and plump.
- Push ingredients aside and add 1 Tbsp. oil to the center of your wok. Add the eggs and quickly stir-fry to scramble.
- Stir to mix the egg with the other ingredients.

Stir-Frying the Rice

- Add the rice, peas, cashews (if using), and stir-fry sauce. Stir-fry all together using a scooping motion (lifting rice from the bottom of the wok). Stir-fry in this way 3 minutes, or until rice and peas are hot.
- Remove from heat and taste test for salt and flavor, adding a little more fish sauce until desired taste is achieved.
- Serve the rice hot from the wok. Sprinkle the sliced green onions over, and serve with Thai chili sauce on the side.

SAFFRON COCONUT RICE

This golden-colored rice is flavorful and also very healthy.

Saffron is a very precious and expensive spice in Asia, and therefore isn't used on an everyday basis in Thai cooking, though you may well see it in some dishes prepared at 5-star hotels and restaurants. Instead, turmeric—also known as "poor man's saffron"—is substituted. As it turns out, turmeric is wonderful for one's health, and also provides that wonderful golden coloring that one associates with saffron-spiced dishes.

At Thai restaurants in North America, the server will normally suggest either coconut or saffron rice as an accompanying dish. The following recipe is actually a combination of the two (so you never have to feel as if you're missing out on one when choosing the other!).

Yield: Serves 2–4

Ingredients

1 tsp. coconut oil or other vegetable oil

1¾ cups chicken or vegetable stock

1½ tsp. sugar

½ tsp. turmeric

2 cups Thai white jasmine-scented rice

2 cups good-quality coconut milk

1½ Tbsp. fish sauce, plus more to taste (vegetarians substitute 1 tsp. sea salt)

¼–½ tsp. saffron threads

Saffron Coconut Rice

- Rub the oil over the bottom of a deep cooking pot. This will help prevent the rice from sticking and possibly burning.
- Add the stock, sugar, and turmeric. Stir to dissolve the sugar and turmeric completely.

RECIPE VARIATION

This recipe can be easily made in a rice cooker, but in this case use 2 cups stock, and 1½ cups coconut milk. Add the same amounts of rice, sugar, turmeric, fish sauce, and saffron. Place everything together in the rice cooker and stir well. Turn on your rice cooker and wait 20 minutes, or until cooker switches to the "warm" mode. Taste test and adjust the salt as instructed.

ZOOM

Saffron is the most expensive spice in the world because the saffron threads are actually stigmas from the saffron crocus flower. It takes roughly 80,000 flowers to make 1 pound of saffron. Saffron was first brought to Thailand by traders from the Middle East. Thais mistakenly referred to these traders as "sultans." There still exists a Thai rice dish called Sultan's Rice—flavored with saffron.

Stir-Frying Ingredients Together

- Add the rice, coconut milk, fish sauce, and saffron threads, and set over medium-high heat. Continue stirring slowly to combine ingredients and help prevent the rice from sticking to the bottom of the pot.
- When the liquid comes to a gentle bubbling boil, reduce heat to medium-low.

Simmering the Rice

- Set lid askew on the pot, allowing ¼ of the steam to escape. Simmer the rice in this way for 20 minutes.
- When the liquid is gone, place lid on tight and turn off the heat (but leave pot on the burner). Allow rice to sit at least 5 minutes, or until you're ready to eat.
- Before serving, do a taste test, adding more fish sauce (or salt) until desired taste is achieved. Fluff rice with chopsticks or a fork, and enjoy.

CLASSIC CHICKEN PAD THAI

This Thai noodle dish is now enjoying worldwide popularity, and for good reason.

Thailand has hundreds, if not thousands of different noodle dishes, from those made with wheat or egg noodles to rice and bean thread noodles. But by far the most popular of these is Pad Thai, a delightfully chewy and slightly sticky rice noodle dish.

There are two keys to creating perfect Pad Thai: first, use a good Pad Thai sauce, and second, do not overcook the noodles. In fact, Pad Thai noodles should never be "cooked" in the sense of boiled; rather, they should merely be soaked in hot water before being fried to perfection.

Yield: Serves 2

Ingredients

1 chicken breast OR 2 thighs, sliced

1 tsp. cornstarch

2 1/2 Tbsp. soy sauce

8 oz. Thai rice noodles (linguini width), or enough for 2 people

2–4 Tbsp. oil for stir-frying

4 cloves garlic, minced

3–4 Tbsp. chicken stock

3 cups fresh bean sprouts

1/8 tsp. white or black pepper

3 green onions, sliced

1 cup fresh coriander

1/3 cup ground or chopped peanuts

Pad Thai Sauce:

3/4 Tbsp. tamarind paste

1/4 cup hot water

2 Tbsp. fish sauce

1–3 tsp. chili sauce, to taste

3 Tbsp. palm sugar OR brown sugar

Classic Chicken Pad Thai

- Slice the chicken into small pieces and place in a bowl. Dissolve cornstarch in the soy sauce and pour over the chicken. Stir well and set aside to marinate.
- To make the Pad Thai sauce, dissolve the tamarind paste in the hot water, then add all other sauce ingredients, stirring to combine and dissolve the sugar.
- This may seem like a lot of sugar, but you need it to balance out the sourness of the tamarind. Set sauce aside.

ZOOM

Tamarind comes from a type of evergreen tree that grows in cooler tropical regions of the world (Thailand is one of them). While it may be tempting to buy fresh tamarind for cooking, be aware that you will first need to de-seed it and turn it into a useable paste. It's much easier to buy tamarind paste already prepared at Asian or Indian food stores.

MAKE IT EASY

Preparing rice noodles for stir-frying is the most important part of making Pad Thai. Always soak rice noodles in a pot of warm to hot water that has been removed from the burner (never leave rice noodles cooking on the stove). Check them often. They're ready when they are soft enough to eat, but still firm and slightly crunchy. Drain and rinse with cold water.

Soaking the Rice Noodles

- Soak the noodles in a pot of pre-boiled water until they are soft enough to eat, but still quite firm and little crunchy. Drain and rinse with cold water.
- Warm a wok over medium-high heat. Add 2 Tbsp. oil plus the garlic. Stir-fry until fragrant (30 seconds).
- Add the marinated chicken and stir-fry 5 minutes, or until chicken is cooked. When your wok becomes dry, add some of the chicken stock, 1 Tbsp. at a time—just enough to keep ingredients frying nicely.

Stir-Frying the Noodles

- Add noodles to the wok, plus the Pad Thai sauce. Using 2 utensils, quickly stir-fry the noodles using a tossing motion (like tossing a salad). Stir-fry 1–2 minutes. If your wok becomes too dry, add a little more oil.
- Add bean sprouts and sprinkle the pepper over. Continue stir-frying 1 minute, or until noodles taste chewy-delicious. For saltier noodles, add more fish sauce.
- Serve immediately with the sliced green onion, fresh coriander, and ground nuts sprinkled over.

PHUKET PAD THAI WITH SHRIMP

This seaside version of Pad Thai is made without tamarind paste.

Although tamarind is normally associated with Pad Thai, originally the dish was made without it. I first tried this type of Pad Thai when I was in Phuket. The woman who made it cooked from a portable kitchen, which she set up daily on the beach. In fact, it wasn't just a kitchen, but an entire restaurant, complete with chairs, tables, and even umbrellas to protect our tender tourist heads from the sun.

In any case, her Pad Thai was extremely delicious despite the absence of tamarind. The following recipe is my attempt to replicate it as I remember it, with the shrimp caught fresh from the sea that very morning.

Yield: Serves 2–3

Ingredients

8–10 oz. Thai rice noodles (linguini width), or enough for 2–3 people

3 Tbsp. fish sauce

3 Tbsp. rice vinegar

3 Tbsp. soy sauce

1 tsp. palm sugar OR brown sugar

3–4 Tbsp. oil for stir-frying

3 cloves garlic, minced

1–2 red chilies, minced

8–12 medium or large raw shrimp, shells removed

2–3 Tbsp. chicken stock

1 egg

2–3 cups bean sprouts

1/3 cup roasted peanuts, ground

1/2 cup fresh coriander

1/2 lime, cut into wedges

Phuket Pad Thai with Shrimp

- Bring a pot of water to the boil and remove from heat. Dunk in the rice noodles. Soak them 5–10 minutes, or until soft enough to eat, but still firm and slightly crunchy. Drain and rinse the noodles with cold water.
- Mix together the fish sauce, vinegar, soy sauce, and brown sugar, stirring to dissolve the sugar. Reserve this sauce for later.
- Warm a wok over medium-high heat. Add 1–2 Tbsp. oil plus the garlic and chilies. Stir-fry 1 minute.

ZOOM

Chicken stock makes a great substitute for oil when stir-frying. However, when stir-frying rice noodles, it's important not to add any more moisture to the wok than is absolutely necessary. If your wok becomes too dry and sticky when stir-frying, add a little more oil instead; otherwise, the rice noodles will absorb the liquid and become soggy.

MAKE IT EASY

Preparing peanuts for Pad Thai needn't take long. If you have a pestle and mortar, this is probably the fastest way to do it, crushing the nuts until they are coarsely ground. You can also use a mini chopper or coffee grinder—just be careful not to over-grind, or you will end up with peanut paste. Some Thai cooks chop the peanuts with a knife instead of grinding them, which is even quicker.

Stir-Frying the Shrimp

- Add the shrimp and stir-fry 1–2 minutes, or until shrimp are pink and plump. When your wok becomes dry, add a little chicken stock, 1 Tbsp. at a time to keep ingredients frying nicely.
- Push ingredients aside and add 1 more Tbsp. oil to the center of the wok. Crack the egg into this space and quickly stir-fry to scramble.
- Add the drained noodles and the sauce you made earlier, pouring it over the noodles.

Stir-Frying the Noodles

- Use 2 utensils to stir-fry the noodles 2–3 minutes, or until they turn soft but are still chewy. If the noodles are sticking to the wok, add a little more oil.
- Add the bean sprouts, stir-frying briefly to mix in.
- Remove wok from heat and taste test the noodles, adding more fish sauce until desired flavor is reached.
- Top with ground peanuts and fresh coriander. Serve with wedges of fresh lime, and enjoy.

FRIED RICE VERMICELLI NOODLES

This simple noodle dish makes a pleasant weekday meal.

These days, one can buy vermicelli-type rice noodles at nearly any major supermarket, and even at smaller grocery and convenience stores. These rice noodles are thin but "wiry," and, when cooked correctly, have lots of texture and taste to them.

In Thailand as in many Southeast Asian countries, vermicelli rice noodles are fried up with a variety of meats or seafood, or might simply be tossed with stir-fried vegetables. They can also be added to soups or used as a filling for spring rolls or fresh rolls.

In the following recipe, these thin rice noodles are cooked up with bite-size pieces of chicken, plus mushrooms and galangal (or ginger), all stir-fried together in a pleasantly tangy-spicy Thai sauce that's very easy to put together.

Yield: Serves 2–4

Ingredients

1½ tsp. cornstarch
4 Tbsp. soy sauce
1–2 chicken breasts OR 2–4 thighs, sliced
10–12 oz. vermicelli rice noodles
2–3 Tbsp. oil for stir-frying
3 cloves garlic
1 Tbsp. grated galangal OR ginger
1 cup fresh shiitake mushrooms, sliced
¼ cup chicken stock
2–3 cups fresh bean sprouts
¼ cup fresh coriander
Wedges of lime for garnish

Stir-Fry Sauce:

2 Tbsp. soy sauce
1 Tbsp. fish sauce
1 tsp. sugar
1 Tbsp. lime juice
¼ cup chicken stock
1–2 tsp. chili sauce

Fried Rice Vermicelli Noodles

- Stir the cornstarch and soy sauce together until the cornstarch dissolves. Pour this mixture over the chicken and stir well. Set in the refrigerator to marinate while you prepare the other ingredients.
- Bring a large pot of water to a boil, then remove from heat. Soak noodles in the hot water for 5–12 minutes, or until soft enough to eat, but still firm and chewy. Drain and rinse with cold water.
- Combine all stir-fry sauce ingredients and set aside.

• • • • RECIPE VARIATION • • • •

To make this recipe vegetarian/vegan, substitute vegetable stock for the chicken stock, and 1½ Tbsp. soy sauce for the fish sauce. Substitute 1 cup tofu for the chicken, marinating it as instructed. Stir-fry the tofu only as long as it takes for the mushrooms to be cooked. Adjust the taste by adding more soy sauce or more lime juice.

ZOOM

For the best possible quality and taste, it's always a good idea to buy vermicelli rice noodles at an Asian food store. While most grocery stores stock this type of noodle, Western-made vermicelli rice noodles are much thinner and break easier. Good-quality vermicelli rice noodles are firmly packed into "squares" (like instant noodles) and are white rather than off-white in color.

Stir-Frying the Chicken and Mushrooms

- Warm your wok over medium-high heat. Add 2 Tbsp. oil and swirl around, then add the garlic, ginger, marinated chicken, mushrooms, and a few tablespoons of stock. Stir-fry 5–6 minutes, or until chicken and mushrooms are cooked.
- If the wok becomes dry, add a little more chicken stock, 1–2 Tbsp. at a time—enough to keep the ingredients frying nicely.

Adding the Noodles and Stir-Fry Sauce

- Add the noodles plus the stir-fry sauce. Using 2 utensils and a tossing motion (like tossing a salad), stir-fry until sauce is well distributed throughout the noodles (2–3 minutes).
- Add bean sprouts and stir-fry 1 more minute.
- Remove from heat and taste test, adding more fish sauce if not salty or flavorful enough. If too salty, add a squeeze of lime juice.
- Sprinkle with fresh coriander, and garnish with wedges of fresh-cut lime. Serve with extra Thai chili sauce on the side, and enjoy.

GLASS NOODLES IN A SAVORY SAUCE

Because glass noodles are made from bean flour, they are particularly healthy.

Glass noodles—also known as cellophane noodles—are exactly as their name suggests: beautifully translucent. Made of mung bean flour, or a combination of mung bean and green pea flours, these noodles start out very thin but expand up to twice their size once soaked in water and cooked. They vary in texture from soft to chewy according to the dish and how long you cook them.

In the following recipe, glass noodles are stir-fried in a savory Thai sauce together with chicken, mushrooms, and red pepper.

Yield: Serves 2–3

Ingredients

6-8 oz. bean thread noodles, or enough for 2-3 people (note: noodles will expand)

1-2 chicken breasts, sliced into small pieces

1 cup shiitake mushrooms, sliced

1 red bell pepper, sliced

1/4 cup fresh basil

Sauce:

1 cup good-quality chicken stock

1/2 cup water

1 Tbsp. ground bean sauce

3 cloves garlic, minced

1 Tbsp. grated galangal OR ginger

1/2 cup coriander leaves and stems

4 Tbsp. soy sauce

1 tsp. dark soy sauce

1 Tbsp. fish sauce

1-3 tsp. Thai chili sauce

Glass Noodles in a Savory Sauce

- Soak noodles in a pot of warm water. If the noodles won't stay immersed (they float easily), weigh them down with a heavy bowl.
- Soak approximately 20–30 minutes, or until soft enough to eat, but still fairly firm. The noodles will absorb much of the water and expand—they will also magically turn from white to transparent.
- Drain and rinse with cold water. Set noodles aside.

ZOOM

Ground bean sauce (also known as brown bean sauce) is a thick dark brown sauce. It is made from ground fermented soybeans (not to be confused with Japanese miso). This Chinese-inspired sauce has a strong, salty flavor that goes well with a number of dishes, giving more flavor and richness to foods. Note that ground bean sauce is suitable for both vegetarians and vegans.

MAKE IT EASY

Glass noodles are very "wiry" and do not break easily. While this can be a plus, for this dish, the noodles may remain too clumped together to be easily mixed with the sauce. Use a pair of clean scissors to cut them into easier-to-manage lengths. This can be done directly in the wok without removing or touching the noodles (in Asia, scissors are a common kitchen tool with myriad uses).

Making the Chicken & Mushroom Sauce

- Place stock in a wok over high heat. Bring to a boil. Add all other sauce ingredients plus chicken and mushrooms, and stir well.
- Reduce heat to medium. Cover and simmer 5–10 minutes, or until chicken is well cooked. Add the bell pepper and simmer an additional 2–3 minutes, or until red pepper has softened.

Cooking the Noodles

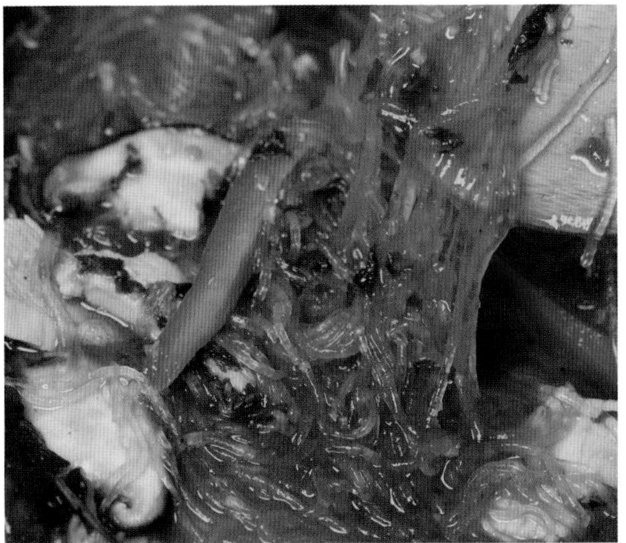

- Add the drained noodles. Use 2 utensils to turn them in the sauce for 2–3 minutes.
- Serve noodles immediately for a saucier dish, or continue to cook them gently over low heat until all the sauce has been absorbed and the noodles are drier and slightly sticky.
- Taste test the noodles for salt, adding more fish sauce if not salty enough. If too salty, add a little lime juice. Serve with a sprinkling of fresh basil and Thai chili sauce on the side.

THAI DRUNKEN NOODLES

Enjoyed by Bangkok's late-night revelers, these spicy noodles are meant to wake you up.

Noodles such as these are a common sight on the streets of Bangkok, and can be purchased all day as well as all hours of the night. Noodles are also enjoyed for breakfast in Thailand.

There are numerous Thai dishes whose names contain the word drunken. In this case, noodles are usually sold to those who are up carousing late at night, in which case the spicy, flavorful sauce is meant as a kind of stimulant to sober you up. But I find they are good any time of day (or night).

Yield: Serves 2–3

Ingredients

8-10 oz. wheat or egg noodles, enough for 2 people
2 Tbsp. oil
2 shallots, diced
4 cloves garlic, minced
1 Tbsp. grated galangal OR ginger
4 kaffir lime leaves, cut into thin strips
½–¾ package medium or firm tofu
2-3 Tbsp. sherry (or cooking sherry)
1 head broccoli, cut into florets
3 tomatoes, cut into bite-size pieces
2-3 cups bean sprouts
½ cup fresh coriander
½ cup fresh basil

Stir-Fry Sauce:

1½ Tbsp. ground bean sauce
1 Tbsp. rice vinegar
1 Tbsp. fish sauce
2 Tbsp. freshly squeezed lime juice
2 Tbsp. palm sugar OR brown sugar
1-3 tsp. Thai chili sauce, to taste

Thai Drunken Noodles

- Place noodles in a pot of boiling water over medium-high heat. Stir until noodles have separated and are soft enough to eat, but still firm (they will be stir-fried later, so avoid over-cooking them at this point).
- Drain and rinse with cold water to prevent sticking. Set aside.
- Combine all stir-fry sauce ingredients in a cup, stirring well to dissolve the sugar. Set near the stove.

• • • • RECIPE VARIATION • • • •

This recipe can be made with non-vegetarian protein sources. Instead of the tofu, substitute 1½ cups shrimp or chicken. If using chicken, marinate it first in a mixture of 3 Tbsp. soy sauce plus 1 tsp. cornstarch. Increase your stir-frying time to 3–4 minutes, or until shrimp are pink and plump, or chicken is well cooked. Continue with the rest of the recipe as written.

ZOOM

In Bangkok, day or night, you can find entertainment as well as an abundance of food. Noodles are a favorite midnight snack, but one can also find everything from satay to fried insects, considered a delicacy among Thais. There are numerous types of insects eaten, usually deep-fried and flavored with spices. Fried insects are enjoyed with beer as a Westerner might enjoy peanuts.

Stir-Frying the Tofu and Broccoli

- Warm a wok or large frying pan over medium-high heat. Drizzle a few Tbsp. oil into the pan and swirl around, then add the shallots, garlic, galangal (or ginger), lime leaf, and tofu.
- Stir-fry 1 minute, or until fragrant. When the wok becomes dry, add a little sherry, 1 Tbsp. at a time—just enough to keep ingredients frying easily.
- Add broccoli and stir-fry another 1–2 minutes, or until broccoli is bright green and slightly softened. Add a little sherry if wok becomes dry.

Frying the Noodles with Other Ingredients

- Add the stir-fry sauce plus the noodles and tomatoes. Stir-fry 1–2 minutes, turning the noodles as you fry them in order to incorporate the sauce.
- Remove from heat and add the bean sprouts and coriander. Toss in the wok to combine.
- Taste test the noodles, adding more fish sauce if more salt or flavor is desired. If too salty for your taste, add another squeeze of lime juice.
- Sprinkle with fresh basil and serve with Thai chili sauce on the side.

EASY BASIL NOODLES

A Thai fusion dish made with rice noodles tossed in a fresh basil-garlic sauce.

In the world of Thai cooking, when it comes to authenticity, there seem to be two separate camps. The first says that nothing that is not authentically Thai should be referred to as Thai; the second uses Thai ingredients and cooking methods freely, claiming there is no such thing as authenticity anymore in a world that is growing smaller by the day. While both perspectives have their strong points, there is no denying the wonderful taste of a dish which, when cooked well, is actually a creative fusion between several disparate cuisines.

Such is the case here, where Thai-style rice noodles are fried up with an Asian version of Italian pesto.

Yield: Serves 2–3

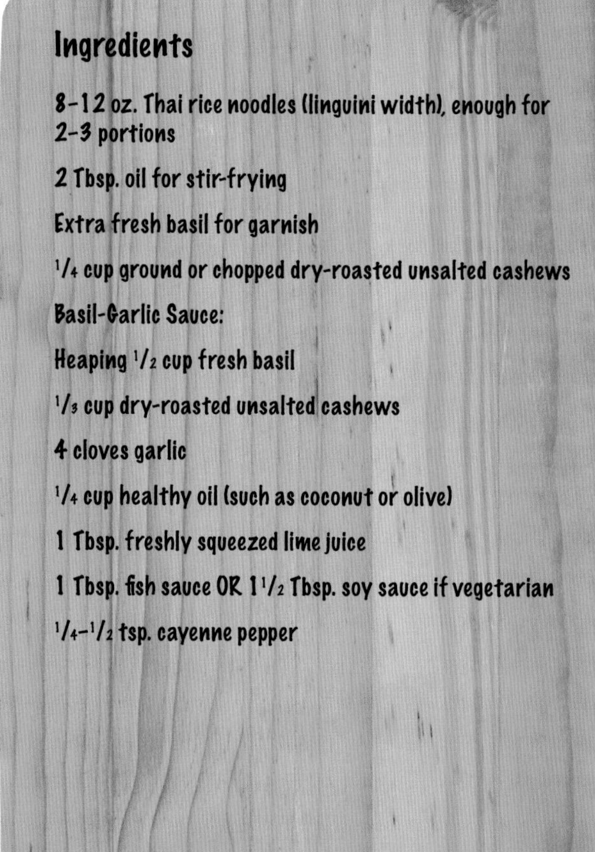

Ingredients

8–12 oz. Thai rice noodles (linguini width), enough for 2–3 portions

2 Tbsp. oil for stir-frying

Extra fresh basil for garnish

1/4 cup ground or chopped dry-roasted unsalted cashews

Basil-Garlic Sauce:

Heaping 1/2 cup fresh basil

1/3 cup dry-roasted unsalted cashews

4 cloves garlic

1/4 cup healthy oil (such as coconut or olive)

1 Tbsp. freshly squeezed lime juice

1 Tbsp. fish sauce OR 1 1/2 Tbsp. soy sauce if vegetarian

1/4–1/2 tsp. cayenne pepper

Easy Basil Noodles

- Bring a large pot of water to a boil, then remove it from the burner. Dunk in the rice noodles, ensuring they are fully submerged in the hot water.
- Allow noodles to soak 6–12 minutes (depending on the thickness of the noodles).
- Rice noodles are ready when they are soft enough to eat, but are still firm and a little crunchy (they will be stir-fried later, so avoid over-softening them now).
- Drain and rinse the noodles with cold water to keep them from sticking.

YELLOW LIGHT

Many Thai noodles dishes can be made wheat-free. If you have celiac disease, Thai cuisine offers numerous ways of cooking rice noodles, all of them delicious. Just be careful about the sauces used to flavor the noodles. Fish sauce is gluten-free, but soy sauce is not, so be sure to buy wheat-free soy sauce. Also check the labels of other sauces used in Thai cooking, such as ground bean sauce, as many contain wheat.

MAKE IT EASY

Rice noodles tend to stick to the bottom of nearly any wok or pan, even those with a non-stick coating. This is normal—just keep loosening them with your spatula and gently turning them. A little oil can be added, but it is best not to add any other liquid ingredients while frying rice noodles than is indicated in the recipe; otherwise the noodles will turn soggy as opposed to chewy-delicious.

Making the Basil-Garlic Sauce

- Combine basil-garlic sauce ingredients together in a mini chopper or food processor (one that can process finely). Blitz to create a brilliant green sauce. Set aside.
- Warm a wok over medium-high heat. Add oil and swirl around to cover the bottom and sides of the wok, then add the noodles. You will hear them sizzle when they hit the hot pan.
- Using 2 utensils, quickly turn the noodles in the oil for 1 minute, or use a tossing motion (like tossing a salad).

Stir-Frying the Noodles

- Add 2 Tbsp. of the basil-garlic sauce and stir-fry the noodles 2–3 minutes.
- If noodles remain firm rather than chewy, add another Tbsp. of sauce and continue stir-frying 1 more minute, or until the desired chewy texture is reached.
- Remove from heat. Add all remaining basil-garlic sauce and toss.
- Taste test the noodles, adding a little more fish sauce (or soy sauce) if not salty or flavorful enough.
- Serve with toppings of fresh basil and ground cashews.

GREEN CURRY CHICKEN

For superior results, this curry starts with a homemade Thai green curry paste.

Green curry is one of the most famous of all Thai dishes. The green appearance of this curry comes from several fresh ingredients: green chilies, fresh coriander, and fresh basil. Coconut milk is an important ingredient in green curry, with the highest quality of canned coconut milk being preferred.

But the real key to cooking up a good Thai curry is in the type of paste that is used. These days, you can easily purchase a ready-made Thai green curry paste. However, there is nothing like fresh paste to make the flavors in your curry come alive. So unless you are very pressed for time, take a few minutes to blitz up my homemade green curry paste.

Yield: Serves 2–3

Ingredients

1 can coconut milk, divided
1–2 Tbsp. oil
1–1½ lbs. chicken thighs, chopped
1 zucchini, cut into thick chunks
8 kaffir lime leaves, cut into thin strips
½ cup fresh basil

Green Curry Paste:
4 green chilies
1 shallot, diced
4 cloves garlic, minced
1 Tbsp. grated galangal OR ginger
1 stalk minced lemongrass
1½ tsp. ground coriander
1 tsp. shrimp paste
½ cup coriander leaves and stems
1 tsp. ground white pepper
1 Tbsp. soy sauce
2 Tbsp. fish sauce, plus more to taste
1 tsp. sugar

Green Curry Chicken

- Place all green curry paste ingredients in a food processor. Also add 2-3 Tbsp. of the coconut milk. Blitz to create a fragrant green curry paste. Set aside.
- Warm a wok or large frying pan over medium-high heat. Add 1–2 Tbsp. oil and swirl around.
- Add all of the green curry paste. Stir-fry briefly to release the fragrance (30–60 seconds).

ZOOM

In Thailand, coconut milk is freshly squeezed from ripe coconuts; but here in North America, canned must suffice. When shopping, be sure to look for the highest quality, preferably organic. The best coconut milk comes naturally separated into coconut cream (which rises to the top of the can and is fairly solid), and coconut water (which remains at the bottom).

MAKE IT EASY

Homemade green curry paste can easily be made ahead of time, or you can double the recipe and store the extra for future use. It can be kept in a jar in your refrigerator for up to 1 week; thereafter, store it in the freezer. If you like adding just a touch of green curry to dishes, consider freezing it in an ice cube tray. Then just pop out as many curry paste cubes as you need.

Adding Coconut Milk

- Add ¾ of the remaining can of coconut milk, setting the rest aside for later. Stir-fry together with the paste, blending the two.
- Add the chicken, stirring to incorporate. When the curry sauce begins to boil, reduce heat to a simmer.
- Cover and simmer 3–5 minutes, or until chicken is cooked through. Stir occasionally.
- Add the zucchini plus the strips of lime leaf, stirring well to incorporate. Simmer another 2–3 minutes.

Adjusting the Flavors

- Remove from heat and taste test, looking for a balance of salty, spicy, sweet, and sour. Add more fish sauce until desired saltiness and flavor is reached. If too sour, add a little more sugar. If it's too sweet or salty, add 1 Tbsp. lime juice.
- Portion out into individual serving bowls, topping each one with a generous sprinkling of fresh basil. Finally, drizzle over 2–3 Tbsp. (per bowl) of the reserved coconut milk.
- Serve with jasmine-scented rice, coconut rice, or sticky rice, and enjoy.

SHRIMP CURRY WITH PINEAPPLE

This saffron-golden curry makes a beautiful dish to serve guests.

A Thai chef once told me, in a secretive kind of whisper, that the best Thai dishes look like a terrible mess, but taste like heaven. While this is true for many a Thai curry and noodle dish, it isn't the case here. This yellow seafood curry is both beautiful to serve and exquisitely delicious.

The curry sauce in this recipe is saffron-golden in color, which then appears to be jeweled with the plump pink shrimp, chunks of bright yellow pineapple, and instances of bright red cherry tomatoes. Top the dish off with a sprinkling of toasted coconut and fresh coriander, and you have a gourmet-style Thai curry that both looks and tastes like heaven.

Yield: Serves 3–4

Ingredients

12–14 medium to large raw shrimp
1/3 cup dry shredded coconut
4 kaffir lime leaves, torn
1 1/2 cups pineapple chunks
1 1/2 cups cherry or grape tomatoes
1/4 cup fresh coriander
Curry Sauce:
1 can coconut milk
1 stalk lemongrass, minced
1–3 tsp. Thai chili sauce, to taste
1 shallot
4 cloves garlic, sliced
1 Tbsp. galangal OR ginger, sliced
1/2 tsp. shrimp paste
3/4 tsp. turmeric
1/2 tsp. ground coriander
2 Tbsp. brown sugar, to taste
1 Tbsp. tomato ketchup
2 Tbsp. fish sauce

Shrimp Curry with Pineapple & Lime Leaf

- Remove shells from the shrimp, except the tails. "Butterfly" them by making a shallow cut down the length of the spine. Remove any veins you find and give the shrimp a good rinse. Set in a bowl in the refrigerator while you prepare the other ingredients.
- Place the shredded coconut in a dry frying pan over medium-high heat. Stir the coconut continually until it turns light golden-brown and is fragrant. Remove coconut from the hot pan and leave to cool.

ZOOM

Although canned pineapple will work for this recipe, you won't get the wonderful flavor that fresh pineapple affords. When shopping for a pineapple, test the fruit by picking it up by one of its uppermost leaves. If the leaf breaks off, the pineapple is ready to be eaten. Note that the skin of the pineapple should be quite firm and changing from green to yellow in color.

MAKE IT EASY

Kaffir lime leaves can be prepared a number of ways according to how much flavor you wish to add. To add a hint of lime flavor, gently tear the leaves in half. For even more flavor, use scissors to cut the leaves into thin strips, discarding the stems. In this case, the leaves will be eaten, so be sure to cook them long enough to soften them.

Making the Curry Sauce

- Place all curry sauce ingredients together in a food processor, blender, or large food chopper. Blitz to create a golden-colored curry paste.
- Pour the sauce into a wok or large frying pan set over medium-high heat.
- Add the torn lime leaves, and stir well.

Simmering the Curry

- When the sauce begins to bubble, reduce heat to medium. Add the pineapple, cherry tomatoes, and shrimp, stirring well. Simmer 6–8 minutes, or until the shrimp are pink.
- Remove curry from heat and add half of the toasted coconut, stirring well.
- Taste test the curry, adding more fish sauce if not salty or flavorful enough, or more sugar if you'd prefer it sweeter.
- Top the curry with fresh coriander and remaining toasted coconut. Serve with plain or coconut rice and enjoy.

RED CURRY CHICKEN

This delicious curry chicken is incredibly quick and easy to make.

In Thailand, most curries are simmered in a wok, but here in North America it's considered much easier to simply stir a few ingredients together and pop them in the oven.

While some Thai curries are best simmered in the traditional way, the following recipe turns out just as delicious when baked in the oven.

Red curry is one of the three most popular Thai curries, the other two being green and yellow. The red color comes from the use of red chilies plus chili powder, suggesting a very spicy curry. However, if you use regular American chili powder (as opposed to Thai or Indian), this dish will turn out mild enough to please everyone at your dinner table.

Yield: Serves 2–4

Ingredients

1/2 medium chicken, cut into parts

4 kaffir lime leaves, torn in half

1 cinnamon stick OR 1/2 tsp. cinnamon

1 red bell pepper, chopped

3 medium tomatoes, chopped

1/2 cup fresh basil leaves

Red Curry Sauce:

1/2 can coconut milk (reserve other 1/2)

1 shallot, minced

1 Tbsp. grated galangal OR ginger

3 cloves garlic

3 Tbsp. fish sauce

1 Tbsp. chili powder

1 Tbsp. ground cumin

1 Tbsp. ground coriander

2 heaping tsp. brown sugar

2 tsp. shrimp paste

1–2 red chilies, minced, OR 1–3 tsp. chili sauce

Red Curry Chicken

- Preheat oven to 350 degrees F. Have ready a large casserole dish for the curry (you will also need a lid).
- Place all curry sauce ingredients together in a food processor or blender, adjusting the chili content to suit your taste.
- Blitz to create a fragrant red curry sauce.

RECIPE VARIATION

This dish can also be made in a slow cooker. Place the chicken pieces, vegetables, torn lime leaves, and cinnamon stick in the slower cooker. Make the red curry sauce and pour it over the other ingredients, stirring well. Switch your slow cooker to the "low" setting and cook all day. Follow the taste testing instructions at the end of this recipe, and finish the dish with a sprinkling of fresh basil.

ZOOM

Cinnamon is one of the oldest spices in existence. There are two types of cinnamon: that from the bark of the cinnamon tree (native to Sri Lanka), and that from the bark of the cassia shrub. The latter is the most common cinnamon in use throughout North America, and it is also used in Thai cooking. Look for cinnamon sticks at your supermarket or gourmet food store.

Baking the Curry Chicken

- Place chicken in the casserole dish and pour the curry sauce over. Gently stir, ensuring each of the chicken pieces is covered with sauce.
- Add the torn kaffir lime leaves and cinnamon stick, mixing these into the curry.
- Cover and bake 45 minutes at 350 degrees F.
- Remove dish from the oven and add the vegetables, stirring them into the sauce. Cover and return to the oven for 15 minutes more, or until both chicken and vegetables are cooked to your liking.

Adjusting the Flavors

- Taste test the curry. If not salty or flavorful enough, add more fish sauce. If it's too sour for your taste, add more brown sugar; if too spicy, or if you'd prefer more sauce, add the remaining ½ can coconut milk. If not spicy enough, add more fresh-cut chili or Thai chili sauce.
- To serve, top curry with a generous sprinkling of fresh basil, and serve with plenty of jasmine rice, coconut rice, or sticky rice.

YELLOW CURRY CHICKEN

This dish is similar to other yellow curries from around the world, but with decidedly Thai flavors.

Yellow curry is a favorite dish across many cultures and traditions, and is made in various ways according to the country or region. In Thailand, yellow curries are created both with curry powder (usually Indian-type) and without. The following dish is an example of the latter type, wherein all the spices that might be contained in a curry powder are added individually, resulting in robust flavors and an entirely Thai taste.

Though lemongrass is not always included in yellow curry, I find it provides yet another layer of flavor and also makes the dish more aromatic. If you're in a hurry or can't find fresh lemongrass, feel free to substitute frozen prepared lemongrass.

Yield: Serves 4

Ingredients

1/2 chicken, chopped into pieces
2 potatoes, chopped into small chunks
4 kaffir lime leaves, torn in half
1/2 cup fresh coriander
1/2 cup fresh basil

Curry Sauce:

1–2 yellow, red, or green chilies
1 stalk lemongrass, finely sliced
1 can coconut milk
2 shallots, diced
4 cloves garlic
1 Tbsp. grated galangal OR ginger
1 tsp. ground coriander
1 tsp. ground cumin
1/2 tsp. cinnamon
3 Tbsp. fish sauce
1 tsp. turmeric
1 Tbsp. brown sugar
1 Tbsp. fresh lime juice
1 Tbsp. ketchup

Yellow Curry Chicken

- Preheat oven to 350 degrees F.
- Chop the chicken and potatoes, and place in a large casserole dish.
- Place all curry sauce ingredients together in a food processor or blender. Blitz to create an aromatic Thai yellow curry sauce.

RECIPE VARIATION

To make Thai yellow curry paste, place all curry sauce ingredients in a food processor; however, instead of 1 can coconut milk, add only ¼ cup. Also add 3–4 lime leaves, snipped into thin strips. Blitz to create the paste. Store in the refrigerator for 1 week, or freeze up to 6 months. Yellow curry paste can easily be thinned out to create a curry sauce by adding coconut milk or vegetable stock.

ZOOM

Thai yellow chilies are not as easy to find in North America as red or green chilies. Yellow Thai chilies are small and close to golden-orange in color. If you can't find them, substitute Hungarian hot wax yellow chilies, or yellow habanero chilies. Just be careful not to use too many since they are some of the hottest chilies in existence!

Baking the Curry

- Pour the curry sauce over the chicken and potatoes. Also add the torn lime leaves, stirring to mix them in.
- Cover and bake the curry at 350 degrees F for 1 hour.
- After 1 hour, remove curry from oven and check to see if chicken is cooked. Test one of the thicker pieces, cutting down to the bone. If meat is white and tender, curry is done. If the meat is still red or pink, return to the oven for 10–15 minutes.

Finishing the Dish

- Taste test the curry. Add 1–2 Tbsp. more fish sauce if not salty or flavorful enough. If too salty for your taste, add a little more lime juice. If the curry is too spicy, add a little more coconut milk; if too sour, add a little more brown sugar.
- When you're happy with the taste, top the curry with the fresh coriander and basil.
- Serve with jasmine rice, coconut rice, or Thai sticky rice, and enjoy.

EASY FISH CURRY

A delightful way to cook nearly any type of fresh or frozen fish.

Fish isn't normally associated with curry, but it should be! Curry sauce makes a wonderfully rich and tasty way to cook milder fillets of fish, and can make even less expensive types of frozen fish taste gourmet good.

For this recipe, use any type of filleted fish or fish steaks (fresh or frozen), so long as they are white-fleshed (such as tilapia, perch, sole, snapper, or trout).

The curry sauce for this recipe isn't based on one of the traditional Thai three (red, yellow, or green), but is rather a combination of all three. It's a quick and easy recipe to make, and because fish cooks up so quickly compared to chicken or red meats, you'll find the dish is ready in no time.

Yield: Serves 2–4

Ingredients

1 cup fresh shiitake mushrooms, sliced
1 red bell pepper or sweet pepper, diced
3–4 white-fleshed fish fillets or steaks
1 medium tomato, diced
1/2 cup fresh coriander
1/3 cup fresh basil
Optional: Freshly cut lime or lemon wedges

Curry Sauce:
1 can good-quality coconut milk
1/2 cup coriander leaves and stems
1 Tbsp. grated galangal OR ginger
4 cloves garlic
2 1/2 Tbsp. fish sauce
1 Tbsp. chili powder
2 tsp. ground cumin
2 tsp. ground coriander
1 Tbsp. brown sugar
4 kaffir lime leaves, cut into thin strips
1/2 tsp. turmeric
1 tsp. shrimp paste
1 fresh chili, minced, OR 1-3 tsp. Thai chili sauce

Easy FishCurry

- Place all curry sauce ingredients in a food processor or blender. Process well to create a smooth and aromatic sauce.
- Pour the sauce into a wok or large frying pan set over medium-high heat.
- Bring to a boil, then reduce heat to medium. Add the mushrooms and red pepper, stirring well to incorporate.

RECIPE VARIATION

To make a mixed seafood curry, use only 2 fish fillets. When the curry is made and the fish has simmered for 2–3 minutes, add ¼–½ lb. cleaned mussels, 1 cup small bay-type scallops, and 6–8 medium shrimp. Cover and continue simmering until the mussels open and the shrimp are pink and plump (3–4 minutes). Taste test the dish according to the instructions, and top with coriander and basil.

MAKE IT EASY

If using frozen fish for this recipe, be sure to thaw it first. This can be done at the last minute by dunking the fish in a bowl filled with lukewarm water. Allow fish to sit for 1 minute in the water (the water will become very cold). Drain off the water and add more. Repeat until the fish is thawed and ready to be used. Be sure to drain the fish well and pat or shake dry before cooking.

Simmering the Fish and Vegetables

- Cover the curry and simmer 2–3 minutes.
- Add the fish and tomatoes, gently stirring them in. Cover once more and continue simmering the dish another 4–5 minutes, or until fish is cooked.
- Fish is done when the inner flesh is opaque (rather than translucent) and flakes easily.

Adjusting the Flavors

- Taste test the curry for salt and sweetness, adding more fish sauce (instead of salt), or more sugar if too sour. If too sweet or too salty, add 1–2 Tbsp. fresh lime (or lemon) juice.
- Portion out the curry into serving bowls. Top each one with fresh coriander and basil. You can also garnish with freshly cut lime or lemon wedges.
- Serve hot with plenty of Thai jasmine-scented rice, Thai coconut rice, or Thai sticky rice on the side.

SCALLOPS IN A RICH RED CURRY

This curry dish is very sumptuous and makes an elegant entrée to serve guests.

These days, red curry paste is used by many chefs (and not just Thai ones) in connection with various seafood dishes, from salmon to shrimp and scallops. There's just something about the taste of a good red curry paste that works with fresh seafood, enhancing and enriching the already rich flavors.

The following recipe is a good example of this combination of flavors, with medium to large scallops simmered in a rich Thai red curry sauce.

If you can't find fresh sea scallops, look for the largest bay scallops you can find, preferably fresh rather than frozen.

Yield: Serves 2 as a main entrée

Ingredients

15–18 medium-sized bay scallops OR 8–10 large sea scallops

1–2 Tbsp. oil

1–2 whole star anise (plus more for garnish)

1/4 cup fresh coriander

Optional: Freshly cut lime or lemon wedges

Red Curry Paste:

1/2 cup coconut milk

1 shallot, diced

1 Tbsp. grated galangal OR ginger

3 cloves garlic

1/8 tsp. white pepper

2 Tbsp. fish sauce, plus more to taste

2 tsp. chili powder

2 tsp. ground cumin

1 tsp. ground coriander

1–2 Tbsp. brown sugar, to taste

1 tsp. shrimp paste

3 kaffir lime leaves, cut into thin strips

1–3 tsp. Thai chili sauce, to taste

Scallops in a Rich Red Curry

- Place all curry paste ingredients in a food processor or blender. Blitz to create a fragrant red curry sauce.
- Place 3–4 Tbsp. of this sauce in a mixing bowl. Add the scallops and gently toss until well coated. Set in the refrigerator to marinate 5–10 minutes.

ZOOM

Like other types of shellfish, scallops cook quickly. In order to retain their natural tenderness, be careful not to overcook them. To test whether a scallop is cooked, make a cut into the center: the inner flesh should be opaque rather than translucent. Also, when scallops are ready to be eaten, the outside of the scallop forms "cracks" (the equivalent of a fish flaking).

GREEN LIGHT

Sea scallop populations in the Atlantic are considered healthy; however, the dredging methods used to harvest them affect other endangered species (such as sea turtles). It's best to buy farmed scallops, which are environmentally green and sustainable. Scallops are healthy to eat, since they simply cannot tolerate toxic conditions. And because scallops remove carbon dioxide from their surroundings, they help reduce greenhouse gases!

Simmering the Scallops in the Curry Sauce

- Warm a wok or frying pan over medium-high heat. Add 1–2 Tbsp. oil and swirl around, then add the curry sauce plus the whole star anise. Stir the sauce until it starts to bubble, then reduce heat to medium. Simmer 3–4 minutes.
- Now add the scallops. Cook the scallops by gently stirring and turning them in the simmering curry sauce for 4–5 minutes.
- Large scallops may need slightly longer to cook, while smaller ones may need only a few minutes.

Finishing the Dish

- When scallops are cooked, remove from heat.
- Taste test the curry, adding more fish sauce if not salty or flavorful enough, or more sugar if too sour. If the sauce is too spicy or strong-flavored, add more coconut milk.
- Transfer the scallops to a serving dish and pour the sauce over the top. Garnish with fresh coriander, plus a couple of whole star anise and wedges of fresh-cut lime or lemon, if desired. Serve with jasmine-scented rice or coconut rice, and enjoy.

GREEN PAPAYA SALAD

Green papaya salad, or Som Tam, is the most popular salad in Thailand.

Green papaya salad, or Som Tam, is extremely popular in Thailand. In fact, many Thais eat it on a daily basis. In other parts of the world, however, this salad is still somewhat of a novelty. With its zingingly delightful flavors and abundance of textures, green papaya salad is definitely one of the best salads the world has to offer.

In Thailand, it is made a variety of ways. It might be tossed up with vegetables or made with a variety of seafood, which is added as a protein source. Feel free to experiment with the dish and see how best you like your Som Tam!

Yield: Serves 2–4

Ingredients

2 tomatoes

3 green onions

1 red chili, de-seeded and finely sliced

2 cups bean sprouts

1/2 cup fresh coriander

Optional: 1 cup cooked seafood, such as crab or shrimp

1 small or medium-sized green papaya (to make about 4 cups grated papaya)

1/3 cup fresh basil

1/2 cup plain or honey-roasted peanuts

Dressing:

2 Tbsp. coconut or olive oil

1/2 tsp. shrimp paste

1 Tbsp. fish sauce

1 Tbsp. soy sauce

2 Tbsp. lime juice

1–2 tsp. honey OR substitute sugar

Green Papaya Salad

- Get out a large salad bowl for mixing and tossing the salad.
- Prepare the tomatoes by cutting them into wedges, then slicing into long thin strips. Place in the bowl.
- Cut the green onion into matchstick-like pieces and add them to the bowl as well.
- Finely slice and mince the fresh chili (scrape out the seeds for less heat). Add the chili plus the bean sprouts, coriander, and seafood (if using) to the salad bowl.

• • • • RECIPE VARIATION • • • •

To make this recipe vegetarian, add a little ground bean sauce instead of fish sauce and shrimp paste. Ground bean sauce is made from fermented soy beans, giving you the salty taste of fish sauce as well as a good kick of added flavor. If you'd like to add some protein to your salad, add some sliced boiled egg or, if vegan, some deep-fried tofu.

ZOOM

Asian green papaya is not exactly the same as an unripe papaya you might find at your local supermarket (which comes from Hawaii or the Caribbean). These papayas, if green in appearance, are probably merely on their way to ripening, whereas Asian green papayas are purposely picked young and are pleasantly sour. For this reason, buy your green papaya at an Asian food store or market.

Grating or Shredding the Papaya

- Slice the papaya down the middle, from one end to the other, and crack it open. Scrape out seeds with a spoon and discard.
- Chop papaya into manageable pieces and peel or slice off the skin and discard it.
- Use a large-size grater to grate the papaya, or shred it the way they do in Thailand: by making many long, deep cuts into the flesh, then, holding your knife flat against the papaya, very shallowly slicing off the surface layers.
- Add the grated or shredded papaya to the salad bowl.

Making the Dressing

- Place all dressing ingredients together in a cup. Stir well to dissolve the honey or sugar.
- The dressing should taste salty, sour, and a little sweet. Adjust the sweetness to suit your taste by adding a little more honey or sugar.
- Pour the dressing over the salad and toss well. Top with the basil and peanuts (left whole or ground), and serve immediately.

GREEN MANGO SALAD

A scrumptious Thai salad that is uniquely refreshing.

Similar to green papaya salad, Thai green mango salad offers both sweet and sour flavors together in a delightfully crunchy dish. Unlike green papaya salad, you needn't venture outside your local supermarket for the required ingredients for this salad, green mangoes being readily available in most stores nearly any time of the year.

The refreshing taste of this salad makes it an excellent accompaniment to hot Thai curries and spicy stir-fries. It is also delicious enough to stand on its own if you're in the mood for a lighter meal. Like Green Papaya Salad, various protein sources can be added to make this dish a nutritionally complete lunch or dinner.

Yield: Serves 3–4 as an appetizer or side dish

Ingredients

3 green onions

3/4 cup fresh coriander

3 cups bean sprouts

1/4 cup dry shredded coconut

2 firm green mangoes

1/3 cup fresh basil

1/3 cup peanuts or cashews, left whole, roughly chopped, or ground

Salad Dressing:

3 Tbsp. fish sauce OR vegetarian fish sauce (OR substitute 3 1/2 Tbsp. soy sauce)

3 Tbsp. lime juice

2 Tbsp. brown sugar

1–2 fresh red chilies, de-seeded and minced, OR 1–2 tsp. Thai chili sauce

Green Mango Salad

- Mix all the salad dressing ingredients together in a small bowl or cup, stirring well to dissolve the sugar. Set aside.
- Get out a large salad or mixing bowl. Slice the green onions into matchstick-like pieces and place in the bowl.
- Roughly chop up the coriander. Add this herb plus the bean sprouts to the bowl.

RECIPE VARIATION

To make this salad into a main entrée, add 1 cup cooked shrimp at the end of the recipe, tossing well to mix in. Other protein sources that can be added include 1 cup cooked crab meat; 1 cup leftover roasted chicken or turkey; or, for vegetarians, 1 boiled egg (sliced and added to the top of the salad). For vegans, add 1 cup deep-fried tofu, cut into small cubes and tossed in with the other ingredients.

ZOOM

When shopping for green mango, make sure the the fruit is very firm and either entirely green on the outside, or a combination of green and red. If the mangoes are too ripe, you won't be able to grate them. The mango should feel hard as an apple. When the skin is peeled off, the inner flesh should be a pale yellow.

Toasting the Coconut

- Place the coconut in a dry wok or frying pan over medium-high heat.
- Stirring continually, "dry-fry" the coconut 3–5 minutes, or until it turns light golden-brown and is fragrant. Tip the toasted coconut onto a plate to cool.
- When cooled slightly, add ½ the toasted coconut to the salad bowl.

Grating the Green Mango

- Peel the green mangoes. Using a medium to large-size grater, grate the flesh (note that mangoes have a flat stone in the center).
- Add the grated mango to the salad bowl. Pour the dressing over and toss well.
- Taste test the salad. If you prefer more flavor or more salt, add 1 Tbsp. fish sauce. If you prefer it sweeter, add a little more sugar. Add more chili for a spicier salad.
- Top with the basil, nuts, and the remaining toasted coconut, and enjoy.

SALAD WITH COCONUT DRESSING

This salad can be made quickly for everyday eating, or dressed up for special occasions.

This recipe for tossed green salad can be easily whipped up for everyday eating. For more formal occasions, it can easily be transformed into a beautiful entree in its own right by slicing the cucumber differently, and by garnishing with some pretty edible flowers.

In Thailand, flowers are a common garnish to many dishes (whether those flowers are edible or not). In fact, the Thais are known for their beautiful presentation of dishes, especially in the genre of Thai food known as "Palace-style" (dishes prepared for the royal family).

Yield: Serves 3–4 as a side dish

Ingredients

4–5 cups lettuce or garden greens

3 green onions

½ cup fresh coriander

Optional: 1 fresh red chili, minced

1 cucumber

¼ cup fresh basil

Optional: A few slices of star fruit

Optional: A few edible flowers, such as pansies, nasturtiums, or rose petals

Salad Dressing:

¼ cup coconut milk

1 Tbsp. lime juice

1 Tbsp. fish sauce (OR substitute 1½ Tbsp. soy sauce)

1 clove garlic, minced

1–2 tsp. brown sugar, to taste

Easy Tossed Green Salad with Coconut Dressing

- Place the lettuce or garden greens in a large salad bowl.
- Cut the green onion into matchstick-like pieces and add them to the bowl. Roughly chop the fresh coriander and add it to the bowl as well.
- If using fresh chili, finely slice and mince it, scraping out and discarding the seeds. Sprinkle these bits of chili over the salad.

ZOOM

There are various types of edible flowers, including nasturtiums, pansies, violas, and roses. Growing your own is the best way to ensure they are free of herbicides; otherwise, prepare a "bath" with warm, soapy water (use a vegetable wash or environmentally friendly dish soap). Hold the flowers by their stems and gentle plunge them into the soapy water several times. Rinse and set aside to dry.

GREEN LIGHT

Try to use organic produce for Thai salads. Not only will the salads taste better (organic produce has more flavor because the growing conditions are superior), but also, for dishes like this tossed green salad, you needn't worry about ingesting toxins in the skins. By buying organic cucumber, you can leave the skin on and enjoy some extra nutrients and taste worry free.

Making the Dressing

- Combine the salad dressing ingredients together in a cup, stirring until the sugar dissolves.
- Taste test the dressing, adding more sugar if you'd prefer it sweeter, or more fish sauce (or soy sauce) if you'd like it saltier.
- For a thicker dressing, simply chill in the refrigerator while you prepare the other ingredients (the cold will naturally thicken the coconut milk).

Preparing the Cucumber

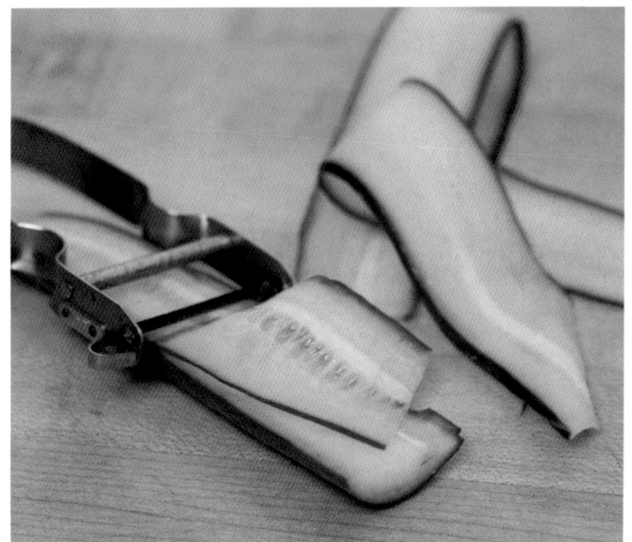

- Simply slice the cucumber as you would for a regular salad, or leave on the skin and peel the cucumber into long, thin, ribbon-like lengths (a regular potato peeler works fine for this).
- If the ribbons are too long or wide to eat easily, cut them in half or into thirds.
- Add the cucumber to the salad bowl. Pour the dressing over and toss to combine.
- Top the salad with the fresh basil. If desired, garnish with star fruit plus a few edible flowers.

FRESH PAPAYA SALAD

This fresh fruit and seafood salad makes a pretty dish for a party.

Papaya is a wonderful-tasting fruit that can be eaten a variety of ways. When still green, its tart flesh can be enjoyed like a vegetable (as in Green Papaya Salad); when ripe, its sweet flesh marries beautifully with myriad savory ingredients, including seafood and salad greens.

In the following dish, papaya is combined with cooked shrimp or prawns, cucumbers, tomato, and star fruit for a beautiful platter that is like a fresh food feast. Drizzled over the dish is a coconut milk dressing that enhances the exotic taste of all these tropical wonders.

While Hawaiian papaya will work for this recipe, the Caribbean variety is preferred for its thicker, sweeter fruit.

Yield: Serves 2 as a dinner salad, 4–6 as a side dish

Ingredients

1 large platter-size bed of greens

1 cup cooked shrimp (tails left on)

1 cup small to medium cooked scallops

1 cucumber, sliced

1–2 tomatoes, sliced

A few star fruit slices, de-seeded

1 large ripe papaya

Fresh coriander for garnish

Optional garnish: A few edible flowers such as nasturtiums, pansies, or violas

Dressing:

1/4 cup coconut milk

1 Tbsp. coconut oil (or olive oil)

2 Tbsp. fish sauce

1 Tbsp. freshly squeezed lime juice

2 heaping tsp. brown sugar

1–2 tsp. chili sauce, to taste

Fresh Papaya Salad

- Prepare a large platter by covering it with a bed of lettuce or garden greens.
- Arrange the cooked shrimp on one section of the platter. Do the same with the cooked scallops.
- Add slices of cucumber and tomato (either all around the edge of the platter, or also in their own "sections").
- Do the same with the star fruit.

RECIPE VARIATION

Grilled Seafood Papaya Salad. Instead of laying the salad ingredients out platter-style, cut all ingredients into bite-size pieces and toss in a bowl with the dressing. In a cup, dissolve 1½ tsp. cornstarch in 4 Tbsp. soy sauce. Pour this mixture over 1 cup fresh shrimp and 1 cup bay-type scallops. Brush the grill with a little oil. Grill just until cooked and serve over the tossed salad.

ZOOM

Papaya was called the "fruit of the angels" by Christopher Columbus. Sweet, juicy, and healthy, papaya is one of the world's favorite tropical fruits. When shopping for a papaya, look for skin that is turning from green to yellow. You should be able to indent the skin with your thumb. When eating papaya, drizzle with some fresh-squeezed lime juice, which brings out the sweetness and flavor.

Preparing the Papaya

- To prepare the papaya, lay the fruit down on a clean surface and slice it down the middle (lengthwise). Crack the papaya open.
- Use a spoon to scrape out the seeds, discarding them. Then turn the papaya over (skin side up). Use a large knife to slice up the papaya as you would watermelon. Peel off the skin from each slice.
- Arrange the papaya slices on the platter next to the seafood.

Making the Dressing

- Combine all the dressing ingredients together in a cup or small bowl.
- Taste test for sweetness, saltiness, and spice, adding more sugar for a sweeter dressing, or more lime juice if too sweet or too salty. Add more coconut milk if it's too spicy for your taste.
- Drizzle the dressing over the platter and garnish with the coriander. If desired, add a few edible flowers to finish the dish.

CUCUMBER SALAD

This salad is quintessentially Thai in flavor.

If you're looking for an authentic Thai salad that can be tossed up in a hurry, this simple recipe will hit the mark every time. Cucumber salad is a classic Thai dish that is commonly served as an accompaniment to other dishes.

After sharing this recipe with several of my friends, I was told it had actually helped one of them lose weight. This made perfect sense to me, as not only is this salad low in calories and fat, it is so high in taste that one large portion more than satisfies. Also, consuming chili actually boosts your metabolism (in this respect, it is similar to coffee, tea, and other natural stimulants).

Yield: Serves 4

Ingredients

2 medium to large cucumbers

1 shallot, finely chopped

2 green onions, cut into matchsticks

1/4 cup fresh basil

1/4 cup fresh coriander

1 fresh red chili, de-seeded and finely sliced

1/4 cup ground unsalted dry-roasted peanuts

Dressing:

2 Tbsp. fish sauce

2 Tbsp. freshly squeezed lime juice

1/2 tsp. shrimp paste

1 Tbsp. soy sauce

1/4–1/2 tsp. cayenne pepper

1 Tbsp. palm sugar OR brown sugar, to taste

Cucumber Salad

- For a beautiful presentation, use a peeler to peel the cucumbers into long, ribbon-like strips. Be sure to wash the outside of the cucumber well, as the ribbons look best with the skin left on.
- If your cucumber ribbons are too wide or long to be easily eaten, slice them into smaller strips.
- Alternatively, using the largest size grater you have, grate the cucumber into a mixing bowl.

RECIPE VARIATION

Cucumber Relish. This salad can easily be made into a Thai-style relish, which can be added onto the side of grilled fish or seafood, or nearly any other Thai dish. Instead of slicing or peeling the cucumber, finely dice it. Finely chop up the other ingredients and toss with the cucumber. Add the dressing and stir well. Follow the taste testing instructions and serve with your favorite Thai entrée.

ZOOM

The oil from chili peppers can, despite numerous washings, remain on your skin for hours. Touching your eyes or face after handling fresh chili can be painful. To prevent this, wear rubber gloves, or get yourself a box of silicon gloves from the pharmacy. Wear the gloves while slicing up and transferring the chili to your wok. Set your knife and cutting board in the dishwasher after use.

Making the Thai Dressing

- Stir together the dressing ingredients in a cup, stirring until sugar dissolves.
- Note that this dressing has a very pungent smell and flavor, but will taste wonderful once it is combined with the salad greens.
- Set dressing aside for a minute, allowing the flavors to mingle.

Tossing the Salad with the Dressing

- In a salad bowl, combine the cucumber together with the shallot, green onion, basil, coriander, and chili. Pour the dressing over and toss well.
- Taste test the salad. If you'd prefer it saltier, add a little more fish sauce. If it's too salty or too sweet for your taste, add a little more fresh lime juice; if too sour, add a little more brown sugar. Toss well to incorporate these additions.
- Portion into salad bowls or onto plates, top with the ground peanuts, and enjoy.

TROPICAL FRUIT SALAD

This fresh fruit salad makes a pretty dessert or side dish for a party.

There are few things more beautiful or more delicious than a fresh fruit salad, and this is especially the case with the following recipe. Tropical fruit has a natural "wow factor" that makes this fruit salad stand apart. If you can, try to use all fresh (rather than canned) fruit for the best possible taste and texture.

These days, even your local supermarket might well be selling exotic Thai fruits like papaya, pineapple, star fruit, and even dragon fruit. Lychees may be more difficult to find, though a quick trip to your local Asian food store or market will likely result in your finding not only lychees, but various other tropical wonders, some of which may be refreshingly new to you.

Yield: Serves 8–10

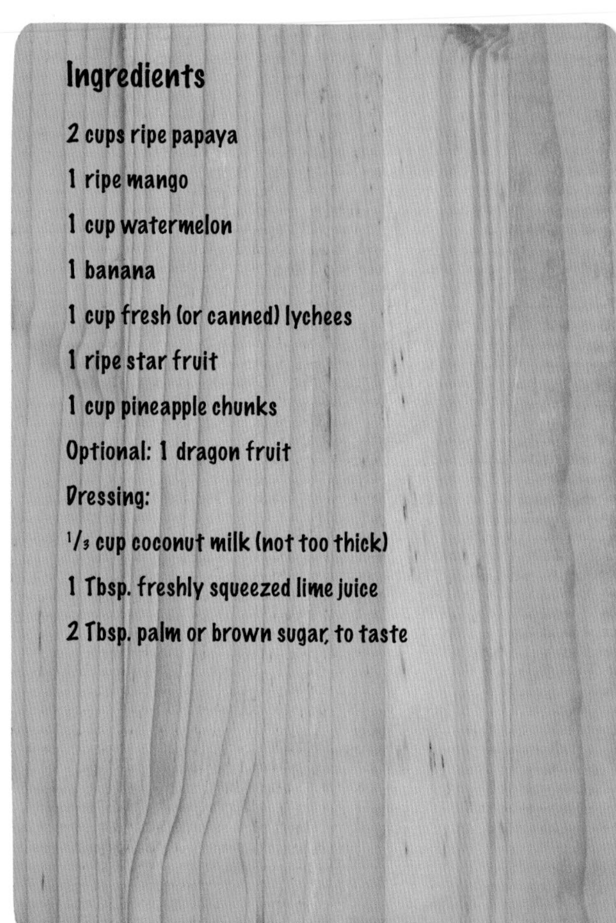

Ingredients

2 cups ripe papaya

1 ripe mango

1 cup watermelon

1 banana

1 cup fresh (or canned) lychees

1 ripe star fruit

1 cup pineapple chunks

Optional: 1 dragon fruit

Dressing:

1/3 cup coconut milk (not too thick)

1 Tbsp. freshly squeezed lime juice

2 Tbsp. palm or brown sugar, to taste

Tropical Fruit Salad

- In a cup or small mixing bowl, combine the dressing ingredients.
- Stir well to dissolve the sugar. Set aside.

ZOOM

Dragon fruit looks like a kind of prehistoric pod. It is bright pink and oval in shape. Dragon fruit is actually the fruit of a climbing cactus that grows in tropical regions. If you can't find it at your supermarket, look for it at Asian stores or markets. Dragon fruit tastes like a cross between kiwi and pear. Simply cut it in half and scoop out the fruit.

MAKE IT EASY

Star fruit is available in most supermarkets these days, and is simple to prepare. The fruit is ripe when turning from green to yellow (avoid buying fruit that is very yellow and/or browning. To prepare star fruit, shallowly run your knife down each of the five "points" on the fruit to remove the dark tips. Then turn the fruit on its side and slice to create star-shaped pieces. Remove seeds and enjoy.

Preparing the Fruit

- Cut the fresh papaya, mango, and watermelon into cubes of fruit. Slice the banana and cut each of the lychees in half. Also cut up the star fruit, reserving a few of the more beautiful whole slices for the garnish.
- If using dragon fruit, slice the fruit in half and scoop out the fruit; then cut it up into cubes.
- Use a large mixing bowl or salad bowl to combine all the fruit.

Tossing the Salad

- Pour the dressing over the fruit and toss well to mix.
- If desired, transfer salad to a serving bowl, and top with one or two of the reserved star fruit slices. If not eating right away, squeeze a little lime juice over the star fruit slices to keep them from turning brown.
- Enjoy this fruit salad on its own as a side dish, or with a little whipped cream for a light and delicious dessert.

CLASSIC MANGO STICKY RICE DESSERT

Mango sticky rice pudding is probably the best known of all Thai desserts.

When this dessert was first served to me, I wasn't expecting anything special. This is because a Thai friend (and inexperienced cook) had made it for me, and she put very little effort into the presentation. I was merely handed a bowl of rice and a few slices of mango with some kind of white sauce. But the unappealing sight of the pudding only served to astound me even more when I took my first bite of this incredible dessert. I was taken with the tropical flavors and mixture of textures: the stickiness of the rice combining with the sweetness of the coconut milk and the fresh taste of the mango—it really was love at first bite.

Yield: Serves 4

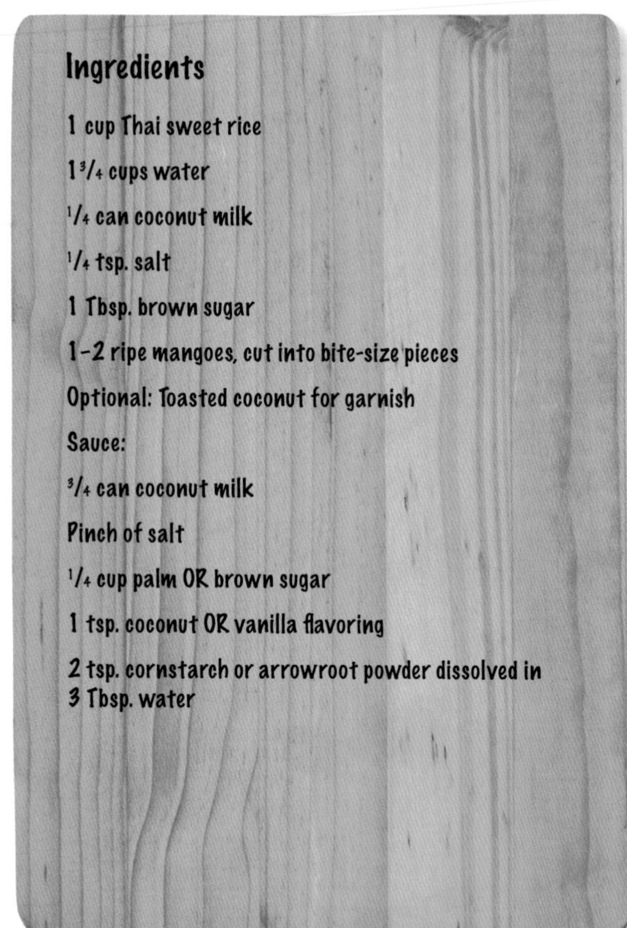

Ingredients

1 cup Thai sweet rice

1¾ cups water

¼ can coconut milk

¼ tsp. salt

1 Tbsp. brown sugar

1–2 ripe mangoes, cut into bite-size pieces

Optional: Toasted coconut for garnish

Sauce:

¾ can coconut milk

Pinch of salt

¼ cup palm OR brown sugar

1 tsp. coconut OR vanilla flavoring

2 tsp. cornstarch or arrowroot powder dissolved in 3 Tbsp. water

Classic Mango Sticky Rice Dessert

- Place rice in a pot and cover with 1 cup water. Soak 30 minutes.
- Add ¾ cup water, ¼ can coconut milk, ¼ tsp. salt, and 1 Tbsp. brown sugar. Stir well.
- Set pot over high heat and bring to a gentle boil, then reduce to medium-low. Simmer 20 minutes, until the coconut water has been absorbed.
- Turn off the heat but leave the pot on the burner and place lid on tight. Let rice sit 10 minutes, or until you're ready to serve.

• • • • RECIPE VARIATION • • • •

In Thailand, this dessert is served with the rice on the bottom of a plate, bowl, or banana leaf, and the coconut milk spooned over. Here is another more flavorful way to serve it: Add scoops of rice directly to the sauce pot and stir over low heat, gently breaking apart larger lumps. Now add the mango pieces and gently stir until warmed through. Portion out into bowls.

ZOOM

When choosing a ripe mango, here are a few tips to keep in mind. Look for skin that is turning from green to orange or yellow. Use your thumb to gently press on the skin: if the flesh indents slightly, the mango is ripening. Most important, look for a fragrant mango smell (as opposed to little or no smell at all). If the mangoes have dark patches, do not buy them.

Preparing the Sauce

- To make the sauce, warm over medium heat the remaining ¾ can of coconut milk together with the pinch of salt, sugar, and flavoring.
- When this mixture starts to simmer, add the cornstarch and water mixture, stirring to combine. As the sauce thickens, reduce heat to low.
- Remove sauce from heat and taste test it for sweetness, adding a little more sugar if you prefer. Note that the sauce will taste less sweet once it is combined with the other ingredients.

Putting the Dessert Together

- To serve, place scoops of the warm sticky rice into bowls.
- Ladle a generous amount of warm coconut sauce over the rice to create an "island" of sticky rice.
- Top the rice and coconut sauce with pieces of fresh mango, and enjoy.
- If desired, a final sprinkling of toasted coconut can be added as a crunchy topping.

THAI CRÈME CARAMEL

This Thai version of the classic French dessert is easy to make and lactose free.

If you're looking for an easy and delicious dessert, try this simple recipe. A variation of the famous French dessert, this crème caramel is made with coconut milk instead of milk or cream, and is therefore lactose free. It's also gluten free, so it makes a wonderful dessert for anyone with dietary restrictions.

Another plus is that you can make this dessert ahead of time if you're expecting company (up to 2 days in advance). Just cook it up and refrigerate until you're ready to serve it.

If you can find pandan paste for this recipe, so much the better. If not, substitute vanilla flavoring.

Yield: Serves 6–8

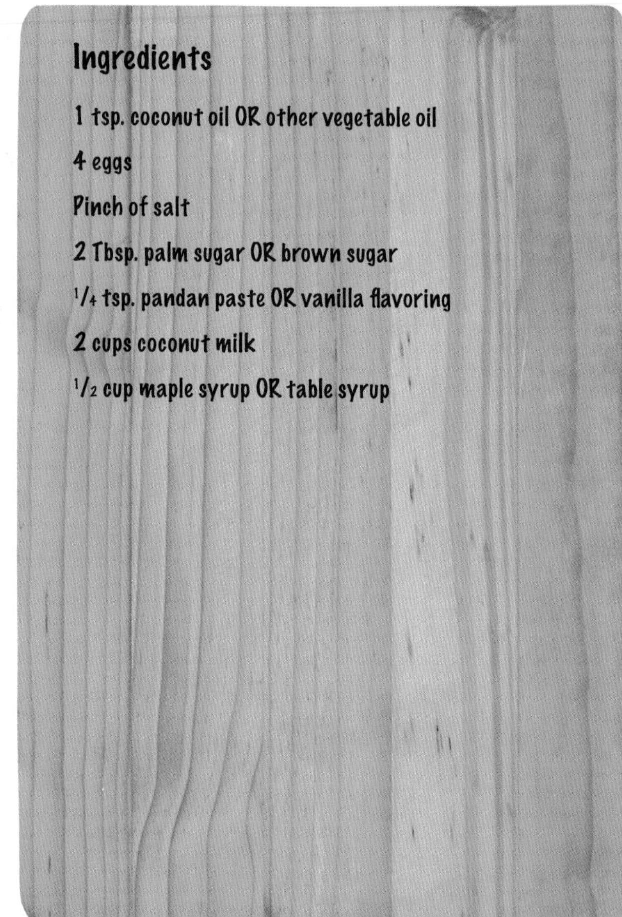

Ingredients

1 tsp. coconut oil OR other vegetable oil

4 eggs

Pinch of salt

2 Tbsp. palm sugar OR brown sugar

1/4 tsp. pandan paste OR vanilla flavoring

2 cups coconut milk

1/2 cup maple syrup OR table syrup

Thai Crème Caramel

- Preheat oven to 350 degrees F.
- Prepare 6–8 ramekins (depending on the size) by lightly greasing with oil.
- Also, prepare a dish to hold the ramekins, such as a glass lasagne-type dish.

ZOOM

Pandan paste (or pandan essence) is a Southeast Asian flavoring made from pandan leaves. Pandan is a tropical plant also known as screwpine, with long leaves that are fragrant and have a sweet flavor. Pandan essence is green in color, and will turn anything you are cooking bright green as well. It can be purchased at most Asian food stores; look for it in very small bottles.

MAKE IT EASY

This dessert can easily be made ahead of time—just cook up a batch and refrigerate until ready to serve. It is wonderful cold, especially on a warm summer night, but during the winter months, you might prefer to serve it warm. Another make-ahead tip: Stir together the custard ahead of time and set in the refrigerator. When company arrives, simply ladle it into the ramekins and bake.

Making the Custard

- Beat the eggs quickly by hand with a whisk or a fork for 1 minute.
- Add the salt, sugar, pandan or vanilla flavoring, and the coconut milk, stirring everything together. Note that the pandan will turn this dessert light green.
- Pour a little syrup into the bottom of each ramekin: enough to cover the bottom plus 1 Tbsp. more.
- Now ladle the egg mixture into each ramekin up to ¾ full. Do not stir—the syrup will remain at the bottom of the ramekin.

Baking the Crème Caramel

- Set ramekins in the baking dish. Carefully pour some water into the dish (around the ramekins). Water should reach halfway up the sides of the ramekins. Carefully set in oven.
- Bake for 30 minutes, or until an inserted fork comes out clean. Remove ramekins from the hot water and set on the counter to cool.
- Run a knife around the inner rim of each ramekin, then overturn onto dessert plates. The pudding will fall out easily, with the syrup dripping down over the custard.

EASY MANGO SORBET

This delicious frozen dessert is actually a cross between sorbet and ice cream.

Surprisingly, you do not need an ice cream maker or sorbet machine to create this dessert; rather, all you need is a food processor or blender. An even more surprising fact is that it only takes minutes to whip up this dessert—and there's no need for a lot of stirring after you set the sorbet in the freezer. In other words, this is the easiest recipe for sorbet you're likely to encounter, and also one of the tastiest.

For the best tasting sorbet, be sure to use only the freshest, ripest mangoes you can find. Note that frozen mango will not give you the delicious results you're looking for.

Yield: Serves 6+

Ingredients

2 fresh ripe mangoes

1 cup white sugar

$^1/_4$ cup coconut milk

2 tsp. lemon juice

1 cup whipping cream (heavy cream)

Easy Mango Sorbet

- Hold a mango on its side and cut it into 3 parts, being careful to slice on either side of the central (flat) stone.
- You will end up with 2 rounded pieces of mango (either side of the fruit) and the flat, central slice, which contains the stone. Using a tablespoon, scoop out the fruit from the end pieces.
- Peel off the skin around the stone and use a knife to cut off any remaining fruit.
- Repeat for the second mango.

RECIPE VARIATION

Mango-Strawberry Sorbet. For this variation, use the fruit of only 1 ripe mango. Place mango fruit in your food processor together with 2 cups fresh strawberries. Blitz to create a puree. An optional step (if you don't like mango fiber) is to run this puree through a strainer. Continue on with the remainder of the recipe as written. Your sorbet will be light pink in color and taste wonderful!

MAKE IT EASY

If you prefer a smooth sorbet (without mango fiber in it), after making the mango puree, strain it through a mesh strainer placed over a bowl. Use a spatula to press the pulp against the strainer to wring out every last ounce of mango juice. This will result in a smooth, fiber-free consistency. (Note: the fiber can also be left in, as it is healthy and also contributes to the taste of this dessert.)

Making the Mango Puree

- Place the fresh mango (as well as any juice) in a food processor or blender.
- Add the sugar and blitz for 1 minute, or until you have a smooth and delicious mango puree.
- Add the coconut milk and lemon juice, and pulse to combine.
- Remove this mango mixture and reserve in a bowl or other container. Scrape out the sides of the processor or blender with a spatula.

Combining the Puree with the Whipped Cream

- Now pour the whipping cream into your processor or blender. Blitz until the whipped cream is firm, not runny.
- Now add the mango puree to the processor or blender and blitz 5–10 seconds, or until you get a good mango-cream consistency (avoid overprocessing).
- Transfer this delicious concoction to a large covered ice cream tub or empty yogurt containers. Freeze at least 7–8 hours, or until sorbet is firm. This dessert keeps in the freezer for several months if covered tightly.

TAPIOCA PUDDING

A scrumptious tapioca pudding that isn't anything like your mother's.

Do you remember your mother's (or grandmother's) tapioca? She would cook it up with eggs, milk, and a little vanilla, and it would taste, well, alright.

If you weren't a fan of this style of tapioca, take heart. The following recipe tastes completely different. It is tropical and exotic tasting—in fact, words cannot adequately describe how delicious it is. The tapioca itself isn't overcooked, so you can still taste its naturally chewy, sticky texture.

If you are avoiding refined sugars, or if you follow a gluten-free or lactose-free diet, this dessert is perfect for you. It is also naturally vegan.

Yield: Serves 4–6

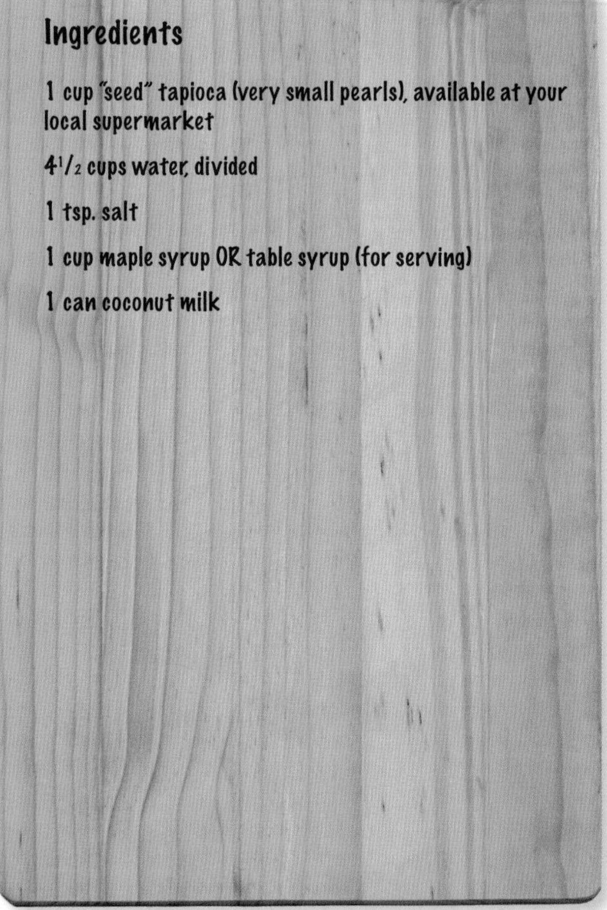

Ingredients

1 cup "seed" tapioca (very small pearls), available at your local supermarket

4 1/2 cups water, divided

1 tsp. salt

1 cup maple syrup OR table syrup (for serving)

1 can coconut milk

Tapioca Pudding

- Measure tapioca into a pot and cover with 2 cups water. Soak for 10 minutes (the tapioca will absorb much of the water).
- Add another 2½ cups of water. Also add the salt and stir.

• • • • RECIPE VARIATION • • • •

Mango Tapioca Pudding. This dessert is made in exactly the same way, except that fresh mango is cut up and served together with the pudding. Simply slice up a fresh, ripe mango. When you scoop out the tapioca into serving bowls, add a generous topping of fresh mango pieces or slices. Then drizzle over the syrup and coconut milk, and enjoy.

ZOOM

Tapioca comes from the root of the cassava plant, which grows in tropical areas. It is inexpensive and easy to cultivate, and has, therefore, become one of the top 3 sources of carbohydrates in the world. During wartime in Southeast Asia, many people actually lived on tapioca. It is naturally high in iron, and also contains calcium. Tapioca is gluten free.

Cooking the Tapioca

- Bring the tapioca-water to a boil, then reduce heat to medium.
- Simmer 15 minutes, stirring occasionally to lift any tapioca stuck to the bottom of the pot. If tapioca becomes too thick to simmer, add a little more water.
- After 15 minutes the pearls will be a mixture of opaque and translucent. Remove from heat and cover with a lid. Let sit for 10 minutes, or until ready to serve (any opaque pearls will finish cooking in the residual heat of the pot).

Putting the Dessert Together

- To put the dessert together, scoop desired amount of tapioca into bowls. Add a generous drizzle (2–3 Tbsp.) of maple syrup—or set syrup in a pitcher on the table and have each person add his or her own. Top with the coconut milk (similar to milk on cereal).
- Before eating, give the pudding a stir and enjoy this refreshing dessert.
- Tapioca can be served warm (nice in the winter) or cold (wonderful in the summer).

HOMEMADE COCONUT ICE CREAM

Creamy homemade coconut ice cream—without an ice cream maker.

You needn't own an expensive ice cream maker to create wonderful homemade ice cream. For the following recipe, all you need is a food processor or blender.

One of the wonderful things about making your own homemade ice cream is the fact that you have complete control over what goes into it—or, more important, what doesn't go into it (these days, commercial ice creams tend to be filled with unhealthy oils, fillers, and preservatives). In fact, if you'd like to make your ice cream even healthier, consider using only organic ingredients.

There are few tropical treats more delightful or refreshing after a spicy Thai meal than coconut ice cream. Enjoy it plain, or pair it with some tropical fruit, such as fresh mango.

Yield: Serves 6+

Ingredients

¼–⅓ cup dry shredded coconut (sweetened or unsweetened)

4 eggs

1 cup white sugar

2 cups heavy whipping cream

2 cups good-quality coconut milk

1 tsp. vanilla flavoring

2 tsp. coconut flavoring

Homemade Coconut Ice Cream

- Place shredded coconut in a dry wok or frying pan over medium-high heat. Stir continuously until coconut turns light golden-brown and is fragrant.
- Remove the toasted coconut from the pan and set aside.
- Place eggs and sugar in a food processor, electric mixer, or blender. Blitz 1 ½–2 minutes.

• • • • RECIPE VARIATION • • • •

For an easier version of coconut ice cream, simply whip 2 cups of whipping cream in your food processor or blender until stiff. Add 1 cup good-quality (thick) coconut milk plus ¾ can sweetened condensed milk, and 2 tsp. coconut flavoring. If desired, add ¼ cup dry shredded coconut. Blitz briefly until well blended and transfer to tubs or clean yogurt containers to freeze.

ZOOM

In Thailand and across much of Southeast Asia, ice cream is sold in carts pushed along the side of the street, or, more recently, in small freezers attached to motorcycles. Tourists are often surprised to see myriad favors, including sweet corn, durian, sweet potato, purple yam (called "ube" in the Philippines), chili pepper, and red bean, among others.

Cooking the Egg Mixture

- Pour the egg mixture into the top of a double-boiler and place over medium-high heat. Cook 8–10 minutes, stirring continuously with a whisk until the mixture thickens and becomes creamy (it should look like a smooth custard).
- Place custard in the refrigerator to cool.
- Now pour the heavy cream into your food processor, blender, or mixer. Blitz until cream becomes very thick (not runny) and stiff peaks form—about 1 minute.
- Scoop the whipped cream into a large mixing bowl.

Adding the Coconut Milk

- Fold the coconut milk into the whipped cream, stirring just enough to combine.
- Add the cooked egg and sugar mixture from the refrigerator, plus both flavorings and the toasted coconut. Gently stir everything together by hand.
- Pour this batter-like mixture into a tub or clean yogurt containers. Be sure to cover with tight-fitting lid(s) and freeze at least 8 hours.
- Although it contains no preservatives, this ice cream stores well in the freezer for many weeks.

FRIED BANANAS

Because there is no messy batter involved, these fried bananas are especially easy to make.

Fried bananas are a favorite dessert across much of Southeast Asia, and Thailand is no exception. Each cook makes fried bananas his or her own way, usually with a thick batter that includes a number of different flours (rice, tapioca, and sometimes even corn flour) plus egg, water and/or coconut milk, and sometimes even butter.

As you can tell from this description, cooking up fried bananas is normally a messy business—unless you use the following recipe.

Pair the hot, just-fried bananas with some vanilla or coconut ice cream for a heavenly treat.

Yield: Serves 2–4

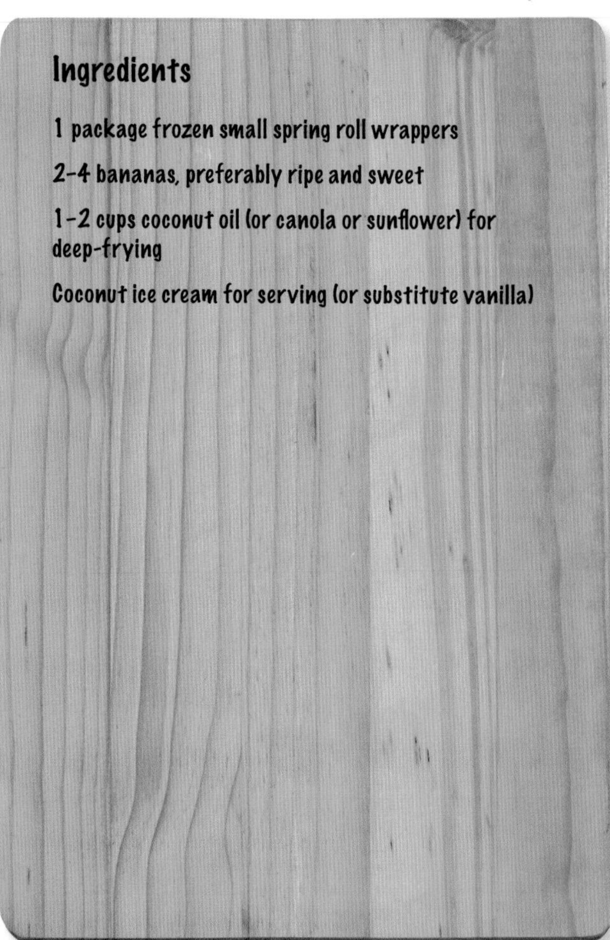

Ingredients

1 package frozen small spring roll wrappers

2–4 bananas, preferably ripe and sweet

1–2 cups coconut oil (or canola or sunflower) for deep-frying

Coconut ice cream for serving (or substitute vanilla)

Fried Bananas

- Remove the spring roll wrappers from the freezer and allow to thaw at least 30 minutes before use (they need to be well-thawed, or they will tear).
- Prepare a clean working surface for rolling the bananas. You will also need a small bowl of water for dipping your fingers.
- Peel the bananas and break them in half.

ZOOM

There is some contention among Asian cooks as to which type of banana is best for making fried bananas. Some say any will do, while others insist it must be a banana known as "raja" (the "king" of bananas). This banana grows in Indonesia, Thailand, Malaysia, and other Southeast Asian countries, and has slightly orange-tinted flesh. If you can't find it, regular bananas will do fine.

MAKE IT EASY

To deep-fry the bananas, it's best to use a wok or small frying pan (this way you will use less oil). To test whether oil is hot enough, dip one end of a wrapped banana into the pan—if it begins to sizzle and cook, the oil is ready. Be careful not to overheat the oil, or it will splatter. Once the bananas are frying, reduce heat to just above medium (otherwise the oil will continue to get hotter).

Wrapping the Bananas

- Place a spring roll wrapper on the diagonal in front of you (so that the square wrapper is diamond-shaped).
- Place half of a banana across the middle of the wrapper. Grasp the sides of the wrapper and fold over either end. Bring up the bottom of the wrapper and tuck over the banana. Roll to the end.
- Secure by wetting the end of the wrapper with your fingers, and pressing firmly to seal.
- Wrap all the banana halves in this way.

Frying the Bananas

- Heat the oil in a wok or small frying pan over medium-high heat (oil should be at least 1 inch deep).
- When oil is hot enough, carefully place the wrapped bananas in the wok.
- Use tongs to turn and cook bananas on both sides. Bananas are done when spring roll wrappers are golden-brown and crispy. Drain on paper towel or a clean tea towel.
- Serve immediately, either on their own, or with vanilla or coconut ice cream. Enjoy.

THAI ICED TEA

This iced tea tastes both familiar and exotic.

Thailand is known for its sweet, refreshing iced tea that is a dark reddish-orange in color. On the streets of Bangkok, it is often sold in plastic bags with a straw for easy sipping.

If you've enjoyed the iced tea you've had in Thai restaurants, try making your own version at home. It's easy to do, and because you're making it yourself, it's also healthier, with no artificial colors or flavorings added.

Though the following recipe is made with orange pekoe, feel free to experiment with other types of tea. Assam, Ceylon, and English breakfast are examples of other black teas you could use. Or try a combination of teas (green or white tea may also be added).

Yield: Serves 2

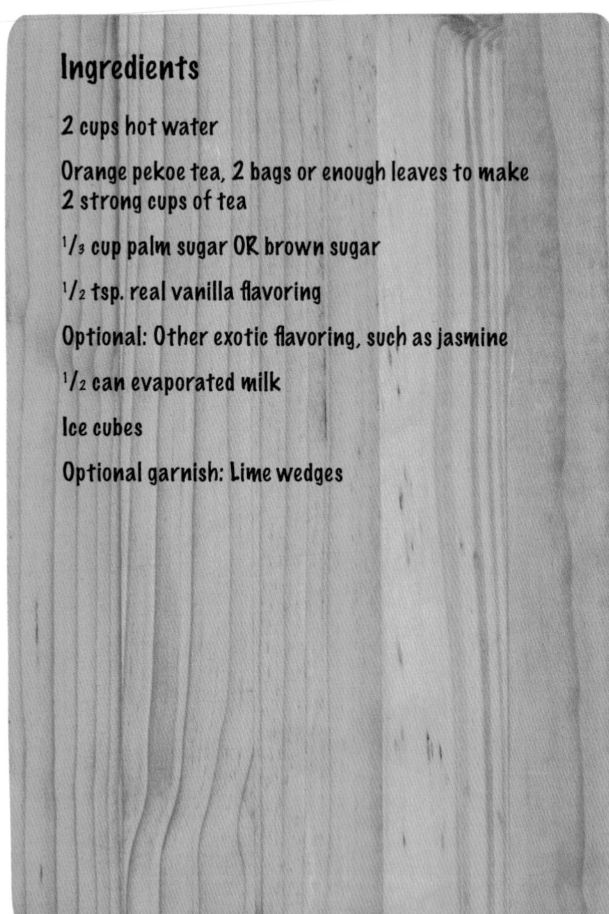

Ingredients

2 cups hot water

Orange pekoe tea, 2 bags or enough leaves to make 2 strong cups of tea

1/3 cup palm sugar OR brown sugar

1/2 tsp. real vanilla flavoring

Optional: Other exotic flavoring, such as jasmine

1/2 can evaporated milk

Ice cubes

Optional garnish: Lime wedges

Thai Iced Tea

- Make the tea very strong. Remove tea bags or put through a strainer to remove the leaves.
- Add the sugar and vanilla, stirring well to dissolve. For very cold iced tea, set the sugared tea in the refrigerator to chill 1–2 hours.

ZOOM

Instead of just plain vanilla, Asian cooks have a variety of exotic flavorings at their disposal, such as banana flavoring, pandan essence (from pandan leaves), or even flavorings that come from flowers, such as jasmine and rose essences. If you'd like to experiment with such flavorings, look for very small bottles of these essences at your local Asian food store.

GREEN LIGHT

The iced tea in Thai restaurants is often served in two distinct layers, with the tea on the bottom and the milk floating on top. This is because they use a syrupy tea mixture that is very thick (it usually comes in a bottle or package). The recipe presented here is actually more natural and healthier for you, while offering the same great Thai taste.

Filling the Glasses

- Before you pour out the tea, taste test it, adding more sugar if you prefer it sweeter. Also add 2–3 drops of jasmine essence, if desired.
- When you're happy with the taste (it should be quite strong), place a few ice cubes in two glasses. Fill ¾ of each glass with the tea mixture.

Adding Evaporated Milk

- Top up each glass with the evaporated milk.
- Adjust the amounts of tea and milk to suit your taste.
- If desired, garnish with wedges of fresh-cut lime. Then just stir and enjoy!

THAI ICED COFFEE

This iced coffee makes an easy summer drink any time of the day (or night).

There are few drinks more energizing on a hot day than cold iced coffee. Traditionally, Thai iced coffee is made right in the glass, but it's just as easy to stir up a jug of iced coffee and keep it in your refrigerator (wonderful on a hot morning instead of regular coffee). In fact, if you happen to have leftover coffee from breakfast, this recipe makes a great way to use it up.

Aside from being a refreshing breakfast drink or afternoon pick-me-up, this Thai-style iced coffee is equally delightful as a kind of after-dinner drink, especially on warm summer evenings. In the latter case, decaffeinated coffee can be substituted for regular, if desired.

Yield: Serves 2

Thai Iced Coffee

- Set a pot of coffee (or a minimum of 3–4 cups) to brew.
- Make sure it is very strong (measure 1 ½–2 rounded Tbsp. ground coffee per cup).
- Prepare 2 tall glasses or regular-sized coffee mugs.

• • • • RECIPE VARIATION • • • •

This iced coffee can be made into a wonderful after-dinner drink by adding a little of your favorite alcohol or liqueur. Bailey's, Kahlua, Grand Marnier, or a shot of scotch are all great choices. To make it taste (and look) even more special, pour into tall, clear dessert-type glasses. Add a straw and a topping of whipped cream, plus some chocolate shavings.

GREEN LIGHT

Iced coffee makes a great way to use up leftover breakfast coffee. Simply transfer the coffee to a pot on the stove (be sure to discard any "sludge" from the bottom of the pot). Warm over medium heat, and add desired amount of condensed milk (depending on how sweet you'd like it), stirring until it dissolves. Then pour or ladle the coffee into a glass jug and place in the refrigerator to chill.

Adding the Sweetened Condensed Milk

- While coffee is brewing, place 2 Tbsp. sweetened condensed milk in the bottom of each glass (adjust according to how sweet you prefer your iced coffee).
- Fill the rest of the glass with ice.

Pouring the Coffee

- When coffee is done brewing, slowly pour it into each glass (over the ice).
- Add a long-handled spoon to the glass for stirring, and serve immediately.

MANGO COCKTAIL

A delicious cocktail that is both tropical and celebratory.

If you like mango, this cocktail may turn out to be one of your favorite drinks. Great for a party or any type of celebration, this sparkling cocktail is tropical tasting and pretty to serve, too.

You will need several fresh ripe mangoes for this cocktail. Although frozen mango fruit from your local supermarket could work in a pinch, it won't give you the wonderful mango taste that you'll get with fresh mangoes.

Unless you're in the mood to splurge, you can save a few dollars by using a less expensive sparkling white wine for this recipe (instead of champagne). When paired with the delicious mango puree and a few other ingredients, you'll hardly be able to tell the difference.

Yield: Serves 6+

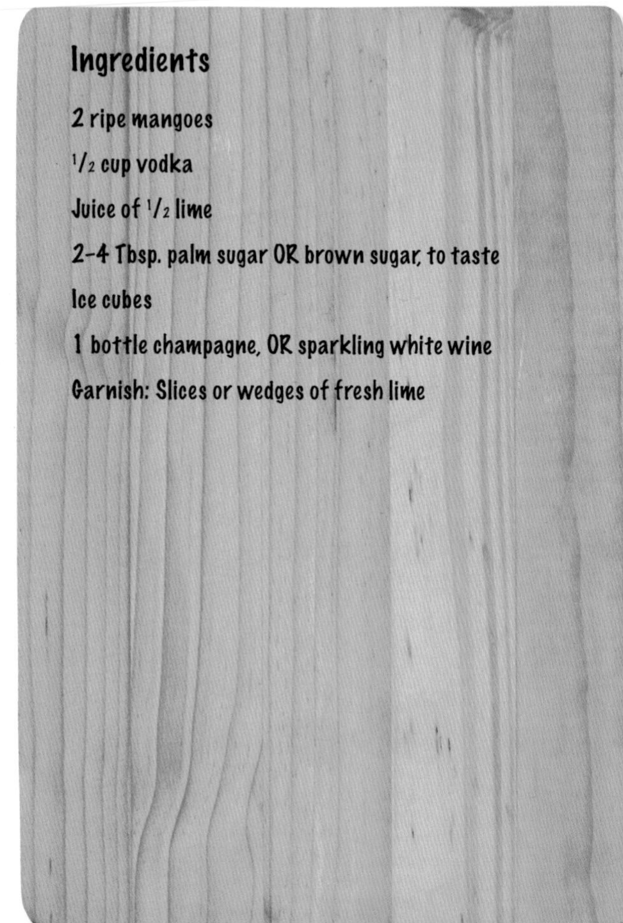

Ingredients

2 ripe mangoes

1/2 cup vodka

Juice of 1/2 lime

2–4 Tbsp. palm sugar OR brown sugar, to taste

Ice cubes

1 bottle champagne, OR sparkling white wine

Garnish: Slices or wedges of fresh lime

Mango Cocktail

- Cut each mango into 3 parts, being careful to slice on either side of the central stone. Using a tablespoon, scoop out the fruit from the 2 largest pieces.
- Peel the skin from around the stone and use a knife to cut off any remaining fruit from around the outside.

• • • • RECIPE VARIATION • • • •

Virgin Mango-Coconut Cocktail. Follow the recipe as written to create the fresh mango puree, but omit the vodka. Pour into glasses, filling them halfway. Add to each glass 3–4 Tbsp. coconut milk, then top up with some sparkling mineral water (sparkling lime-flavored water works well too). Add your choice of tropical garnishes, as suggested at the end of the recipe, and enjoy!

MAKE IT EASY

If you're planning on serving this cocktail at your next party, you can do most of the preparation ahead of time. Blend the mango puree up to 1 day in advance, and place (covered) in the refrigerator. Make sure your sparkling wine or champagne is also kept cold in the refrigerator. Then simply put the two together when guests arrive, adding your choice of garnish to the side of each glass.

Making the Mango Puree

- Place the mango fruit in a blender or food processor. Add the vodka, lime juice, and 2 Tbsp. sugar.
- Blend well to create a smooth mango puree.

Now do a taste test, adding more sugar if desired (how much will depend upon the sweetness of your mangoes).

Topping up the Glasses

- Pour the mango mixture into cocktail glasses, filling them halfway. Then top them with the champagne or sparkling wine.
- If desired, add some ice cubes and garnish the glasses with lime slices or wedges, plus any other tropical fruit of your choice (a slice of star fruit looks especially beautiful on the side of a glass). Cheers!

FRESH FRUIT COCONUT REFRESHER

A healthy and energizing drink, perfect for a hot summer afternoon.

For a taste of the tropics, try this fresh fruit drink. Because it's non-alcoholic, the drink makes a great addition to breakfast, or a wonderful treat to savor on a hot afternoon. The combination of mango, papaya, and watermelon is a sweet and refreshing concoction, while the coconut milk thickens and enriches it ever so slightly.

If you enjoy these flavors, you might be inspired to substitute or add other fruits to the mix. Very ripe lychees work well, and these days, bartenders are doing amazing things with dragon fruit.

Of course, all of these fruits can be put through a juicer, but if you use your food processor or blender, you'll reap the health benefits of the fruit fiber, which then remains in the drink.

Yield: Serves 2–3

Ingredients

1 ripe mango (about 1 cup fruit)

1/2 cup fresh papaya

1 cup watermelon

2 Tbsp. palm sugar OR brown sugar (or more to taste)

1 1/2 cups coconut milk

Ice cubes

Garnish: Slices or wedges of fresh lime, plus pieces of watermelon and papaya

Fresh Fruit Coconut Refresher

- Cut the mango into 3 parts, being careful to slice on either side of the central stone. Using a tablespoon, scoop out the fruit from the 2 largest pieces.
- For the papaya, slice the fruit down the center (lengthwise) and crack it open. Scrape out the seeds, then slice up the fruit and peel off the skin.
- Cut the watermelon into pieces, removing any seeds that you find.

• • • • RECIPE VARIATION • • • •

To make this drink into a tropical alcoholic cocktail, follow the recipe as written. Pour 1 cup of the resulting fresh fruit drink into a shaker together with a shot of coconut or mango liqueur and some crushed ice. Shake up and pour into a martini glass. (Alternatively, pour the fruit drink into glasses, then add the coconut liqueur and a little ice.) Garnish with some of the leftover fresh fruit and enjoy.

ZOOM

While coconut milk is considered a healthy fat, it does tend to be high in calories. If you're watching your diet, try substituting "lite" coconut milk, which has about 100 calories per ½ cup (½ cup is all you need to make a nice-size glass of the drink featured here). Another option is to substitute plain yogurt for coconut milk (resulting in what most people call a "smoothie").

Making the Fresh Fruit Puree

- Place 1 cup each of the prepared mango and watermelon, plus ½ cup papaya fruit in a blender or food processor.
- Add the sugar and blitz to create a fresh fruit puree.

Adding the Coconut Milk

- Add the coconut milk and blitz again briefly to blend all ingredients together.
- Pour into glasses prepared with ice cubes.
- Add garnishes of your choice and enjoy.

WHITE LOTUS FLOWER

This beautiful drink is so wonderful tasting, you'll want to make it repeatedly.

Thailand is famous for its beautiful 5-star hotels and spa resorts where gorgeous drinks are served all hours of the day.

This non-alcoholic tropical fruit drink is named after the flower of enlightenment, and when you try it, you'll agree it is pure serenity. The drink is fun to make and to serve. Plus, because it's made with fresh star fruit and honeydew melon, it is also very healthy, refreshing, and energizing.

As with the other tropical fruit drinks featured in this chapter, you don't need a juicer to make it—just a blender or food processor. It's perfect for serving any time of the day or night, and is especially wonderful to make for guests.

Yield: Serves 2–3

Ingredients

1/2 cup fresh star fruit

1 cup honeydew melon

1 Tbsp. freshly squeezed lime juice

1–2 Tbsp. palm sugar OR white or brown sugar, to taste

1/2 cup good-tasting soy milk, such as Soy Dream

1/2 cup coconut milk

Ice cubes

Garnish: Star fruit and lime slices, plus chunks of melon

White Lotus Flower

- Prepare the star fruit by washing it well. Then, sitting it upright, shallowly run your knife down each of the 5 "points" on the fruit to remove the dark tips. Turn on its side and slice to create star-shaped pieces of fruit. Remove the seeds.
- Save some of the smaller "stars" to garnish your glasses. Chop up the larger pieces.
- Slice open the honeydew melon and use a tablespoon to scrape out the seeds.
- Scoop out the fruit.

• • • • RECIPE VARIATION • • • •

Although this drink is just as delicious without alcohol, if you're planning a party, you can easily convert this drink into a cocktail. Simply add 1–2 shots of coconut liqueur when you add the coconut milk. If you don't have coconut liqueur, try 1–2 shots of rum, or the same amount of vodka. Blitz well to blend and garnish with a slice of star fruit.

MAKE IT EASY

Star fruit makes a beautiful garnish for tropical drinks. For best results, use one of the end pieces of the fruit. Once you have a suitable slice, remove any seeds that you find, then make a small cut into the slice with your knife—this will allow it to stay on the glass (the fruit should stand upright on the rim). To prevent star fruit slices from turning brown, just squeeze some fresh lime juice over them.

Making the Fresh Fruit Puree

- Place ½ of the prepared star fruit, plus 1 cup of the prepared honeydew fruit in a blender or food processor.
- Now drizzle the lime juice over the fruit and add 1 Tbsp. sugar.
- Process or blend well to create a fresh fruit puree.

Adding the Coconut and Soy Milk

- Add the soy milk and the coconut milk. Blitz again to create a frothy drink.
- Taste test the drink. Add more sugar if you prefer it sweeter (and blitz again).
- Pour into cocktail-type glasses. Add ice cubes plus a star fruit or other garnishes of your choice, and enjoy this tropical fruit wonder.

FRESH LIME WATER

This non-alcoholic drink is similar to Western lemonade, but refreshingly different.

If you're a cold lemonade fan, try this Asian version of the drink. Very refreshing on a hot day, lime water also provides a quick pick-me-up because of its sugar content.

Limes are naturally less acidic than lemons, which makes them a better choice for those with stomach sensitivities.

The following recipe makes quite a strong lime water drink, so feel free to adjust the lime-to-water ratio as you make it. This is very easy to do—simply taste test it as you go along, adding more water to dilute the strength of the lime juice, or more sugar depending on how sweet you'd like it.

Yield: Makes 1 large jug

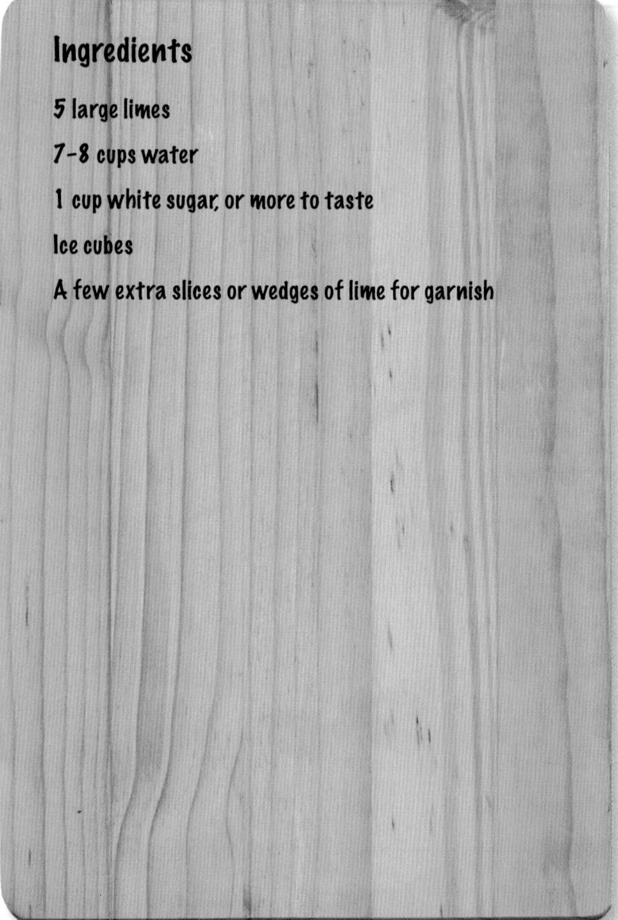

Ingredients

5 large limes

7–8 cups water

1 cup white sugar, or more to taste

Ice cubes

A few extra slices or wedges of lime for garnish

Fresh Lime Water

- For this drink, it's best to use fresh limes. Bottled lime juice has a different taste, and might also give an aftertaste you don't want.
- Using key limes will take a long time, though this is actually the type used in Asia. Larger limes will give you nearly the same taste and are much faster going.

ZOOM

In Thailand as well as in other Southeast Asian countries, key limes are more common than the large limes most of us use here in North America (Florida excepted). However, I have seen street hawkers making this drink with key limes, and it isn't easy. For simpler preparation, use large ripe limes for this recipe—they will give you the same wonderful taste with far less work.

MAKE IT EASY

When shopping for limes, hold the fruit in your hand. Look for flesh you can indent slightly with your thumb (softness indicating ripeness). If the limes are very firm, it will be difficult to squeeze them, and you won't get as much juice out of them. Before juicing, roll limes on your countertop, pressing down on them with the flat of your hand. This "loosens" the juice, making juicing them easier.

Squeezing the Limes

- Squeeze the juice from the limes, either by hand (slicing the limes into wedges and squeezing them), or by using a citrus juicer or press.
- Pour 1 cup lime juice into a large jug, and add the water.

Adding the Sugar

- Add the sugar and stir until dissolved.
- Taste test the lime water, adding more sugar if you prefer it sweeter. Add more water if you find the taste too strong or sharp.
- Set the lime water in the refrigerator to chill for 1–2 hours, or until cold.
- Serve in tall glasses garnished with slices or wedges of lime, plus a few ice cubes if desired.

NAM PRIK PAO CHILI SAUCE

Aside from being a wonderful condiment, this chili sauce is also used in many Thai recipes.

The famous Thai chili sauce nam prik pao is easy to make and goes well with nearly any Thai dish. In Thailand, there are as many different types of chili sauce as there are cooks. The more passionate will insist the only way to make it is to roast the chilies first until they are fairly burnt.

However, doing so is hard on the eyes as well as the lungs. It may also cause your neighbors to call an emergency crew, as happened in London, England, a few years ago when a Thai restaurant was found to be the source of what was thought to be a terrorist plot. In actual fact, the eye-stinging fumes were only chilies being roasted for nam prik pao!

Yield: 1 small bottle of chili sauce

Ingredients

1/4 cup vegetable oil such as canola

2 shallots, minced

4 cloves garlic, minced

3 Tbsp. ground dry-roasted red chilies OR
3 Tbsp. cayenne pepper

3/4 tsp. shrimp paste

2 1/2–3 Tbsp. fish sauce, to taste

2–3 Tbsp. palm sugar OR brown sugar, to taste

1/2 tsp. tamarind paste

3–4 Tbsp. water, divided

Nam Prik Pao Chili Sauce

- Warm a wok or small frying pan over medium-high heat. Add the oil, plus the chopped shallots and garlic.
- Stir-fry until the garlic and shallots have turned a very light golden-brown and are slightly crispy (2–3 minutes).
- Remove garlic and shallots with a slotted spoon and place in a bowl. Remove oil from heat but leave it in the wok, reserving it for later.

ZOOM

In Thailand, people are so crazy about nam prik pao, they'll spread it on toast for breakfast! Obviously most Thais have strong stomachs. On the other hand, if you're one of those people who suffer from a sensitive stomach, you may want to use cayenne pepper instead of regular chilies. Cayenne is actually good for your stomach, helping to heal ulcers and stomach inflammation.

MAKE IT EASY

Chili sauce makes preparation of many Thai dishes easier, and is invaluable to have around when you're cooking. If you run out of fresh chilies for a recipe, nam prik pao makes a good substitution in most instances. Adding a dollop to your recipe is so much easier than slicing up a fresh chili (plus you needn't worry about burning your eyes after handling the fresh chili skin or seeds).

Processing the Ingredients

- Place the ground chili or cayenne, shrimp paste, fish sauce, sugar, tamarind paste, and 2 Tbsp. water in a mini chopper or food processor. Also add the fried garlic and shallots.
- Process well to create a thick paste.
- Note that this step can also be accomplished using a pestle and mortar, gradually adding the liquid after all the ingredients have been pounded together.

Stirring the Sauce

- Combine this mixture with the reserved oil in the wok or frying pan. Set over low heat and lightly simmer, stirring continuously.
- Adjust the chili sauce in terms of consistency, adding 1–2 more Tbsp. water for a runnier sauce, or more oil if you prefer it "shinier."
- Taste test the sauce. Add more fish sauce if not salty enough, or more sugar if it's too sour.
- Pour the chili sauce into a jar and refrigerate. Nam prik pao will keep for a month or longer in this way.

REAL PEANUT SAUCE

Unlike a lot of recipes for peanut sauce, this one is made with real peanuts.

Most peanut sauce recipes start or end with peanut butter. Not only is peanut butter not a Thai ingredient, it also makes for a rather poor peanut sauce. And because most peanut butters contain ingredients like icing sugar and hydrogenated oils, the resulting sauce also tends to be unhealthy as well.

The following recipe starts with real peanuts and is one of the easiest peanut sauces you're ever likely to make—it may also be one of the tastiest.

Serve this sauce with chicken or pork satay (or other grilled meats), fresh rolls or dumplings, or even as a dip for fresh vegetables.

Yield: Serves 6+

Ingredients

1 cup fresh-tasting dry roasted peanuts, unsalted

2 cloves garlic, minced

2 Tbsp. fish sauce (vegetarians substitute 2½ Tbsp. soy sauce)

½ tsp. dark soy sauce

½ tsp. tamarind paste OR 1 Tbsp. lime juice

2 tsp. sesame oil

2 Tbsp. brown sugar

1–2 tsp. Thai chili sauce OR ½–¾ tsp. cayenne pepper, to taste

¼ cup water

½ cup coconut milk

Real Peanut Sauce

- Place peanuts in a food processor or blender.
- Pulse until nuts are ground to preferred consistency: coarsely ground if you prefer a chunkier sauce, or more finely ground for a smoother sauce.

ZOOM

Strangely enough, you won't find peanut sauce served often in Thailand. "Thai peanut sauce," as we know it, actually hails from Indonesia and Malaysia. However, it goes so well with satay that it has become part of North American Thai food culture. The Thais do have a satay sauce that calls for peanuts, but the nuts are merely added on top.

MAKE IT EASY

When shopping for peanuts for this recipe, look for crunchy, fresh-tasting dry roasted nuts. Bulk peanuts are usually fine, so long as they are crisp on the outside (not soft). Also, note that this sauce tends to thicken as it sits. Just add a little more water or coconut milk to bring it back to your preferred consistency.

Blending the Peanuts with Other Ingredients

- Add all the other ingredients to the food processor or blender and blitz to create a delicious peanut sauce.
- If you prefer a runnier sauce, add a little more water or coconut milk.

Adjusting the Flavors

- Taste test the sauce, adding more fish sauce if you prefer it saltier, more sugar if you prefer it sweeter, or a squeeze of lime juice if it's too sweet or too salty.
- Serve at room temperature or lightly warmed, as desired.
- This sauce is excellent served with satay or fresh spring rolls, or tossed with noodles and vegetables for a cold noodle salad.

FRESH MANGO SAUCE

This sauce makes an excellent dip for shrimp, fresh rolls, and other Thai treats.

This mango sauce pairs beautifully with a number of Thai dishes, from fresh rolls or spring rolls to battered shrimp, crab cakes, or calamari. It tastes delicious with nearly any type of grilled seafood, and can also be drizzled over salad greens for a delightfully different kind of dressing.

Though it may be tempting to buy frozen prepared mango from your local supermarket, only fresh ripe mango will give you the kind of delicious results you're looking for.

A nice optional ingredient in this recipe is chili (either chili sauce or cayenne pepper), which makes for a more interesting spicy-sweet taste combination.

Yield: Serves 6

Ingredients

1 ripe mango

1–2 Tbsp. palm sugar OR brown sugar, to taste

1 Tbsp. fish sauce (OR 1 1/2 Tbsp. soy sauce if vegetarian)

1 Tbsp. lime juice

2–4 Tbsp. good-quality coconut milk

Optional: 1/2 tsp. cayenne pepper OR 1 tsp. Thai chili sauce

Fresh Mango Sauce

- Hold the mango on its side and cut it into 3 parts, being careful to slice on either side of the central (flat) stone.
- You will end up with 2 rounded pieces of mango (either side of the fruit) and the flat, central slice, which contains the stone. Using a tablespoon, scoop out the fruit from the end pieces.
- Peel off the skin around the stone and use a knife to cut off any remaining fruit.

RECIPE VARIATION

Grilled Shrimp with Mango Sauce. For this simple recipe, toss some medium to large fresh shrimp in 3 Tbsp. oyster sauce combined with 4 minced cloves garlic, and 1½ Tbsp. brown sugar. Marinate 10 minutes, then cook the shrimp over a hot grill until pink and plump (the shrimp can be skewered onto satay sticks if small). Serve with the fresh mango sauce drizzled over.

Thai-style Mango Salsa. Omit the coconut milk from the recipe, and reduce the sugar to just 1 tsp. Place all other ingredients in a food processor, including the chili. Add ⅓ cup fresh coriander, and 2 minced cloves garlic. Pulse to create a delicious mango salsa that is wonderful served over fresh grilled fish, or as an accompaniment to other Thai or international dishes.

Making the Mango Puree

- Place all the mango fruit and sugar in a blender or food processor. Blitz to create a smooth mango puree.
- Add the remaining ingredients and blitz again (add more coconut milk for a runnier sauce).

Adjusting the Flavors

- Taste test the sauce, adding more sugar if too sour, or more chili sauce if you prefer it spicier. If too sweet or salty, add another squeeze of lime juice.
- For a thicker sauce, simply refrigerate for an hour or two (both the coconut milk and mango will thicken in cooler temperatures).
- If desired, garnish with a little fresh coriander, and enjoy as a dip with a variety of Thai appetizers or dishes of your choice.

EASY COCONUT DIP

This simple dip can be put together in just minutes.

This coconut dip is very easy to make, and with any luck, you probably already have all the ingredients on hand.

Coconut dip goes well with a variety of Thai appetizers, such as deep-fried calamari, coconut-battered shrimp, or Thai fish cakes, crab cakes, or corn cakes. It can also be thinned out and used as a fresh and delicious salad dressing—or try using it as a dip for fresh fruit and vegetables. Grilled tropical fruits (such as grilled pineapple) are especially wonderful with it.

As always, good-quality coconut milk will give you better results (thicker is better, so unless you're planning to make this recipe into a salad dressing, avoid using "lite" coconut milk, which will give you a runny rather than a thick sauce).

Yield: Serves up to 6 people as a dip

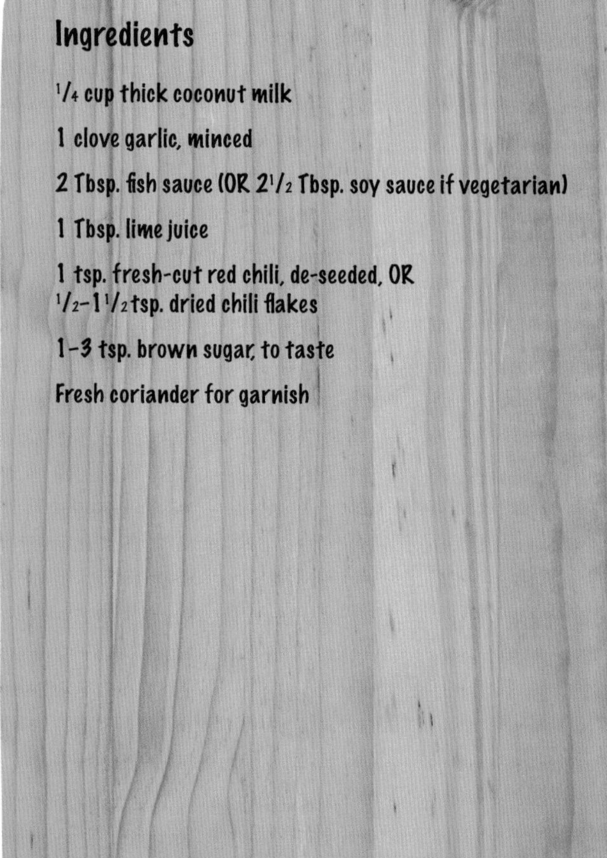

Ingredients

1/4 cup thick coconut milk

1 clove garlic, minced

2 Tbsp. fish sauce (OR 2 1/2 Tbsp. soy sauce if vegetarian)

1 Tbsp. lime juice

1 tsp. fresh-cut red chili, de-seeded, OR 1/2–1 1/2 tsp. dried chili flakes

1–3 tsp. brown sugar, to taste

Fresh coriander for garnish

Easy Coconut Dip

- For this dip, it's best to use good-quality coconut milk. If your coconut milk includes a layer of cream on the top of the can, be sure to include at least 2 Tbsp. of this (plus 1 Tbsp. of the coconut water), as it will give you the best coconut flavor.
- Place coconut milk in a mixing bowl.

• • • • RECIPE VARIATION • • • •

Grilled Pineapple with Coconut Dip. Make the coconut dip but omit the chili. Set aside. Marinate fresh-cut pineapple spears in the following: ½ cup coconut milk, pinch salt, and 3 Tbsp. brown sugar. Marinate for at least 20 minutes, then either grill as is, or pierce with satay sticks (to make a kind of fresh fruit lollipop). Grill until pineapple has grill marks and is bright yellow. Serve with the coconut dip.

To make this recipe into a coconut salad dressing, reduce the sugar to ½ tsp. Add all other ingredients, plus 2 Tbsp. chopped fresh coriander. Include or omit the chili, as desired. If a lighter dressing is preferred, use "lite" instead of regular coconut milk. Stir well and taste test the dressing, adding more sugar or fish sauce for a sweeter or saltier flavor. For a thicker dressing, refrigerate 30 minutes.

Stirring Ingredients Together

- Add the garlic, fish sauce, lime juice, chili, and 1 tsp. of brown sugar.
- Stir together and taste test the dip, adding more fish sauce if not salty enough, or more lime juice if too salty or too sweet.
- If you find the sauce is too thin, simply place in the refrigerator for 30 minutes (the coconut milk will naturally thicken with the lower temperature).

Adding Fresh Chili and Coriander

- Add fresh coriander as a garnish, and sprinkle over a little more fresh chili (or chili flakes) if desired.
- Enjoy this dip with Thai appetizers and finger foods.
- Store covered in the refrigerator for up to 6 days.

HOT SWEET THAI SAUCE

This sauce goes well with grilled meats as well as dumplings and fresh rolls.

This sauce is typical of what is served alongside a freshly grilled steak or other broiled or grilled meats. But the sauce is also wonderful with fresh rolls, spring rolls, or steamed or pan-fried dumplings. The spicy, salty, and sweet flavors are typical of Thai flavorings, making for a zinging combination.

As with all Thai sauces and condiments, the recipe for this sauce can be adjusted to suit your taste. While some people prefer sweet more than sour or spicy, others like a saltier flavor to dominate. See which you prefer—or whether, like most Thais, you'd rather have a balance of all possible flavors.

Yield: Serves 2–4

Ingredients

2 Tbsp. soy sauce

1/2 tsp. cornstarch

1/4 cup good-quality chicken stock

1 Tbsp. fish sauce

1 fresh-cut red chili OR 1–2 tsp. Thai chili sauce OR 1/2–3/4 tsp. cayenne pepper, to taste

1-2 green onions, sliced finely

1 Tbsp. freshly squeezed lime juice

2 Tbsp. palm sugar OR brown sugar

Hot Sweet Thai Sauce

- Measure the soy sauce into a cup. Add the cornstarch and stir until it dissolves completely.
- This will be the thickener for your sauce. Set this mixture aside, near the stove.
- Get out a saucepan and pour in the chicken stock.

RECIPE VARIATION

Vegetarian/Vegan/Gluten-free Hot Sweet Thai Sauce. Substitute simulated chicken stock or a good-tasting vegetable stock for the chicken stock. Instead of fish sauce, use 1½ Tbsp. soy sauce. If you have celiac disease, use only wheat-free soy sauce and wheat-free stock. If you would rather not use cornstarch as a thickener, sprinkle 1 tsp. to 1 Tbsp. rice flour over the sauce and whisk to blend.

ZOOM

In Thai cooking, nearly everything that isn't already cooked in a sauce is served with one. Often a dish will be marinated and cooked in the same sauce that will accompany it. In this case, be sure to make lots of sauce, reserving ½ or ⅓ for serving. The sauce used for marinating can also be used for basting, but should then be thrown away (so as not to confuse it with the serving sauce).

Heating the Sauce

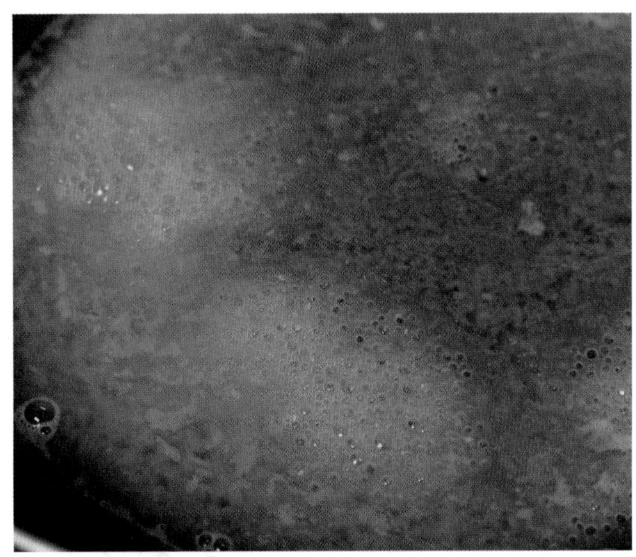

- Add the fish sauce, chili, onion, lime juice, and sugar to the saucepan. Bring to a boil.
- Reduce heat to medium and add the reserved soy sauce/cornstarch mixture.
- Stir occasionally until sauce thickens (1–2 minutes). Remove from heat.

Adjusting the Flavors

- This sauce should taste spicy, sweet, and salty. If not salty enough, add a little more fish sauce. If you'd prefer it sweeter, add more sugar. If not spicy enough, add more chili; and if too spicy, add a little more stock.
- Serve warm with Thai grilled fish or meats, or with fresh spring rolls or dumplings.

CHILI & GARLIC SAUCE

This versatile sauce can be used as a dip, side sauce, or stir-fry sauce.

Chili and garlic are used both individually and together in Thai cuisine. Nearly every Thai recipe begins with garlic (as the start of a stir-fry or curry) and ends with chili (sprinkled over as a garnish).

In the following recipe, the two come together beautifully in a spicy chili-garlic sauce. The sauce can be used as a dip for a variety of Thai appetizers and main course offerings, such as fresh rolls, deep-fried ribs, or steamed or fried dumplings, among other dishes. Feel free to experiment and see what dishes you like it served with.

Yield: Makes approximately ½ cup sauce

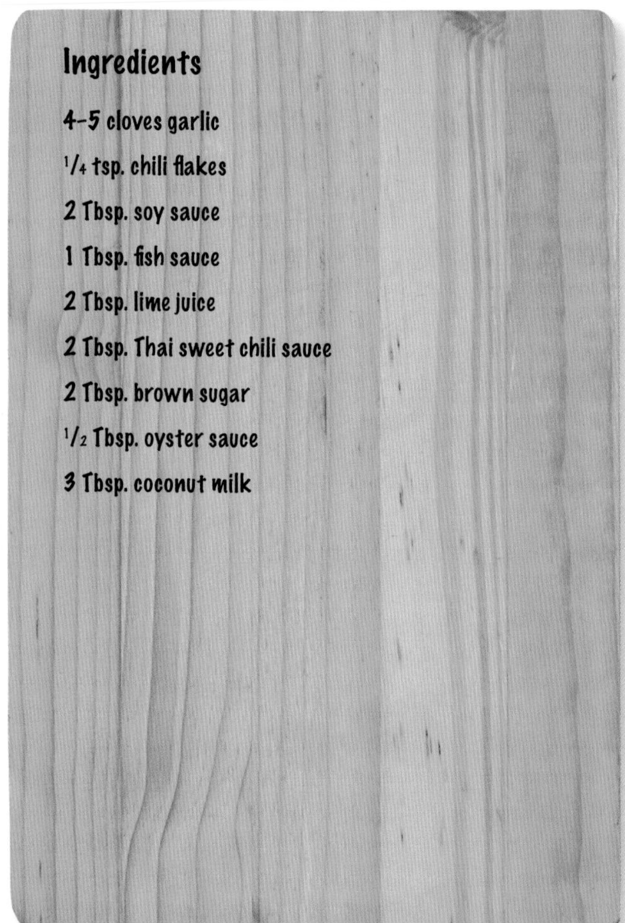

Ingredients

4–5 cloves garlic

¼ tsp. chili flakes

2 Tbsp. soy sauce

1 Tbsp. fish sauce

2 Tbsp. lime juice

2 Tbsp. Thai sweet chili sauce

2 Tbsp. brown sugar

½ Tbsp. oyster sauce

3 Tbsp. coconut milk

Chili & Garlic Sauce

- Mince the garlic by processing it in a mini chopper, or by using a garlic press. You can also chop it up very finely with a knife. Set aside.
- Combine all other ingredients together in a bowl, stirring to dissolve the sugar. Set aside.

RECIPE VARIATION

To make this condiment into a stir-fry sauce, double the recipe, combining all ingredients in a mixing bowl and stirring well to dissolve the sugar (be sure to add the garlic uncooked). Taste test for sweetness and spice, adding more sugar if too sour, or more chili and/or garlic if you prefer it spicier. This sauce is now ready to be stir-fried with your favorite foods.

Garlic Shrimp. Stir together all the ingredients in a bowl as written. Remove the shells (except tails) from 10–12 medium to large-size shrimp. Toss shrimp in ½ the sauce, reserving the rest. Marinate shrimp 10 minutes. Heat 1 Tbsp. oil in a wok, and add marinated shrimp. Stir-fry 1 minute, then add remaining sauce. Stir-fry until shrimp are cooked (2–3 more minutes). Taste test and adjust the flavors to your liking.

Stir-frying the Garlic

- Heat 1–2 Tbsp. oil in a wok or small frying pan over medium-high heat.
- Add the minced garlic and stir-fry until fragrant, but not so long that it turns brown or bitter (1 minute).
- Reduce heat to low. Add the previously combined ingredients, stirring well.

Adjusting the Flavors

- Taste test the sauce for sweetness and spice, adding more sugar if too sour, or more chili if you prefer it spicier. It not salty or flavorful enough, add more fish sauce. If too sweet or too salty, add more fresh lime juice.
- Serve the sauce with your choice of Thai finger foods, or grilled meats, fish, or seafood.

WEB SITES & VIDEOS

Quick information and tips for cooking Thai.

It's quite easy these days to get cooking help and advice on nearly any type of cuisine, and Thai is no exception. Going online is the fastest and easiest way to get information and cooking tips as well as additional Thai recipes. Online videos are also an excellent resource, providing visual step-by-step guidance; they're also a fun way to get some great cooking tips and information on Thai ingredients.

If you're looking for an answer to a specific question, online message boards and forums can help. Answers may come from other learners, experienced cooks, or from an expert in the field of Thai cooking, depending on which board you post your question.

Thai Cooking Web Sites

About.com's Thai Food Site

http://thaifood.about.com/

- The companion Web site to the book you are presently reading, this Web site is continuously updated with new and exciting Thai food recipes. Also contains additional information on regional Thai cuisine, Thai ingredients, cooking techniques, and more.

Joy's Thai Food

www.joysthaifood.com/about/

- This site features authentic Thai recipes created by a wonderful Thai cook who lives and works in Thailand.

Thai Food Recipes

www.thaifoodrecipesite.com/

- A Web site containing a number of authentic Thai recipes with simple, straightforward instructions.

ImportFood.com

http://importfood.com/recipes.html

- This Web site features 125 authentic Thai recipes that are simple and quick to make. Also contains links to online supermarkets selling all types of Thai ingredients.

Temple of Thai

www.templeofthai.com/

- A complete Thai Web site that includes not only Thai recipes, but also cookware and utensils, ingredients, cookbooks, and more.

Thai Food & Travel

www.thaifoodandtravel.com/ingredients.html

- A terrific resource for Thai ingredients, this Web site contains information on all the basic Thai pantry staples and explains each one thoroughly. You will also find information on Thai sauces and condiments, as well as Thai herbs and vegetables.

Thai Cooking Videos

About.com Food Videos

http://thaifood.about.com/od/thairecipesstepbystep/p/cooking videos.htm

- This site offers numerous Thai cooking videos that can teach you to cook Thai food in just a few minutes. Learn to easily make everything from Thai curry to salads and famous Thai desserts.

Thai Food Tonight

www.thaifoodtonight.com/thaifoodtonight/recipes.htm

- A site that is dedicated to teaching you how to cook Thai food by watching an expert Thai cook. Also contains information about ingredients and utensils.

Thai Recipe Videos

www.thairecipevideos.com/

- Another site dedicated to cooking videos rather than printable recipes. Learn the basics with the videos on this "cooking school" Web site.

iFood.tv

www.ifood.tv/r/thai/recipes/videos

- This Web site contains numerous Thai cooking videos as well as recipes. Most are rated by users and include comments that can assist you in choosing which videos or recipes to try.

ImportFood.com: Street-side Thai Food

http://importfood.com/vendor_video/thai_street_vendor_videos.html

- On this Web site you'll find videos of authentic street cooks in Thailand cooking up a variety of Thai favorites, including old-fashioned Pad Thai and Shrimp Fried Rice.

Thai Message Boards

Thaifood.about.com

http://forums.about.com/n/pfx/forum.spx?nav=messages&webtag=ab-thaifood&lgnF=y

- Write to the author of this cookbook with your questions and comments, or get information from other Thai food fans.

Thai-Food.com

www.thai-food.com/

- Contains information on cooking and eating Thai food in addition to a useful forum.

- Yahoo Answers http://answers.yahoo.com/dir/index;_ylt=ApwLIQIPfBjCr6_.nkeLrOdJxQt.;_ylv=3?link=list&sid=396545367

- A great message board to post any question on Thai cooking. Or search through the answers that are already posted.

THAI COOKBOOKS

Some of the best Thai cookbooks available today.

Quick and Easy Thai Cookbooks

The Original Thai Cookbook by Jennifer Brennan. Perigee Trade, 1984

- A simple and very clear Thai cookbook that also gives the English spellings for most Thai dishes. The recipes are simple but authentic.

Real Vegetarian Thai by Nancie McDermott. Chronicle Books, 1997

- Simple Thai recipes especially created for those who are vegetarian or vegan. Most Thai recipes contain some kind of shrimp or fish base (fish sauce is used in nearly every dish), but the recipes in this book show you how to achieve true Thai taste without resorting to any meat, fish, or seafood products.

Simple Thai Cookery by Ken Hom. BBC Books, 2007

- Forty of the most popular Thai dishes prepared with step-by-step instructions. This is a great book for those who like mouth-watering pictures.

Simply Thai Cooking by Wandee Young and Byron Ayanoglu. Robert Rose Inc., 2003

- Features fairly simple Thai recipes with clear instructions. Most of the classic Thai dishes are represented in this book, plus there are a few Thai fusion recipes.

Quick & Easy Thai: 70 Everyday Recipes by Nancie McDermott and Alison Miksch. Chronicle Books, 2004

- For those who wish to try cooking Thai, this book offers a good start. Highly recommended for beginners or those who prefer Thai versions of more familiar Western-type dishes.

Quick and Easy Thai Cuisine: Lemon Grass Cookbook by Panurat Poladitmontri. Japan Publications Trading, 2002.

- Easy to make Thai dishes with real Thai taste. Simple and easy to follow recipes, plus many of the ingredients are described in detail.

Intermediate to Advanced Thai Cookbooks

Cracking the Coconut: Classic Thai Home Cooking by Su-mei Yu. Willow Morrow Cookbooks, 2000

- Recommended for advanced cooks of Thai and Asian cuisine, this book contains numerous and unique Thai recipes from an experienced Thai chef. Also features cultural background and personal stories that center around many of the featured dishes.

Keo's Thai Cuisine by Keo Sananikone. Ten Speed Press, 2004 (Revised Edition)

- A true Thai chef provides numerous authentic Thai recipes along with beautiful photographs. Recommended for those who are intermediate to advanced Thai cooks.

100 Great Thai Dishes by Mini C. Cassell Illustrated, 2008

- A wonderful collection of classic and new Thai dishes by a Thai chef living and cooking in Britain. Many of these beautifully illustrated recipes were created by the chef for her London restaurant.

Thai Food by David Thompson. Ten Speed Press, 2004

- Quick and easy Thai recipes from an Australian chef, restaurant owner, and Thai food scholar. A great resource for authentic Thai recipes that call for real Thai ingredients.

Vatch's Thai Street Food by Vatcharin Bhumichitr. Kyle Books, 2007

- Thai street cuisine taken to a whole new level. This book of authentic Thai favorites is beautiful to look through and contains authentic Thai street recipes. A must-have for any Thai food enthusiast.

THAI COOKING EQUIPMENT & FOOD RESOURCES

Find kitchen equipment and Thai food ingredients through the following online sources.

Thai Cooking Equipment & Utensils

Temple of Thai

www.templeofthai.com/cookware/

- Whether you're looking to buy a wok or pestle and mortar set, this Web site can help you out. Features authentic Thai cookware and utensils at reasonable prices.

Import Food

www.importfood.com/thaicookware.html

- This online source features various Thai kitchen utensils and equipment, including woks, steamers, specialty tools, and even ceramic dishware.

Gourmet Sleuth

www.gourmetsleuth.com/citems.asp?c=18

- An online catalog with some of the best Asian kitchen tools and equipment, from basic woks to coconut graters and clay pots.

Amazon.com

www.amazon.com/b?ie=UTF8&node=370776011

- A secure source for ordering all the basic necessities for your Thai kitchen. Features top of the line Thai and Asian kitchen equipment, along with appliances, tools, and accessories.

Shopping for Thai Ingredients

My Thai Mart

www.mythaimart.com/

- An online Thai store based in San Jose, California. Offers all types of Thai ingredients as well as snack foods, rice and noodles, sauces, and instant packaged meals.

Temple of Thai

www.templeofthai.com/food/

- A good source for specialty Thai ingredients that may be difficult to find elsewhere, such as Thai spices, curry pastes, different types of rice, and even Thai beverages.

Grocery Thai

www.grocerythai.com/

- Another online store physically located in California, this source makes shopping for Thai ingredients easy. Also features some vegetarian Thai products.

Asian Wok.com

www.asianwok.com/store/pc/viewCategories.asp?idCategory=18

- On this site you'll find numerous Thai ingredients and products, from fish sauce to banana leaves to your favorite type of Thai instant noodles.

GLOSSARY

Key Thai ingredients explained.

Banana Leaves

- Leaves from the banana tree are often used in the Thai kitchen for various purposes. They can take the place of both foil and parchment paper in nearly all your Asian cooking and baking needs, and are environmentally friendly. They are available in Asian stores, either in fresh packages or frozen.

Basil

- This herb is commonly used in Thai cuisine, usually as a final topping over curries, noodles, soups, and other types of Thai dishes. Nearly any type of basil will work for most Thai recipes, although Thai basil will give you the most authentic results. Thai basil has narrower leaves than sweet basil, and features purplish stems and flowers.

Chilies

- The most common type of Thai chili is a thin, bright red variety known as "bird's eye chili" because the place where the dark stem attaches to the chili resembles a bird's eye. If you find that fresh chilies are too spicy for your taste or stomach, try substituting dried crushed chili or cayenne pepper from your local supermarket spice aisle. This type of chili (both are made from cayenne pepper) is actually good for your stomach and can help heal rather than irritate a sensitive digestive system.

Coconut Milk

- While in Thailand nearly every cook buys freshly squeezed coconut milk, here in the West we are forced to rely on the canned variety. Unless you are watching your calorie intake, regular thick coconut milk is recommended ("lite" coconut milk tends to be very thin and lacking in taste). And try to buy organic whenever possible.

Coriander

- Also known as cilantro or Chinese parsley, fresh coriander is another herb commonly found in Thai cuisine. However, it isn't only used in its fresh form. All parts of the coriander plant are made use of in the Thai kitchen, including the root, stem, leaves, and seeds (both whole and ground coriander are commonly used).

Cumin

- Dry, ground cumin is a common spice added mainly to Thai curries. You can either buy your cumin already ground, or grind whole cumin seeds yourself with a coffee grinder or pestle and mortar.

Fish Sauce

- One of the most important Thai ingredients to have on hand, fish sauce is an absolute must for most Thai recipes. You'll find a good selection of fish sauces at any Asian food store. Look for tall bottles with "Fish Sauce" and the ingredients displayed on the label (anchovy or other fish extract, salt, and water—other ingredients aren't necessary). Look for fish sauce made in Thailand or Vietnam. If you are vegetarian, look for vegetarian fish sauce (available at Vietnamese food stores).

Galangal

- Galangal is a type of ginger used in the Thai kitchen as well as in other Southeast Asian cuisines. Also referred to as Siamese ginger, it has a milder, sweeter taste than North American ginger, and can be distinguished by its slightly reddish skin. Look for galangal at your local Asian market (fresh or frozen) or grocery store. Note that galangal can also be purchased in its dried, ground form; however, like ground ginger, the dried version does not have the same quality of flavor or nutrients as the fresh.

Green Peppercorns

- Green peppercorns are unripe peppercorns. You can find them in cans or bottles in gourmet and Asian food stores. If possible, try to buy them fresh (they look like small green berries still on the vine), although the pickled variety is an excellent substitute.

Jasmine Rice

- This is the most popular type of Thai rice, also known as jasmine-scented rice. Jasmine rice is well known the world over for its high quality and health benefits. Be sure to source your jasmine rice at an Asian import food store for the highest quality. When you open the bag, you should be able to detect the subtle fragrance of jasmine.

Kaffir Lime Leaves

- The leaf of a type of dark green fruit distinctly different from the limes we commonly see in North America. These limes are easily distinguished by their knobby skin. In Thai cuisine, it is mainly the leaves that are used, adding a unique lime flavor to soups, curries, and sauces. These leaves are available at most Asian specialty stores, and can be purchased fresh, dried, or frozen. I recommend buying either fresh or frozen for more intense flavor and aroma.

Lemongrass

- Lemongrass provides a fragrant and distinct lemon flavor to many Thai dishes. Thai cooks use the lower half of the lemongrass stalk, first slicing and then usually pounding or crushing it before adding it to spice pastes, soups, or curries. Whole bruised lemongrass stalks, cut into lengths of three or four inches, are often added to soups and curries for extra flavor.

Limes

- Fresh limes are used more often in Thai cooking than lemons. In Thailand, the smaller key lime variety are popular, but regular limes work just as well for most Thai dishes. In a pinch, grated lime zest can be used as a substitute for kaffir lime leaves.

Oils for Thai Cooking

- Because Thai cooks do all their cooking over a stovetop or fire, cooking oil is required for nearly every hot Thai dish. Thai cooks commonly use coconut or palm oil, both of which have a low smoke rate and do not break down easily. They are also surprisingly healthy if purchased organic and non-GMO. Other good alternatives include safflower, sunflower, corn, peanut, and other nut oils. Note that olive oil should not be used for high-temperature frying (including stir-frying), as it breaks down easily and may even turn toxic. Enjoy olive oil at room temperature in salads and with breads, or for roasting vegetables at oven temperatures under 300 degrees F.

Oyster Sauce

- Oyster sauce, which is a Chinese influence, has become a common Thai ingredient in recent years. There are many types of oyster sauces available in stores and markets, all of them with varying levels of sodium—therefore, some are saltier than others. For this reason, when using oyster sauce, be sure to always taste test as you go to make sure your dish isn't overly salty. (Note that a squeeze or two of fresh lime juice can always remedy a too-salty dish). Note: Vegetarian oyster sauce can be found in larger Asian food stores.

Palm Sugar

- Instead of sugar from the sugarcane, palm sugar comes from the sweet sap of the date palm, which grows in many Southeast Asian countries including Thailand. Palm sugar can be purchased in hard round cakes in Asian stores (usually sold in clear packets). However, brown sugar makes a good substitute.

Pandan Leaves or Paste

- Pandan is a herbaceous tropical plant with long green leaves. In Southeast Asia, pandan leaves are used to lend a unique taste and aroma to many Thai desserts and some drinks. Pandan leaves can also be used to wrap savory foods, such as chicken. Pandan paste is used mainly in cakes and desserts, as it is sweet and imbues foods with a bright green color. It can be purchased in very small bottles at Asian specialty stores. If purchased fresh, pandan leaves should be pounded into a paste before using, adding water sparingly.

Shallots

- Instead of cooking onions, shallots are commonly used in Thailand and come in all sizes and colors, including purple. If shallots aren't available at your local grocery store or are too expensive for your budget, a good substitute is purple onion, or a combination of white cooking onion and garlic. Or use only the white parts of spring onions.

Shrimp Paste

- Shrimp paste is used to add depth of flavor and a unique taste to many Thai dishes, including noodles, soups, and curries. It is made from fermented shrimp, which are dried under the hot Thai sun and then pounded or processed to a paste. Shrimp paste comes in bottled form and is available at most Asian grocery stores. As it is salty and highly concentrated, be sure to use it sparingly (½ tsp. is usually all you need).

Soy Sauces, Light and Dark

- Soy sauces, light and dark, are a mainstay in all Asian cuisines, including Thai. "Light" refers to regular soy sauce, while "dark" is literally darker and stronger in flavor. Vegetarians should note that light soy sauce can be substituted for fish sauce in most recipes (1 Tbsp. fish sauce = 1½ Tbsp. soy sauce). Thai chefs also use Thai sweet soy sauce in certain dishes, or as a dipping sauce—look for it in specialty Asian stores.

Tamarind

- Tamarind is a kind of sour tropical fruit that grows in a pod. While some cuisines use tamarind to make desserts and even candy, in Thai cooking it is used mostly to flavor savory dishes. While pods of tamarind—or its dried counterpart—are available in many Asian stores, it is more convenient to purchase tamarind puree or paste (and it tastes just as good). In this form, it resembles molasses. Look for it in jars at your local Asian or Indian food stores.

Tapioca

- Tapioca is made from the cassava root and, when combined with coconut, sugar, or rice, forms the basis of many Thai desserts. While regular tapioca is made up of sphere-like granules, Western "minute tapioca" is smaller and cooks faster (though much longer than a mere minute!). For most Thai desserts, seed tapioca is recommended. Tapioca starch is used in Thailand as a thickener instead of cornstarch. It is a good-for-you starch, and is available at Asian specialty stores or health food stores. Note that tapioca is gluten free and vegan.

Turmeric

- Turmeric is one of the healthiest spices you can eat. Turmeric powders are widely available in spice sections of grocery stores and may offer the same health benefits as fresh. Fresh turmeric is harder to find, but well worth the hunt. Like galangal and ginger, turmeric is a kind of root (rhizome) and has a similar appearance, except that it has an orange hue. Turmeric is used frequently in Thai curries and other savory dishes.

Sesame Oil

- The use of sesame oil in Thai cuisine is mainly a Chinese influence. Sesame oil can add extra flavor and richness to certain Thai dishes. Be sure not to "cook" sesame oil, or you will lose all its natural goodness and health benefits. Sesame oil can be drizzled over the finished dish as a final topping, or added to salads, dips, fresh rolls, and other fresh (uncooked) Thai dishes.

Stir-Fry

- To stir-fry means to quickly cook foods in a wok or large frying pan while manipulating them with a wooden spoon or other utensil over high heat.

White Pepper

- In Southeast Asia, white peppercorns and ground white pepper are actually more commonly used than black pepper. White pepper has a sweeter, milder, and altogether different flavor than black pepper. These days, it's possible to find ground white pepper in the spice section of most large supermarket chains. If not, look for it at Asian or gourmet food stores.

INDEX

R

S

T